Praise for *Theod*

"Fascinating… *Theodore Roosevelt for the Defense* is a must read."

—John A. DeFrancisco, New York State senator (1992–2018)

"Many of the questions the trial raised about the effects of money in politics, the dangers of blind allegiance to party politics, and oversize corporate political influence will resonate with contemporary readers. Legal eagles and history buffs will enjoy this one."

—*Publishers Weekly*

"*Theodore Roosevelt for the Defense* reads like a blow-by-blow radio account of a prizefight between two heavyweights."

—*New York Journal of Books*

"A feisty Roosevelt takes center stage in a mostly lively history."

—*Kirkus Reviews*

"Maintaining suspense about the jury's verdict, Abrams and Fisher deliver a fine and timely legal drama."

—*Booklist*

"The reader gets to know the lawyers, the judge, the jurors, the witnesses, the arguments and the rulings–and above all, the indomitable TR.… All are brought vividly to life by Abrams and Fisher."

—*Law360*

"Dan Abrams and David Fisher have penned a thrilling account of a...high-stakes, high-drama, high-profile, yet so far relatively unknown, trial from our nation's history."

—Gregg Tripoli, executive director, Onondaga Historical Association

"Dan Abrams and David Fisher prove that the story of a libel case can indeed make for gripping reading.... Abrams and Fisher are gifted writers, and their prose is neither overly spare nor showy; they're clearly fascinated by the trial, and their enthusiasm for their subject matter shows. *Theodore Roosevelt for the Defense* is a must-read for anyone with a deep interest in the 26th president, or in First Amendment law, but any reader with an affection for American history will find something to admire in this book."

—NPR

"The greatest strength of *Theodore Roosevelt for the Defense* is the detailed play-by-play account of the trial. All of Roosevelt's charm and bluster is on display.... Abrams and Fisher have succeeded in their goal of reestablishing the importance of *Barnes v. Roosevelt* in American jurisprudence.... Students of American legal history and general audiences with an interest in learning more about Theodore Roosevelt will both find *Theodore Roosevelt for the Defense* an engaging read."

—Bowling Green Daily News

Theodore Roosevelt for the Defense

Also by Dan Abrams and David Fisher

Lincoln's Last Trial
John Adams Under Fire

THEODORE ROOSEVELT FOR THE DEFENSE

THE COURTROOM BATTLE TO SAVE HIS LEGACY

DAN ABRAMS

AND **DAVID FISHER**

HANOVER
SQUARE
PRESS

ISBN-13: 978-1-335-62901-2

Theodore Roosevelt for the Defense: The Courtroom Battle to Save His Legacy

First published in 2019. This edition published in 2021.

This edition published by arrangement with Harlequin Books S.A.

Hanover Square Press
22 Adelaide St. West, 40th Floor
Toronto, Ontario M5H 4E3, Canada
HanoverSqPress.com
BookClubbish.com

Printed in U.S.A.

To my wonderful son, Everett, who I hope will develop a love for history that we can share together, along with so much else, for many years to come.

Theodore Roosevelt for the Defense

INTRODUCTION

The first time I heard about the "Trial of the Century" I was a twenty-eight-year-old newly minted lawyer who, only through a series of mishaps and bad luck for other, more qualified journalists, had suddenly been tasked with covering what felt like the nation's most momentous legal story. Not only was I covering it, but I had secured one of a handful of coveted courtroom seats allocated for a cable channel called Court TV. Courtroom cameras were a relatively new phenomenon, cable news was still in its infancy and the defendant, former football great and actor OJ Simpson, was one of the best-known Americans in any field. His defense, that he had been targeted and ultimately framed by a racist Los Angeles police department, only added heat to what already felt like a boiling public cauldron. The result was a nation transfixed by everything from the most consequential to the most picayune moments of his trial for the murder of his ex-wife Nicole Brown Simpson and her friend Ron Goldman.

Waiting outside the courtroom before the first preliminary hearing, as we ended up doing for long stretches, I recall a local Los Angeles TV reporter concluding a live report with his stentorian voice reverberating in the hallway: "Many now saying that this could become the trial of the century." As the case moved forward, that became a common refrain and to many of us living the trial, it felt like there could never have been another that rivaled it in terms of media and public interest.

In retrospect, however, it might have been more accurate to have called it the trial of the decade or even arguably of my lifetime. From the Lindbergh kidnapping case to the Nuremberg and Eichmann trials, to the Scopes and the Leopold and Loeb cases, there have been at least twenty other twentieth-century trials dubbed the "trial of the century," all captivating based on the nature of the crimes or the identity of the defendants or victims. But only one involved a former president of the United States testifying in his own defense for over a week, and with testimony that would expose the underbelly of seedy political backdoor deal making and even profiteering. *Barnes v. Roosevelt* also didn't involve just any former president taking the witness stand. Teddy Roosevelt was one of the most charismatic and entertaining presidents that the nation had, and has, ever seen.

He didn't disappoint, offering animated and at times blistering testimony for an audience that extended well beyond the courtroom. The majority of the other witnesses were a who's who of New York's political leaders, including many household names at the time and others like Franklin D. Roosevelt who would go on to achieve so much more.

Teddy Roosevelt readily admitted that he had written, and then caused to be widely circulated, an article criticizing the political system, its leaders and what he said was their abuse of power. And while he could have been coy and suggested that his condemnation was broad and not specifically meant to single out Republican party boss William Barnes, he chose to stand by every word and sought to prove that Barnes was in fact "corrupt."

As a legal matter, it was a defense far more difficult than it would be today. Roosevelt's attacks on Barnes were determined by the judge to be defamatory or libelous "per se." Before the 1964 *New York Times v. Sullivan* case and its progeny, once that determination was made, if the defendant could not then prove the statements true, the only real issue would be the amount of damages awarded. Today, however, a political leader would have to overcome a far higher legal hurdle to even get to trial over a political jab. This type of public figure plaintiff would now have to demonstrate not just that the statement was defamatory, but would be obliged to prove that it was false and that the defendant knew or suspected it to be so.

While the legal standards have evolved, it's startling to think that over one hundred years later, Roosevelt's claim of corruption still resonates so clearly, and in some cases so directly today. After all, this case was always about much more than just a formal accusation of libel against Theodore Roosevelt. All involved recognized the political system as it existed at that time would be on trial. For Roosevelt, it was about defending a legacy he had carefully crafted and jealously protected.

When the case began in 1915, he was still one of the most influential people not just in the United States but on the planet. Three years earlier, he had left a Republican Party that he felt cheated him out of the 1912 nomination, launched his own party and lost to Woodrow Wilson but only after splitting votes with Republican incumbent William Howard Taft, who received roughly 635,000 fewer votes than did Roosevelt. Not surprisingly, coverage of the trial was ubiquitous and exhaustive. The *New York Times* alone sometimes devoted as many as twelve single-spaced pages to a day's testimony, much of it including transcribed notes from various witnesses. A legion of firsthand accounts allowed us to supplement and animate the words from the trial transcript, as well.

That is probably the most significant difference between this and our previous book: *Lincoln's Last Trial: The Murder Case That Propelled Him to the Presidency*, which used a little-known trial transcript to tell the story of Abraham Lincoln's defense of Peachy Quinn Harrison. There, the handwritten transcription from 1859 included only sworn testimony of witnesses, and while there was extensive media coverage, it involved mostly terse descriptions of witnesses. That comparative dearth of information forced us to make certain presumptions about preparations, reactions and even some of the arguments to the court. Here, everything is directly based on original source material, not just the complete typed transcription of each moment of the case, but rich descriptions and color from outside the courtroom from the nation's finest reporters.

Legally, the difference in American law from Lincoln's days in court to this courtroom only fifty-six years later is also substantial. The system had become far more formalized and regimented. Gone were the footloose days of lawyers traveling on a circuit taking whatever cases came their way. Specific expertise and location of practice had become critical factors in choosing an attorney. But these cases were also very different. The Harrison murder trial involved more limited strategic legal options; while in *Barnes v. Roosevelt*, the variety of choices shaped the entire trial.

Despite those differences, we were amazed to once more find a truly compelling trial and transcript involving one of our great presidents and one that appears to have become a footnote to history. Yet again, our goal was to bring that mostly forgotten trial to life.

There is also some surprising overlap between the Lincoln book and this one. First and foremost, Roosevelt was a great admirer of a central character in *Lincoln's Last Trial*, Robert R. Hitt. Having been Lincoln's trusted transcriber during the Lincoln-Douglas debates and a pioneer in that field, he transcribed the Harrison murder trial, meticulously chronicling Lincoln's precise words in his defense. We told that story through Hitt's eyes and described how he later went on to an illustrious career as a twelve-term member of the United States Congress, serving as chairman of the prestigious Foreign Affairs Committee for a time. In 1904, Hitt was also Theodore Roosevelt's first choice to be his vice president and running mate, writing to his son Theodore Roosevelt Jr.: "I very earnestly hope that Mr. Hitt will be nominated for vice president with me. He would be an excellent candidate and if I should be elected he would be, of all the men the pleasantest to work with."

Alas, it was the very political bosses and party leaders that Roosevelt came to decry who successfully pushed him to agree to the more politically sensible Senator Charles Fairbanks for the role.

While Hitt's relationship with Lincoln was not the impetus to seek him out as his running mate, Roosevelt was a great student and longtime disciple of Lincoln. Mary and Abraham Lincoln had been friendly with Roosevelt's father and went to church with him during the Civil War. Roosevelt regularly referred to Lincoln in speeches, describing him as his "great hero" and the "great heart of public life." After hanging a portrait of Lincoln on his office wall in the White House, he remarked, "I look up to that picture, and I do as I believe Lincoln would have done." Speeches by, and books about, Lincoln were regular reading for Roosevelt, including the entire ten volume *Abraham Lincoln:*

A History, written by Lincoln's personal secretaries John Nicolay and John Hay, who would become Roosevelt's secretary of state. Some of the more humorous moments in this trial come when the plaintiff, William Barnes, claims that Roosevelt pilfered a letter written by Lincoln to Barnes's grandfather, Republican Party pioneer Thurlow Weed.

The most striking connection, however, may be a photo dated April 25, 1865, of the New York City cortege of Lincoln's body. In the 1940s, magazine editor and historian Stefan Lorent identified a home in that photo as that of Cornelius van Schaack Roosevelt, grandfather to Teddy. Two small boys can be seen sitting on a windowsill watching the procession pass. Lorent was able to ask Roosevelt's widow, Edith, who was also a childhood friend of Roosevelt, about it and described it as follows: "She looked at the picture and the two little heads in the window. Her face lighted up as her memories jumped back to that day in 1865. She said, 'Yes, I think that is my husband, and next to him his brother.' And then, chuckling, 'That horrible man! I was a little girl then and my governess took me to Grandfather Roosevelt's house on Broadway so I could watch the funeral procession. But as I looked down from the window and saw all the black drapings I became frightened and started to cry. Theodore and (his brother) Elliott were both there. They didn't like my crying. They took me and locked me in a back room. I never did see Lincoln's funeral.'"

While this book is about the other end of Roosevelt's life, after he too had become a leader many sought to emulate, at the time of the trial he still had big plans that included another possible presidential run. It was a future placed in jeopardy by a case that threatened to humiliate and humble him. Merely responding to an accusation of libel would not suffice; he would be forced to defend his reputation and honor under questioning by one of the finest and toughest lawyers in the country and one who may have even convinced his client to file the suit. Roosevelt's advocate, an equally skilled legal tactician, made this a courtroom showdown that will still serve to inspire any modern-day lawyer.

For everyone involved, the stakes could not have been higher, and for the spectators lucky enough to be inside, an unprecedented opportunity to see the former president up close and unscripted.

They could have made a very good case that they were witnessing the trial of the century. It certainly felt that way in the spring of 1915.

CHAPTER ONE

On Sunday, April 18, 1915, several hundred men and women gathered in a light rain to await the arrival of the Southwestern Limited, due in at 10:05 p.m. in Syracuse, New York. They were joined at the New York Central Railroad station by reporters and photographers from as many as fifty newspapers from across the country. The train steamed slowly through the center of the city, stopping traffic at every north-side intersection. As it pulled into the massive redbrick structure, a muffled commotion slowly transformed into booming hurrahs as the numerous flashlight beams landed on the familiar black slouch hat stepping down onto the platform.

Teddy Roosevelt had come to town.

This was a Theodore Roosevelt the nation already knew well. One of the most recognizable and celebrated Americans alive, the former 26th president of the United States, the hero of San Juan Hill and the daring leader of the legendary Rough Riders. The Republican progressive who as president broke the industrial trusts, regulated the railroads, set aside 230-million acres for national parks and forests and preserves, and who had fought to give the workingman "a Square Deal" through his eight years in the White House. This was T.R., the 1906 Nobel Peace Prize recipient who brokered the end of the Russo-Japanese War and who championed the seemingly impossible dream of cutting a canal through Panama to connect the mighty oceans. The historian, writer and naturalist whose death-defying adventures in the jungles of Africa and South America had captivated the country. The courageous man who had survived an assassination attempt and insisted on delivering his full speech with the bullet still lodged in his chest as his shirt bloodied. Despite being of just average height, his presence and personality were vastly oversize. As the *New York Sun* wrote, he "completely absorbs and occupies the senses of whenever and wherever he is present."

The progressive policies of the Square Deal, which emphasized conservation of resources, controlling monopolistic corporations and attacking economic corruption, had aroused the passions of Americans. In 1908, for example, a riot took place in the small Texas town of Brownfield when residents decided to erect a life-sized statue of the then-president in hunting costume in the town square. "The erection was vigorously opposed by democrats and some republicans," reported the *New York Herald*. The statue had been stolen and buried for a week but finally was recovered. "When the ceremony took place a band of cowboys made a rush and met a determined crowd. Revolvers, clubs and fists were freely used, but the statue was not disturbed." In the melee one man was killed and nine others wounded. When he learned about it, Roosevelt wondered, "Who with a sense of humor and a real zest for life would not be glad to be prominent in American politics at the outset of the 20th century?"

"I have never known such a man as he," wrote the great journalist William Allen White. "He overcame me…he poured into my heart such visions, such ideals, such hopes, such a new attitude towards life…and patriotism and the meaning of things, as I never had dreamed."

"The Colonel," as he was known affectionately, had visited Syracuse many times previously, beginning in 1898 during his term as governor of New York and always with exuberance and often in celebration. He had even come to "the Salt City" as president and throughout his visit, spectators remembered, "the president's face wore the broadest smile, the president's teeth flashed continuously and the president indulged in the heartiest laughter of any member of his party." But this time was different. This time he had come to Syracuse to defend his honor, and perhaps complete one last seemingly quixotic quest to reclaim his political prestige.

This visit to Syracuse was for a trial, in which Teddy Roosevelt was the accused. Sued by the former head of the state Republican Party, Mr. William Barnes, for libel. The supposed offense that brought him here: while endorsing a nonpartisan candidate for governor more than a year earlier, Roosevelt had railed against two-party political boss rule, claiming Republican and Democratic political bosses had worked together to "secure the appointment to office of evil men whose activities so deeply taint and discredit our whole governmental system." The result, he said, is a government "that is rotten throughout in almost all of its departments" and that this "invisible government…is responsible for the maladministration and corruption in the public offices" and the good citizens of the state would never "secure the economic, social and industrial reforms…until this invisible government of the party bosses working through the alliance between crooked business and crooked politics is rooted out of the government system."

Coming from a lesser man, this attack might easily have been overlooked, but T.R. remained one of the most influential men in the entire world. This was nothing less than an assault on the American political structure, and for party boss William Barnes, who harbored dreams of running for governor himself, it was potentially devastating to his aspirations. To save his reputation from these "false and malicious attacks designed to damage (his) reputation and career," Barnes sued Roosevelt for libel, demanding the princely sum of $50,000.

This attack on Barnes from Teddy Roosevelt was hardly surprising. He had spent much of his political career publicly fighting political corruption. As a twenty-three-year-old Republican freshman New York State assemblyman in 1882, he had written,

"A number of Republicans, including most of their leaders, are bad enough, but over half the Democrats, including almost all the City Irish, are vicious, stupid-looking scoundrels with apparently not a redeeming trait…a stupid, sodden vicious lot, most of them being equally deficient in brains and virtue."

During that early phase of his career, he reported seeing bags of cash handed over to politicians to kill legislation that might have adversely affected business. He described powerful Republican leader John Rains as a man who had "the same idea of public life and civil service that a vulture has of dead sheep."

Ironically, this fight against corruption had indirectly led him to the White House. He had won election as New York State's Progressive governor in 1898, and only two years later practically had been forced to run for vice president with President McKinley by New York state political leaders who desperately wanted to replace him in that office with a more compliant man.

He continued his crusade even after ascending to the presidency following the assassination of McKinley. In a 1906 speech, for example, he popularized the word *muckraker*, which he appropriated from John Bunyan's 1678 allegory *Pilgrim's Progress* to critique journalists who used their "rake" to dig in the mud and muck. But until William Barnes took legal action in 1914, no one had dared challenge him like this.

As fate would have it, Roosevelt and Barnes actually arrived in the city on that same Sunday-night train, although in contrast to the raucous crowd that greeted the former president, few people even recognized the Albany boss, who hung back toward the rear of the train shed. While photographers were busy snapping pictures of the Colonel, Barnes exited the station unnoticed. Although the two men ignored each other on the platform, there had been an incident along the way that might easily have served as the plot of a nickelodeon flicker. The former president had boarded the train in New York City, settling into a stateroom in car 51—the same car in which Barnes had booked space. No one knew if this was simply a coincidence or an intentional insult, and Roosevelt did not comment about it. Barnes learned of this slight when the train arrived in Albany and discovered his place was taken. He had it out with the conductor directly below what was now the Colonel's compartment, arguing loudly with him on the platform as Roosevelt quietly watched the skirmish from the disputed room. Barnes eventually settled for seats in the adjoining car.

Years earlier, Roosevelt's insults might have been resolved on a plain with pistols or swords, but now civilized gentlemen dueled in the courtroom. The stakes were enormous for both men, and a case of this magnitude, receiving prolific and ubiquitous media attention, would test the public's faith in the American legal system, as well. What had started two centuries earlier as a ragged combination of British laws adapted to local necessities, had developed into the United States' unique system of fed-

ONONDAGA HISTORICAL ASSOCIATION

By 1915 Syracuse was a bustling manufacturing center with a population of more than 110,000. The last stagecoach line in "the Salt City" had become obsolete eight years earlier, replaced by great locomotives steaming through the center of the city and a rapid street-trolley system.

eral, state and local rules and regulations necessary to govern everyday life in this amazingly diverse country. The circuit riding judges and lawyers who decades earlier had brought the skeleton of law to the frontier by carriage and on horseback, when necessary setting up court in barrooms and bedrooms, had been replaced by an organized and efficient structure. National standards for legal training and the conduct of a trial had been established. A great body of precedent, settled law, now existed to guide jurists through the maze of human conflicts that had to be settled in a courtroom.

Respect for the law was central to the concept of democracy, and there was good reason that the most imposing structure in virtually every city and town was the courthouse. Perhaps symbolically, these classical buildings were centrally located on the main street or green, and from the birth certificates to death certificates filed there, the life of the city took place around it.

At issue in this case was far more than just the specific allegations in the lawsuit. For William M. Ivins, the head of Barnes's legal team and a prestigious New York City attorney: "the very existence of law depends upon the determination of each individual to maintain his rights and property when willfully, wantonly, and ruthlessly attacked…" Failing to do so, he continued, "If generally adopted by all men, would mean the destruction of society itself."

Barnes v. Roosevelt would demonstrate that US law had reached its maturity. The former president of the United States, only years earlier the most powerful man in the country, had been called to answer charges no differently than a lowly pushcart vendor. Both sides would be ably represented by several of the most experienced, respected and knowledgeable attorneys in the country, and after all the arguments were heard, judgment would rest in the hands of twelve common men.

William Barnes was fully aware what he was risking by attacking the enormously popular Roosevelt. In fact, he had been repeatedly cautioned against bringing the lawsuit. State Republican leader Cornelius Collins observed, "I warned Barnes that he was dragging Roosevelt out of the political graveyard when he brought this suit. He replied that his honor had been assailed and he must defend it."

While Barnes had never held elective office, as the grandson of legendary political kingmaker and Republican Party pioneer Thurlow Weed, and owner and publisher of the powerful *Albany Evening Journal*, he had become a mighty political leader, serving as chairman of both the Republican National Committee and the Republican Committee of New York State. Always ambitious, there was considerable speculation he intended to follow Roosevelt's model and run for governor and then the White House. A loss in this trial, however, would likely scotch those dreams, while a victory over the revered Roosevelt might well serve as a springboard to a far more celebrated future. But beyond the political ramifications was his personal disdain for the former president. He wanted to make Roosevelt eat those bitter words.

The stakes were equally high for Roosevelt; a loss in the courtroom could forever taint the reputation he had spent his lifetime building, as well as ending any hopes he had of reviving his dormant political career—in addition to the potential financial impact. But if he could win this court battle, the renewed national attention could help him regain his political footing. As Indiana's Democratic *Anaconda Standard* suggested, "The Colonel has reached a stage in his career where he experiences difficulty in keeping himself prominently before all of the country all of the time. But Mr. Barnes helps..." Roosevelt's objective, he wrote to a good friend, was to expose "the most thorough-going and authoritative exposure of political crookedness that we have yet seen." Publicly he claimed absolute confidence, promising his testimony would "satisfy every fairly intelligent and decent man that I am right." But privately Roosevelt was well aware that this was a trial that had the potential to get ugly, and personal.

Roosevelt and Barnes had once been political allies, if not friends, but their relationship had been broken beyond repair at the 1912 Republican National Convention in Chicago when Barnes had maneuvered successfully to thwart T.R.'s presidential bid for an unprecedented third term. In response, he had founded the Progressive (Bull Moose) Party, and as its presidential candidate he received more votes than the Republican President William H. Taft; but the split enabled Democrat Woodrow Wilson to win with only 41.8 percent of the popular vote. Roosevelt's subsequent condemnation of the political bosses who had denied him that nomination had often focused on the ambitious Barnes.

The trial initially had been scheduled to take place in Barnes's backyard, the state capital of Albany, but Roosevelt's attorneys had argued successfully for a change of venue, claiming it would be impossible for T.R. to get a fair trial in a city practically controlled by Barnes's political operation. Eventually the appellate court agreed with him and ordered it moved to the state supreme court in Onondaga County, located in downtown Syracuse.

That decision immediately raised a hullabaloo in Syracuse, then the thirtieth largest city in America with a population of just over one hundred thousand people. This "lawsuit without precedent in the history of the United States," according to the *Syracuse Journal*, had brought renewed national attention to the rapidly growing manufacturing center. The prospect of the generally beloved, pugnacious former president of the United States taking the witness stand to defend his honor and his legacy was irresistible. The Colonel had charged into heavily armed Spanish troops on the San Juan Heights, he had braved the uncharted dangers of Brazil's River of Doubt and stood tall against the great charging beasts of Africa; the prospect of doing battle with antagonistic, slick New York lawyers was, as the Colonel himself might say, "DEE-lightful!" One thing that everybody agreed on: there were going to be fireworks in that courtroom.

It was just about the only topic of conversation in the saloons and barbershops and the churches of Syracuse. One lawyer in town predicted, "There's sure to be testimony that will make your hair curl." The most prominent newspapermen in the country poured into the city to cover the remarkable spectacle. Among them were Louis Seibold of the *New York World*, Hambige of the *Times*, Montague of the *American* and Williams of the *Evening World*. The *Tribune* sent three men. The *International News Service*'s nationally known crime reporter, L. V.

B. Rucker, wrote that this trial would be even more interesting than the sensational Kansas City, Missouri, murder trial he had covered five years earlier, in which Dr. Bennett Clarke Hyde was accused of killing his wife's rich relatives with the typhus germ and a touch of cyanide and strychnine.

Throughout his public career, Roosevelt and the newsmen had a symbiotic relationship with each profiting from the interactions. Perhaps more than any previous president, T.R. had appreciated the power of the press to deliver his populist message directly to the nation and had given reporters unprecedented access to the White House, even setting aside space for them, creating a rudimentary "pressroom." The newspapers celebrated his transformation of the presidency into his "bully pulpit," and in return his outspoken character and bold decisions sold newspapers. On some days during campaigns, T.R. would give as many as thirty speeches a day, filling column inches with his always loud and often outspoken commentaries. For the newspapers, this trial was an opportunity to put Teddy back on the front page, and they rushed to Syracuse to do just that. The result was a media furor.

"Syracuse is on the tiptoe of expectancy," Hambige reported in the *Times*, and in preparation the popular burlesque house The Barnstable Theatre had booked the renowned "Big Sensation Company" to titillate visitors. Even the local department stores took advantage of the growing excitement, running ads portraying the proper courtroom attire for spectators and jurors.

The city had spent weeks preparing to host the trial in its strikingly beautiful million-dollar courthouse that had opened in 1906. Fifty extra law enforcement officers had been assigned to maintain law and order. Inside the classically designed "Great Marble Temple of Justice," eight-foot-high barriers had been erected to safely control the expected crowds of spectators. Two thirty-foot-long unpainted planks had been set up on the perimeter of the third-floor courtroom for reporters, and a small silk American flag was slotted in front of each seat. This was quite an innovation. Rather than following the common practice of snapping their fingers to alert messenger boys when copy was ready to be dispatched, reporters would wave their flag to signal a pickup. An adjoining room had been set aside for the score of telegraphers who would transmit these stories, and additional telephone and telegraph lines had been run into the courthouse. One hundred fifty spectators were going to be admitted each day to watch the proceedings—but only if they were fortunate enough to obtain one of the coveted yellow tickets, which were offered to the first in line each morning.

The opportunity to see Teddy Roosevelt thundering in the public arena one more time came as a welcome diversion. The world seemed to be descending into chaos. Americans were becoming increasingly concerned the country would be drawn into the bloody European War. The Great War, which had begun the previous August, had steadily engulfed Europe and was spreading into parts of Asia. Daily headlines reported ominous new horrors. A German zeppelin had staged a daring bombing raid outside London barely missing a train crowded with innocent civilians; near the Belgian city of Ypres, where one hundred thousand men had been killed or wounded only five months earlier, hundreds of thousands of reinforcements were preparing for a second and larger battle. The German government was threatening to attack American ships carrying war supplies for England, and the kaiser's submarines were hunting in the Atlantic.

In Washington the Supreme Court had refused to set aside the controversial conviction of Leo Frank, a leader of Atlanta's Jewish community who had been convicted on flimsy evidence and sentenced to hang two years earlier for the murder of thirteen-year-old Mary Phagan. In New York City a riot was averted when police and private detectives escorted black and white demonstrators out of the Liberty Theatre, where the controversial film-play *The Birth of a Nation*, which lionized the KKK, had been interrupted by irate patrons throwing eggs at the screen. And in Syracuse the headless remains of a murdered woman had been discovered, sparking local fears that a twisted killer might be on the loose.

While President Wilson was desperately trying to maintain America's neutrality in the rapidly expanding European war, hoping to serve as a peace broker, Teddy Roosevelt's disdain for the president and his firm belief that the country should enter the fighting alongside Great Britain were well-known.

As he wrote to the noted Egyptologist Arthur Weigall, "We are cursed with a President who is a timid and shifty phrasemaker; and naturally our people, when they are not roused by their official leader, fail to realize their duty, or the real nearness to them of events in the rest of the world." So as court convened on April 19 to begin the trial, there was serious concern within his defense team that his views on the war could alienate any Germans on the jury and cost him their support.

To make his case, both to the jury and the public, Roosevelt had assembled what he would call a "splen-DID" defense team headed by the eminent New York attorney John M. Bowers. In contrast to his boisterous client, Bowers was a publicly restrained, no-nonsense, impeccably dressed gentleman. His perfectly trimmed whiskers, parted in the middle, and clipped mustache reinforced the impression of a man in complete control of his emotions, an unflappably cool customer whose natty appearance barely hinted at the fact that he was one of the wealthiest lawyers in the country. The fifty-six-year-old Democrat had an expansive legal practice, ranging from defending the *New York World* in most of the libel suits brought against that newspaper, serving as counsel to Third Avenue Railroad bondholders and representing the Sugar Trust against government efforts to prevent it from doing business in Pennsylvania.

His primary second was William Van Benschoten, who had represented Colonel Roosevelt two years earlier, when he had been the victorious plaintiff in a libel lawsuit against the *Ishpeming Iron Ore*, a Marquette County, Michigan, newspaper that had claimed in an editorial that the Colonel "gets drunk not infrequently;" a statement they were eventually forced to retract.

The plaintiff Barnes's team was led by the flamboyant and combative, nationally respected litigator William M. Ivins, who seemed to have been cast as the perfect foil in almost every way for the courtly Bowers. A man not the slightest bit intimidated by Roosevelt, on the eve of the trial he confidently told Senator Elihu Root, who had served as Roosevelt's secretary of state, "I'm going to Syracuse tomorrow to nail Roosevelt's hide to the fence."

The wise Root, who butted heads with the president during T.R.'s 1912 bid for a third term, was said to have responded by warning that "I know Roosevelt and you want to be very sure it's Roosevelt's hide that you get on that fence."

Ivins's brilliant legal career had spanned more than four decades, stretching all the way back to the sensational 1875 Tilton-Beecher trial, in which progressive leader Theodore Tilton sued Reverend Henry Ward Beecher, the most celebrated Protestant minister in the country, for adultery and alienation of affections, claiming he had enjoyed an undefined relationship with his wife. The six-month-long trial, during which Ivins served as secretary to Judge Neilson, was likely the last civil case to rival *Barnes v. Roosevelt* in terms of national interest. Eventually Beecher was cleared le-

ONONDAGA HISTORICAL ASSOCIATION

On April 19, 1915, a supportive crowd turned out to join the beloved former American president as he walked confidently to the courthouse to begin his epic battle to save his reputation.

ONONDAGA HISTORICAL ASSOCIATION

Plaintiff William Barnes (center) risked the ire of regular Republicans by providing the politically damaged Roosevelt a national platform, putting him back on the nation's front pages. But Barnes's reputation and his own political ambitions were also at stake.

gally, if not in the mind of the public, and returned to his post in New York's Plymouth Church. Ivins had learned a lot from that notorious trial, and had put his experience to use in many other high-profile trials, as well.

Barnes had complete confidence in Ivins, who had successfully represented him in a previous case in which his political methods had been questioned. In fact, according to newspaper editor Joseph Bucklin Bishop, Barnes had actually "been induced to bring the suit (by Ivins) who had assured him that he would be able to produce evidence that would drive Roosevelt forever from political life."

The heavyset Ivins cut a memorable figure in the courtroom; his daily garb was as unpredictable as his manner. In fact, he was humorously described as "meticulously overdressed," to the point that he might just as easily appear wearing a black cutaway coat and vest with dark striped trousers as a casual suit with a spotted pattern and patched pockets. More often he appeared with a brightly colored cravat secured with an emerald pin rather than a tie above his winged collar, and matching spats. But no matter what dress he wore, his head always was covered with a distinctive pope-like skullcap, which was strictly a fashion choice.

Ivins was renowned for his ready wit, which often appeared as sarcasm during his legendary cross-examinations. He was said to be fluent in six languages and possess a working knowledge of philosophy, finance and foreign affairs. Asked by reporters before the trial how he might describe himself, he claimed that he hadn't seen a baseball game in four decades yet still knew the batting average of every player during that span, that he hadn't been to a horse race but still knew the record of every horse. As for recreation, he said with a twinkle in his eye, "Getting goats." Like Roosevelt's, was the clear implication.

The sixty-four-year-old Ivins was also an experienced politician; he had held several elective offices and had once run unsuccessfully for mayor of New York. A lifelong Republican, and self-proclaimed reformer who had waged a decades-long fight against election fraud by advocating the secret ballot. Although his health was faltering, far more than anyone was aware, he embraced this opportunity. Theodore Roosevelt was a worthy adversary, and he cherished this challenge to bring the great man to ground. His clear intention was to tear open Roosevelt's political career and decimate his reputation.

Ivins's chief lieutenant was the rotund former district attorney for Onondaga County, William L. Barnum. "Large, ponderous and businesslike," described the *Syracuse Herald*, "he would try a suit between a couple of Czars or Kings with no more emotion than a case involving ownership of a tomcat." In contrast to Ivins, who would often take a cleverly circuitous route to home in on his point, Barnum attacked witnesses with the subtlety of a Jack Johnson roundhouse.

The task of maintaining control of this array of characters fell to Judge William S. Andrews. Like both Roosevelt and Barnes, Judge Andrews, the son of the former New York State Chief Judge Charles Andrews, was a Harvard man; he actually was a classmate of the Colonel, although his ability to fairly preside was never in question. He had first been elected to the state supreme court in 1900, and after fifteen years on the bench and more than two thousand trials, at least ten of them capital murder cases, he was considered the leading jurist in the region, respected for his broad knowledge of the law and his ability to apply it evenly and without drama. Lawyers not involved in specific cases were said to sit in his courtroom just for the pleasure of seeing him strip away "legal verbiage and confusing technicalities" to get right at the heart of a case. He was also known to have a quick gavel. Lawyers knew they had to be sharp in Judge Andrews's courtroom; while he might give them some sway to wander through legal points, two bangs of his gavel instantly brought them back to boundaries. Most often he sat on the bench with that gavel in his hand, tapping it lightly on his chin as he listened to the proceedings, ready to pounce when required.

In describing his serious and somber demeanor, the *Herald* wrote, "He drives his own automobile and enjoys that, and when he first owned his car, he studied its mechanism and its workings as though it had been a lawsuit which had come before him for decision." The judge was an avid reader of history and his wife, Mary Raymond Shipman Andrews, was among the best-known writers in the nation. Her work appeared often in *Scribner's Magazine* and her book, *The Perfect Tribute*, a fictional account of Lincoln writing the Gettysburg Address, was one of the most popular books about the president ever published.

The statement at issue in this case was issued by Roosevelt to the media in July 1914 in support of the candidacy of Harvey Hinman for governor, running on a nonpartisan ticket, and subsequently was published in hundreds of newspapers throughout the country. The rancor between Roosevelt and Barnes had been building for years as they battled to control the Republican Party, but it was just as much a clash of political philosophy. T.R. was a progressive, believing that power should be vested in the people and exercised on their behalf by the politicians they elect; conversely, Barnes felt strongly that a highly structured political system, run by so-called bosses, best served the people.

New York state politics was essentially controlled by party bosses who demanded—and generally received—total loyalty to their organization. Barnes's grandfather Thurlow Weed had helped create the Republican Party and, although William Barnes had never been elected to any political office, he had fully embraced his inherited leadership position. Conversely, the opposition Democrats were tightly run by Tammany Hall, whose "Grand Sachem," William "Boss" Tweed, had used his unrivaled political power to become the third largest landowner in New York.

Barnes and Roosevelt had clashed over then–state committeeman Barnes's patronage requests during Roosevelt's brief term as New York's governor. During Roosevelt's second presidential term, they fought bitterly over his strong support for a direct primary bill backed by his fifth cousin, the Democrat state senator Franklin D. Roosevelt, that would allow New York State voters to choose candidates for office rather than having them selected by the party officials. Supposedly under Barnes's direction, the Republican-led legislature twice defeated the proposal. Their feud escalated in 1910, when Roosevelt returned from an African safari, wrested control of the Republican Party from Barnes and successfully gained the New York gubernatorial nomination for his candidate.

It was impossible to know it at that moment, when T.R. seemed to be regaining his hold on power, but this would be his last great political victory. Barnes got his revenge in 1912 when he was instrumental in denying Roosevelt's bid for the Republican presidential nomination. That had led Roosevelt to found the Bull Moose Party, which championed causes like campaign finance restrictions, an eight-hour workday, child labor laws, a social insurance policy, trust-busting and even women's suffrage.

Although the Progressives aligned themselves with the Republican Party, its platform promised to drain power from the bosses. The third battle for party supremacy between Roosevelt and Barnes took place at the Republican state convention two years later, when Barnes's candidate thrashed Roosevelt's choice in the fight to be the party's nominee for governor.

In his endorsement of the independent-minded Harvey Hinman, Roosevelt gathered reporters at his home at Oyster Bay, Long Island, and bitterly attacked the prevailing power structure with remarks that ultimately led to the lawsuit:

"In New York State, we see at its worst the development of a system of bi-partisan boss rule…"

It was classic T.R., letting loose his beliefs in a manner that few other politicians would dare, but with the frankness that had long endeared him to the public. In addition to referring to this "invisible government of the party bosses," he specifically cited Barnes, claiming, "In New York State the two political machines are completely dominated, the one by Mr. Barnes, the other by Mr. Murphy." This stench in state government, he continued, "is directly due to the dominance in politics of Mr. Murphy and his sub-bosses, acting through entirely subservient agents as Governors Dix and Glynn, aided and abetted when necessary by Mr. Barnes and the sub-bosses of Mr. Barnes.

"Mr. Murphy and Mr. Barnes are of exactly the same moral and political type. Not one shadow of good comes from the substituting of one for the other in control of our government. Not one shadow of good comes from perpetuating a governmental see-saw, with first one of them and then the other at the upper end of the plank, while the function of the people of the state is limited to serving as the trestle across which the plank is laid.

"The interests of Mr. Barnes and Mr. Murphy are fundamentally identical, and when the issues between popular rights and corrupt and machine ruled government is clearly drawn the two bosses will always be found fighting on the same side openly or covertly, giving one another such support as can with safety be rendered. These bosses do not hold public office themselves. They act through the holders of public office whom they control.

"Yet they form the all-powerful invisible government which is responsible for the maladministration and corruption in the public offices of the state. By means of electing officers…whose fundamental weakness or insecurity and double-dealing renders them fit instruments through whom the machine masters can work, these machine masters secure the appointment to offices of these evil men, whose activities so deeply taint and discredit our whole government system.

"It is idle for a man to pretend that he is against machine politics unless he will, with straight forward good faith, openly and by name attack Mr. Barnes and Mr. Murphy and pledge himself to do all he can to eliminate them from the control of political affairs, and in destroying them to destroy the system which renders possible such pernicious activities as theirs.

"We Progressives are pledged to work disinterestedly for the good of the whole people…for the overthrow of the two corrupt and boss ruled machines that disgrace the political life of New York State."

Charles "Silent Charlie" Murphy, the Democratic boss then busily transforming Tammany

Hall into a more progressive organization, simply ignored the broadside. Initially Barnes did too, dismissing it as a "diatribe." But by the next day he had changed his mind, perhaps at the urging of Ivins, and eventually served T.R. with a libel lawsuit demanding $50,000 in damages. "When an issue of this kind is raised by a person of such prominence one has but two courses: to enter into an unseemly personal controversy or to appeal to the courts, in order to enable the person who utters the libel the opportunity to produce legal evidence.

"I deny," said Barnes, "the truthfulness of every statement made by Mr. Roosevelt in his publication."

Although there was no explanation of how the $50,000 figure was arrived at, it clearly was meant to emphasize that this was a significant matter, and the alleged libel was serious and harmful. In reality, should Barnes prevail it would be up to the jury to decide the damages. Roosevelt claimed to welcome the lawsuit, responding confidently, "This will give me the chance to put on record under oath in court proceedings far worse matter about Barnes than I have dreamed about putting out on the stump." And he understood completely that this was intended to be a direct challenge to those political beliefs he had defended his entire life. As he told his son Kermit, "If anyone cares to look at it some years hence, when the bitterness had died down" this trial would completely vindicate those beliefs.

The case began with a substantial number of pretrial motions. To buttress his case Ivins demanded from Roosevelt copies of tens of thousands of letters, articles and even books that T.R. had written or received throughout his career covering a vast number of subjects. While seemingly an innocuous request for evidence, what Ivins really intended to do was use these letters to pry into Roosevelt's private dealings throughout his political career, publicly exposing potentially embarrassing or hypocritical words, actions and decisions in an effort to prove that Roosevelt was no less a political survivor than Barnes or Murphy or any boss.

The fact was that Roosevelt was a prodigious letter writer; he estimated that throughout his career he had written as many as one hundred fifty thousand letters. But he didn't flinch at this request; rather, he seemed to welcome it. In 1912, when he was making his run for president as the Bull Moose candidate, the legendary publisher William Randolph Hearst claimed that he had in his possession letters written by T.R. that would prove very damaging if made public. T.R. responded in typically brash fashion, challenging anyone to produce anything he had ever written that he would not want the public to read. Hearst backed down and never produced any letters. In response to Ivins's demand, the defense handed over so much correspondence that an entire room in the courthouse had to be set aside to store and examine them.

The defense filed a 105-page brief asking that the case be dismissed, making an array of legal arguments including that the statement did not defame Barnes personally but only attacked him in his role broadly as a political figure. "The only reference to Mr. Barnes," Bowers wrote, "was such as there was a fair and plausible reason for making, and such reference was made in the course of proper and appropriate criticism concerning the manner in which the affairs of the State Government had been conducted."

It was a well-reasoned brief, citing numerous cases and making important legal points. It addressed a basic preliminary question: Was the statement made and issued by Roosevelt a legally actionable attack on Barnes? Judge Andrews would rule on it after the trial had begun, a ruling that would either end the trial at that point or support the plaintiff's contention that he had been legally maligned. The questions about the scope of the lawsuit, possible damages and even whether the statements were true would only come if, and when, the judge determined the case should move forward.

While technical in nature, the legal ruling would be the first key decision of the trial; it would dictate the legal strategy that each side had to follow and set a tone. But few believed the judge would end the case at that point. The former president of the United States, one the nation's most beloved citizens, had made a direct attack on its political system and one of its leaders. This was a case, a debate, that was going to be tried in a courtroom in Syracuse, New York, and on America's front pages.

CHAPTER TWO

The right of a man to protect and defend his good name was one of the first precepts of settled British law. More than four hundred years ago Shakespeare wrote in *Othello*, "Good name in man and woman, dear my lord, Is the immediate jewel of their souls: Who steals my purse steals trash; 'tis something, nothing; 'twas mine, 'tis his, and has been slave to thousands; But he that filches from me my good name, Robs me of that which not enriches him, And makes me poor indeed."

Long before Shakespeare wrote those immortal words, the value of a man's reputation or that of a woman was considered worthy of legal protection. Slander, defaming an individual through spoken words or gestures, especially members of the ruling classes, was considered "scandalum magnatum" and subject to royal penalty as early as the thirteenth century in England.

Libel was generally defined as "any published or written statement likely to harm a person's reputation," or by extension their livelihood. In either slander or libel, the statement itself was the crime; the truth of the matter was not considered a defense. Until the sixteenth century, these cases most often were tried in an ecclesiastic court. The defendant, the "sinner," would wrap himself in a white shroud and while holding a candle, kneel and acknowledge in the presence of a priest, parish wardens and the offended party that he had brought "false witness" and beg the pardon of the claimant and absolution from the priest. These cases were entered in the official records of the court, which through the centuries proved to be a valuable historical source.

Libel was considered an extremely serious charge. In the 1630s, only a few decades after the Bard wrote those words, a Puritan English politician and lawyer, William Prynn, published *Histriomastix*, a book taken to be a libelous attack on Queen Henrietta Maria, the wife of Charles I. For this offense the court of the Star Chamber, an official body that had been formed to protect and affirm royal authority, sentenced him to spend the rest of his life in prison, to be pilloried and fined £5000, to have both of his ears lopped off and later to be branded on his cheeks, S.L., meaning seditious libeler.

British law stood firm in the American colonies until 1735, when a German immigrant named John Peter Zenger was accused of libeling the governor of New York, Sir William Cosby. In fact, Zenger did not write the anonymous attack on Cosby, he simply printed it in his *New York Weekly Journal*. In that trial the judge cited as precedent the 1605 case in which Lewis Pickering was tried for libeling the Archbishop of Canterbury in a satirical poem, quoting the existing law, "it is not material whether the libel be true."

In a surprise maneuver, the most famous lawyer in the colonies, Andrew Hamilton of Philadelphia, replaced Zenger's court appointed attorney after the trial had begun. Although the judge remained adamant that the jury could consider only whether or not Zenger had published the libel, Hamilton made an impassioned plea that the foundation of all freedoms is the right to speak the truth, declaring, "It is a right which all freemen claim, and are entitled to complain when they are hurt; they have a right publicly to remonstrate the abuses of power in the strongest terms, to put their neighbors upon their guard against the craft or open violence of men in authority, and to assert with courage the sense they have of the blessings of liberty, the value they put upon it, and their resolution at all hazards to preserve it as one of the greatest blessings heaven can bestow."

When warned that he was going too far, Hamilton slyly averred, "All men agree that we are governed by the best of kings, and I cannot see the meaning of Mr. Attorney's caution; my well known principles, and the sense I have of the blessings we enjoy under His present Majesty, makes it impossible for me to err, and I hope, even to be suspected, in that point of duty to my King… I beg leave to insist that the right of complaining or remonstrating is natural; and the restraint upon this natural right is the law only, and those restraints can only extend to what is false… Truth ought to govern the whole affair of libels."

Under the law, Zenger clearly was guilty; he had published the attack and Hamilton admitted as much but appealed to the jury, "It is not the cause of one poor printer, but the cause of liberty," that they were deciding. It took them less than ten minutes to vote to acquit Zenger, taking another step in creating a truly American jurisprudence.

While the elusive definition of exactly what constituted a libel or defamation varied from state to state, the acceptance of truth as a proper defense became a standard in 1803. A twenty-two-year-old Federalist editor named Harry Croswell was charged in New York State with criminal libel and sedition for publishing a series of articles attacking President Thomas Jefferson and other prominent politicians, essentially claiming the president had supported a smear campaign against George Washington. Even decades after the Zenger decision, simply publishing these accusations was a criminal act, and Croswell was declared guilty. He appealed that verdict to the state's highest court, and Alexander Hamilton agreed to defend him. Hamilton argued, "The liberty of the press consists in the right to publish, with impunity, truth, for good motives, for justifiable ends, though reflecting on government, magistracy or individuals… That the allowance of this right is essential to the preservation of a free government; the disallowance of it fatal.

"That the doctrine of excluding the truth, as immaterial, originated in a tyrannical and polluted source, in the court of Star Chamber; and though it prevailed a considerable length of time, yet there are leading precedents down to the revolution, and ever since, in which a contrary practice prevailed." The high court judges deadlocked on Croswell's appeal and his conviction stood, although he was never sentenced or retried for the offense. But a year later the New York State legislature transformed Hamilton's appeal into state law, finally abandoning the British precedent that truth was not a defense. Other states and eventually the federal government adopted Hamilton's doctrine, establishing the legal proposition that a truthful statement cannot be an actionable libel.

As civil law developed, and dueling was outlawed, libel cases became more common. Among the most celebrated was the 1901 case, *Cherry v. Des Moines Leader*. The singing Cherry Sisters were reputed to be the worst act in vaudeville, so bad that before coming on stage they would raise a protective fishnet to catch thrown fruits and vegetables. But when the *Leader* wrote in a scathing review, "The mouths of their rancid features opened like caverns, and sounds like the wailings of damned souls issued there from," they sued for libel. After watching the sisters perform their act in the courtroom, the judge ruled the review was fair comment and protected by the First Amendment. "Surely," decided the judge, "if one makes himself ridiculous in public performances he may be ridiculed by those whose duty or right it is to inform the public…"

From 1904 to 1910 sure-shooter Annie Oakley pursued fifty-five different libel suits, accusing newspapers of reporting she had been imprisoned for stealing money to feed a cocaine addiction. She won or settled fifty-four of them, with estimates of her total payment ranging from $250,000 to $800,000.

In 1907 a muckraking article in *Collier's Weekly* magazine questioned Postum Cereal's claim that Grape-Nuts could cure appendicitis. When founder C. W. Post responded by questioning the sanity of the author of that piece, *Collier's* sued for libel. Post won the case on appeal, but stopped making that claim.

Teddy Roosevelt himself had been involved in two previous libel suits before arriving in Syracuse. In 1908 the *New York World* published a report that a syndicate of Americans, among them relatives of both Roosevelt and President Taft, had received a portion of the $40,000,000 the United States had paid to the French canal company for the land that became the Panama Canal. T.R. vehemently denied it, calling it an "abominable falsehood"; and attacking the newspapers who had republished the story, writing, "The most corrupt financiers, the most corrupt politicians are no greater menace to the country than the newspapermen of the type I have described."

The *World* responded by demanding a "full and complete investigation…" to discover "who got the money," claiming "Theodore Roosevelt…issued a public statement…full of flagrant untruths, reeking with misstatements…"

The furious T.R. called it "a libel upon the United States government" and ordered the attorney general to bring criminal libel charges against the *World* and the *Indianapolis News* in Washington, DC, based on the theory that those papers were distributed there. The litigation was widely viewed as an assault on the First Amendment. "It is the duty of a newspaper to print the news and tell the truth about it," wrote US District Judge Anderson, throwing out the case. "If the history of liberty means anything—if constitutional guarantees are worth anything—this proceeding must fail."

But Roosevelt wouldn't give up, instructing the US attorney from New York's Southern District to bring criminal libel charges against the Press Publishing Company, which published the *World*, and the paper's editor. Many were shocked by Roosevelt's persistence, believing his action to be a direct assault on the fundamental right of the free press and a great danger to the Bill of Rights. It was a bizarre indictment; using language taken directly from the notorious and maligned Sedition Act of 1798 it accused the *World* of attempting to "stir up disorder among the people." The court described the charge as "a novelty," and agreed with the *World* that no federal libel law existed and threw out the case.

The government even appealed the case to the United States Supreme Court. Almost a year later that court agreed with the lower court that the indictment was not authorized by any statute of the

United States and once again dismissed the case. "The decision of the court," sneered the *World*, "yet leaves unanswered the question: Who got the money?" With the end of that lawsuit the *World*'s charges were never confirmed nor disproved.

The Colonel's second libel suit had a far more satisfying outcome for him. For a long time there had been persistent rumors that T.R. had a serious drinking problem. When an Upper Peninsula, Michigan, newspaper, the *Ishpeming Iron Ore*, reported during the 1912 campaign, "Roosevelt lies, and curses in a most disgusting way, he gets drunk too, and that not infrequently, and all of his intimates know about it," he decided to rid himself of that rumor forever and sued for libel.

The headlines created when he filed that lawsuit were magnified, since they came at about the same time an attacker shot him as he prepared to deliver a speech in Milwaukee; the bullet was slowed by passing through T.R.'s steel glasses case and the folded speech in his breast pocket, but lodged in his ribs. The description of the wounded former president still delivering his speech added to his legend.

That libel trial eventually dominated the news. Numerous witnesses—including newspaper reporters who had spent years covering Roosevelt—testified they had never seen him drunk. Roosevelt spent several entertaining days on the witness stand essentially regaling spectators with tales of his great adventures, all of them culminating in the claim that his favorite beverage was milk.

The *Iron Ore* publisher offered no defense, instead

admitting they were wrong. Rather than punishing the paper, Roosevelt stood up and asked for the least possible damages; he was awarded six cents. That was sufficient, he said, as long as his reputation had been restored. When asked as he left the courtroom how he intended to spend his award, he cheerfully responded, "That's about the price of a *good* newspaper!"

That trial served as a warm-up act for *Barnes v. Roosevelt.* A national audience anticipated hearing Teddy once more candidly telling his stories when he took the stand. This time though, the tables were turned and Roosevelt was the accused. While some Syracusans were entranced by the magician Hang Ping Chien then performing at the Temple Theatre, the greatest show in town was about to begin at the new courthouse.

On the morning of April 19, 1915, a large crowd greeted Roosevelt as he left his trial headquarters in the Onondaga Hotel and walked with him in what was described as a "sort of triumphant procession" to the courthouse entrance. The unmistakable click-clicking of Kodak cameras and shouts of support were heard as an unusually subdued T.R. climbed the steps to the State Street entrance. Given a choice of seating reserved for counsel, he settled at the table nearest the empty jury box and put on his thick spectacles.

Barnes arrived several minutes later, dressed in an impeccably tailored blue suit and sat down about ten feet and slightly behind Roosevelt. He gazed at

ONONDAGA HISTORICAL ASSOCIATION

The opposing counselors, William M. Ivins (left) for the plaintiff, Barnes, and John M. Bowers for Roosevelt's defense, here nattily turned out for court, were among the most respected attorneys in the nation, and were known for their keen intellect and biting wit.

ONONDAGA HISTORICAL ASSOCIATION

The $1.2 million "Great Marble Temple of Justice," Onondaga County's fourth courthouse, which had opened in 1907, received national recognition as "a great public structure built without scandal or graft." It took almost five years to build and covered an acre of downtown real estate.

T.R., who set the tone that would exist through the next several weeks by completely ignoring him.

Ivins came in separately, wearing his black silk skullcap and accompanied by his striking secretary, Miss Cassie Doran, the only woman permitted in the courtroom well. This was, as she admitted to reporters, the first time she had ever been in a courtroom.

Among the two hundred people in the gallery was eighty-year-old former state senator Francis Hendricks, who claimed to admire Colonel Roosevelt while not agreeing with his politics. Asked about his presence, he said with no hint of exaggeration, "I just dropped in to be able to say that I was present at one of the greatest trials in the history of the country."

The trial began with jury selection. Barnes wanted to keep obvious Roosevelt supporters off the jury, while Roosevelt was hoping to eliminate any men with pro-German sympathies who might have been angered by his outspoken criticism of that country. As was often done, both the plaintiff and the defense teams had added a local lawyer to question the talesmen. The jury pool consisted of seventy-five men from Onondaga County, the majority of them Republican, but among them a smattering of Progressives.

As the questioning proceeded, Roosevelt and Barnes studiously avoided facing each other, swinging occasionally in their swivel chairs, both of them from time to time making a show of conferring with their attorneys.

Outside the courtroom, a sledgehammer was breaking up the street, its rat-tatting sometimes drowning out the questions. Those questions were monotonously similar, repeated over and over through the morning and into the afternoon. "Would you follow the court's instructions as to any and all questions that might arise in this case," William Barnum, representing Barnes, asked a farmer named Burton I. Crego, "without attempting to use your own judgement about that in any way?"

"As near as I could," Crego responded.

"Do you believe you could do that?"

"I think probably, if there was not too much of it."

Another potential juror, Earnest F. Wagner admitted to Oliver Burden, for the defense, that he was German born, although he had lived in the United States all his life, "excepting two years."

Burden continued, "I want to ask you a question or two along this line. I take it that you as a German have relatives in the old country?"

"I have."

"And you are naturally personally interested in the war?"

"Somewhat, yes."

"Assuming that the defendant in this action, although he has been friendly to Germany at all times, has recently taken the stand that…"

As Judge Andrews was known to do, he cut through to the intent of the question, "Has he any prejudice against the defendant in this case because of any stand he may have taken with regard to the war?"

Burden rephrased his question, "Have you any prejudice in this action because of any stand which has been taken by the defendant, Colonel Roosevelt, with reference to Germany's position in the war?"

"Not in the least."

"Or the alleged violation of the neutrality of Belgium, particularly?"

"No, sir."

"You don't happen to know that he has taken a position on that subject?"

"I don't know anything about it at all, no sir."

Wagner was acceptable to Ivins, but Bowers used one of his six peremptory challenges, the right to dismiss a potential juror without giving any reason, to eliminate Wagner.

Although in theory this was a jury of T.R.'s peers, in fact he had little in common with them. They were farmers and woodworkers and trolley motormen, they delivered coal, worked in factories and clerked in grocery stores. A very few of them were financially well-off, but most were working men; people like farmer Ray Tanner, who lived "two miles west of South Onondaga, nearly the same distance to Cedarvale as to South Onondaga, on the large Chase farm." When asked by Barnum if he knew anything about the lawsuit he said, "I have not heard of it at all." He had read nothing about the case but agreed he could follow the judge's instructions.

"If you were informed by his Honor that the article was in fact libelous, you would not undertake to set your mind or opinion as against what the Court might tell you?"

"Well," he replied, plainspoken as possible, "that would be the way I would think."

When Barnum concluded his questions Burden began, wondering, "If the fact that this defendant had been Governor and President, would that affect you in arriving at a verdict in this case?"

"It would not."

Ray Tanner, a Democrat, became a member of the jury.

Henry Hoag was "at present a clerk in a flour and feed store." As questions were repeated fifty, sixty, seventy-five times, Roosevelt and Barnes sat transfixed, knowing that opinions are formed early and may be hard to change later. Unlike most other prospective jurors, Hoag knew one of the plaintiff's lawyers, who once lived in the same town, but there was nothing about that relationship that would prevent him from being honest and fair. He was, however, one of the few jurors who admitted, "I always take an interest in politics and elections." But, he replied, he had followed the careers of both Roosevelt and Barnes, and harbored no prejudice whatsoever and was "in an entirely fair frame of mind between the two individuals."

He also was one of the few men on the panel who had read the offending article but claimed to have formed no opinion about it. Henry Hoag was added to the jury.

Jury selection steamed on through the morning and into the afternoon. As the *Post-Standard* noted, if men exercised such care in choosing their cigars as these lawyers did in picking a jury, "all imitations of Neapolitan ten and five cent Browns would be promptly rejected." Engineer Charles L.

Griffin was the only candidate to admit his political leanings, explaining to Barnum that he had seen the defendant at the state fair several years earlier and that "I politically differ with him…it is the difference between a Republican voter and a Progressive voter."

Barnum asked, "Then you mean by that that whatever feeling there is is because he is a Republican and you are a Progressive?"

"Exactly the opposite!"

"It is the plaintiff I am speaking about."

"I beg your pardon; I misunderstood you entirely."

The spectators laughed loudly when Barnum pointed out, "Nobody up to today has ever accused Mr. Barnes of being a Progressive!"

Griffin was excused.

Ivins used all six of his peremptory challenges; Bowers used four. It took only five hours to select the jury, which consisted of seven Republicans, three Progressives and two Democrats. Bowers was able to get two of those Progressives on the jury after Ivins had run out of challenges. One Democrat was a coal dealer who might well have harbored resentment against Roosevelt for interfering, while president, in a nationwide coal strike in 1902. The jury was representative of the city; consisting mostly of farmers, clerks, grocers, carpenters and a manufacturer who was so rich, noted the *Herald*, that he had come to court in his own automobile!

After admonishing the jury not to read about or discuss the case, Judge Andrews dismissed the jurors. He then turned to the pretrial briefs that both sides had filed, and oral arguments began. Speaking for Roosevelt, Bowers contended his statements were not libelous, but rather "In a sense calling on the voters of the state to rise...to overthrow the power that had obtained mastery of one or other of such political parties, and had used it for purposes against the interest of the citizens of the state...

"That it is the right and must forever be the right in a republic of every citizen to voice his views upon the government of the nation and the government of the state will not seriously be denied...

"Mr. Roosevelt's article which forms the basis of this action was founded on the assertation on his part, based upon information that he had obtained away back at the time when he was governor of this state, that after all said and done the voters of the state had little to say or do with the administration of the governmental affairs of this state..."

Bowers went through the entire article, paragraph by paragraph, sometimes clause by clause, putting an interpretation on it most favorable to his client: it was simply T.R. exercising his free speech. The statement had been made during "the heat" of a political campaign and therefore was privileged, or by legal definition, made him immune to prosecution. The naming of Barnes and Democratic leader Murphy was simply a matter of timing; the same article could have been written in 1898 and would have included different names. There was no charge in the article that either Barnes or Murphy personally had benefited in any way from the rotten government, only that their actions had permitted it to exist. Colonel Roosevelt simply was being a good citizen attempting to advance the cause of good and honest government. His use of the word *corrupt* was not meant to refer to bribery or illegal transactions but rather was an encompassing term used to describe a bad government. "Is it possible," Bowers wondered, "that a construction can be put upon that language that does not charge Mr. Barnes with being personally corrupt… If so, without an innuendo this complaint must fail." Bowers concluded by making a motion to dismiss the complaint on the ground that the article was not libelous, that "it is capable of innocent meaning…"

The judge listened respectfully then decided, "I have given the matter some attention and consideration already… I am satisfied that the motion to dismiss the complaint must be denied at present, and I will deny it…"

No one was surprised. The fact that the case had gone this far already suggested that these motions would be perfunctory, a little bit of jockeying for position, hoping to find some early advantage rather than ending the trial. After this ruling, John Bowers told reporters the entire brief and ensuing argument were only technical, and should not be taken as an indication his client wanted to avoid a trial. Why, as anyone who knew the Colonel would imagine, he was practically chomping at the bit to tell his story! "The motion having been denied," he told the bevy of reporters, "the defense will now proceed to prove the allegations set up in the answer of Colonel Roosevelt."

By that decision Judge Andrews was ruling that the article, by its nature, was "libelous per se" and therefore actionable. Legally, this meant that the burden shifted to Roosevelt who would now have to effectively prove his innocence, one of the few types of cases in which this was true in American jurisprudence.

The trial would be fought over two issues: justification and mitigation. Justification was the core of it. Was T.R. justified in making these charges? Was William Barnes in actuality a boss who ruled over a corrupt government in coordination with Democrat Charles Murphy? Did his actions deprive the citizens of the state of the opportunity to have the government of their choice? Could Roosevelt really prove the charges he made about Barnes were true?

If the jury concluded that Roosevelt had not been able to do so, and therefore his comments were not legally justified, the second issue to decide would be damages. How much had Barnes actually been hurt by the accusation? Six cents' worth? The whole $50,000 that Barnes was asking for? Maybe more? The facts of a case can mitigate, or limit the damages awarded to the plaintiff. A jury is free to award a victorious defendant any sum it decides is appropriate, although the judge can modify that decision.

Mitigating those damages means reducing the amount of money the defendant would have to pay the plaintiff. The concept of mitigation goes back to medieval times, both in criminal and "tort" or civil law. In criminal law a defendant could claim there were reasons he committed the crime, and a judge was permitted to take that into consideration before passing sentence. It simply meant that not every felon received the same punishment. In civil law it at least goes back to agreements made between landlords and tenants in the late 1500s, a century before there was such a thing as a contract. It simply meant that the plaintiff has to take steps to lessen the damage caused by the other person, that for example if land is left vacant, the landlord has to do as much as he can to find another tenant before calculating his damages.

Theodore Roosevelt had grown up in a wealthy home and inherited a significant sum from his father, but had proceeded to lose a substantial amount of it with a bad investment in cattle in the 1880s. Other investments and revenue from his many books had made him comfortable but not rich. If he lost, he could afford to absorb the damages, but it would be painful.

In a case like this one, the difference between justification and mitigation could sometimes be confusing. Much of the evidence T.R. presented to justify his claims could also be used to mitigate damages should he lose the case. Judge Andrews would attempt to identify how the jurors could and should consider the testimony; for "justification," essentially the defense of the statements themselves, or just "mitigation" of damages, but that is a distinction made by and for lawyers, not jurors.

It meant that certain testimony that might not be technically allowed for justification could still be heard for mitigation, a neat legal loophole that a seasoned lawyer like Bowers might easily exploit.

A decision on any damages would involve speculating on the Colonel's state of mind, a trick that very few men had done successfully. Everyone agreed there had never been anyone quite like T.R. and somehow the jury might have to divine his intent. What was he thinking when he made these statements? What was his motive? Was it political or personal or both?

In the end, there would be two fundamental questions to answer: Did the jurors believe the statements were true, and did they believe Theodore Roosevelt about how and why he made them? Roosevelt was the star of the show, around whom all the supporting characters would be playing their roles. Most people long ago had made up their minds about him. It was possible he could avoid losing this trial solely on the basis of his popularity and accomplishments. Out of twelve workingmen, there always would be at least one or two who would support the war hero, the progenitor of the cuddly Teddy Bear, the president who championed the common man. At worst, the outcome would be a split jury. At least that is what he hoped.

To win this case, Barnes and Ivins knew, Roosevelt had to be reined in. Corralled. Controlled to the point of frustration. Their strategy was clear: get the self-righteous Roosevelt angry and agitated to the point where jurors might get a glimpse, firsthand, of how he could make vindictive comments about an adversary. For them, this contest had to be strictly limited to Roosevelt's allegedly libelous statements. These weren't random or general statements at all, Ivins would argue, but carefully chosen insults. Roosevelt could not be permitted to expand the argument beyond the precise accusations at issue. For example, he had accused Barnes of working together with the Democratic boss Murphy; he had to be challenged on that specific claim rather than on a more general statement that their interests had on occasion coincided.

In addition to preventing Roosevelt from transforming into the beloved "Colonel" in the courtroom, Ivins's team had to deal with the reality that people generally believed that politics was a dirty business and that politicians often were corrupt and cared little for the workingman, just as Roosevelt had claimed. That was going to be a hard pull for Ivins, but he had carefully thought out a fine strategy: he intended to show that Roosevelt was no different from any of the politicians he had attacked; that he had survived a lifetime in politics by making the same deals and compromises everyone else did; that from the time he was governor of New York he had often worked with the same bosses he now criticized; that he had accepted without complaint some of the same behavior he suddenly deemed corrupt—and that this newly enlightened position was nothing more than a charade to disguise his personal attacks on Barnes. It was a daring strategy: Ivins was going to prove that rather than a true reformer, Roosevelt was instead just another manipulative politician.

Ivins would stand alone in the spotlight first thing the following morning.

The magnitude of the challenge faced by Barnes and Ivins was on display that evening. After Judge Andrews gaveled the proceedings to a close, a small crowd accompanied T.R. back to the Onondaga Hotel, where he met briefly with his legal team, then was driven to the home of shipbuilder and steel magnate Horace Wilkinson, where he intended to stay throughout the trial. Wilkinson was a close friend and longtime financial supporter who had left the Republican Party with Roosevelt in 1912 and had been instrumental in founding the Bull Moose Party. He was hosting a small dinner party in honor of the Colonel at his home on Walnut Avenue when an estimated four hundred Syracuse University students gathered in the street and with great enthusiasm and affection began serenading his guest with college songs. T.R. delivered a brief speech from the veranda, praising the university's football team and crew, and telling them that while he was not at liberty to discuss the case he certainly wished "you were all on the jury."

Illustrating the dilemma faced by Ivins, the next day's newspapers all reported this impromptu rally while barely mentioning what Barnes did that night.

CHAPTER THREE

A pile driver was already hard at work, loudly chewing up the street, when court resumed. The hubbub inside the courtroom faded instantly as Judge Andrews entered and placed bowls of carnations on either side of his bench. When he was ready, he nodded toward Ivins and directed him to "lay out the merits of the controversy."

In an opening statement, which at various times in history has been referred to as a "declaration," "narrative," "count" or even a "tale," the attorneys for both the plaintiff and defendant essentially lay out a road map for the jurors, describing the case and evidence they intend to present. The tradition of presenting opening remarks goes back at least nine centuries to the Saxons, when the principals in a trial were permitted to make oral pleadings. It's the first time an attorney gets to directly address the jury; an opportunity to make a first impression.

Ivins stood directly in front of the jury box and in a pleasant tone, as if he were speaking with smart friends, explained, "This is an action for libel. The plaintiff in this case is William Barnes of Albany. The defendant in this case is Theodore Roosevelt, of the United States…

"The scope and function of an opening is in reality the discussion," he said, "of what is proposed to be proved. It is a means for preparing your minds for the reception of the testimony as it may be offered by both sides… The occasion on which this particular libel in question arose was antecedent to the primary elections in this state. Who were the parties? On one hand the defendant. He had been a member of the assembly of this state during the early '80s. He had promptly thereafter and during that time become a prominent author and already had begun to exercise a tremendous influence upon public opinion, an influence…larger than that of any individual or single newspaper in the United States… He had already, as a young man established a reputation as one of our foremost authors and one of our foremost historians. His next appearance in public life was as one of the civil service commissioners in Washington. From that office he passed to the office of police commissioner in the City of New York. From that office he passed to the office of Assistant Secretary of the Navy. From that he passed to the governorship of the state and from that to the presidency of the United States. He held that office for practically two full terms…

"During all of this time he continued to be active with his fluent and his very eloquent pen, and became probably the greatest arbiter of opinion in this country who has been known in history..."

Roosevelt sat mostly still, his elbow leaning on the defense table, his head resting against his palm. Occasionally he would write a brief note or whisper something to one of his attorneys, but surprisingly, wrote Seibold of the *World*, he looked depressed.

Ivins continued, introducing his client to the jury. Barnes was brought up and trained in the same collegiate and educational atmosphere as Roosevelt, "in the same spirit of Americanism and public duty." Rather than going into politics, he had become a newsman by purchasing the *Albany Evening Journal*, a newspaper that had long had great influence in state Republican politics. Their respective positions had resulted in them "working together harmoniously in politics."

Ivins spoke in an even voice, neither raising it nor dropping it; he was a teacher simply explaining a subject of interest to his students, providing the background they would need to truly appreciate the information that was to come. The rift between his client, Barnes, and the other fellow began in 1910, when "the question arose as to who would dominate or control the convention that year for the nomination for the governorship. The result was that Mr. Roosevelt secured control of the party during the election of 1910 and secured the nomination of Mr. Stimson... In that election the

Republican party failed and since then…has been out of power.

"In 1912 there was a national election for the presidency." After Roosevelt failed to receive the Republican Party nomination "he accepted the nomination from the newly created or voluntarily arisen Progressive party, with the historical result that is known to all of you, of the great contest between Mr. Wilson, Mr. Roosevelt and Mr. Taft, in which election Mr. Roosevelt's popularity in this country was so great that he did the altogether unexpected and unprecedented thing of securing at the hands of the people somewhat more than four millions of Votes, from a party theretofore entirely unknown, upon a platform theretofore unpromulgated and based entirely on the belief of those four millions of people in a strength, his ability, his integrity, his intelligence and the desirability of having him for the President of the United States.

"The controversy over the nomination in the Republican convention became acute. Mr. Barnes was a party to that controversy." The unease between the two men continued into the summer of 1914, when the various parties had to nominate a candidate for the governorship. Roosevelt and the Progressives supported Harvey Hinman, who was defeated in the Republican primary by the man Barnes backed, Charles Whitman. "In consequence of this the defendant, Mr. Roosevelt prepared or caused the preparation of a statement and secured the publication of that statement which is precisely the subject matter of our complaint."

Ivins then laid out the standard for determining whether Roosevelt had defamed Barnes: "The question fundamentally, the elementary question which is going to arise with you will be this: Are the assertations and allegations contained in this statement true or are they false? If the statements are true, the plaintiff has no standing in court because the truth is never libelous. On the other hand, if the statements are false, the court will charge you with regard to the extent, character and meaning of the law with regard to the question of damages, compensatory or vindictive; that if a statement be libelous in fact, libelous on its face and the truth of it not be proved in detail, substantially, in whole or part, that then it will be your duty, the evidence being before you, to pass merely upon the question of damages, so the matter which you as a jury will have to determine under the rulings of the court as to the admissibility of the evidence, will be purely and simply the question of the truth or the falsity of the statement Mr. Roosevelt then made."

Ivins, the elite New York City attorney, was careful not to speak down to this Syracuse jury, making every effort to talk to them as educated citizens regardless of their backgrounds. The jury focused on the meticulously and expensively dressed attorney as he read out loud and in its entirety, Roosevelt's publication.

Then he continued in that same friendly tone, "Having written it and having done it with that mastery of English which characterized him and which for years has made me respect him as a historian and as a writer of one of the best contributions to American history, his book on *The Winning of the West*, the same character, the same thought, the same calculation was put together with the result of his political experience... That article was published in its entirety in communities outside the state of New York, in places to which Mr. Barnes had no political relation and bore no political duty..." Published in more than sixty newspapers, Ivins contended, with a combined circulation of at least 2,600,000.

Ivins had laid his groundwork, and now some hyperbole began to creep in as he steered this opening statement to argument, showing jurors the harm Roosevelt's statement had done to Barnes, who had dared defeat him in a political dispute. This article "was directly by publication and indirectly by suggestion instilled in the minds of millions of people...by the most powerful and potent intellectual factor then existing in the United States, seeking an attack upon and the political destruction of the plaintiff... When this was done it is inconceivable that any man could have lived under it...in the atmosphere of a remnant of self-respect and in touch in the community with his fellow citizens, unless he did that which the law offered him the opportunity to do, compelled him to do, namely to say, 'Sir, you have made these charges, there is a law in the land, unless the citizens themselves enforce the law, the law itself will die...'"

After almost an hour and a half, Ivins began wrapping up. "You are called upon to consider what…in your own minds is the nature and value of the reputation. The extent which a man may suffer through an attack on his reputation…

"By a mere coincidence it happens that this trial was begun yesterday on the 140th anniversary of that battle (on the fields of Lexington and Concord, Massachusetts), when the shot of the embattled farmer was heard around the world in aid and support of the principle of the right of an individual, his life, his liberty, his happiness, his freedom of speech, his property and the good will of his neighbor. We have come into court…as a duty to society, to make a man who sees fit through his great power to regard himself as the director, the arbiter of the morals of a nation, to substantiate by proof what he has seen fit to say because of the immensity of his reputation and the tremendousness of his influence on the public mind."

Never once during his entire presentation had Ivins looked at Roosevelt, instead making and maintaining eye contact with each member of the jury. But suddenly, having seemingly concluded, he turned dramatically and faced Roosevelt and said in a loud and accusatory voice, "You have made these charges against the plaintiff and it is up to you to prove them!"

The Colonel caught Ivins's hard stare and held it, then nodded slowly in response. His meaning was clear to everyone in the courtroom. That was exactly what he intended to do.

Now the defense would begin. But rather than Bowers, a partner in his New York law firm, William H. Van Benschoten, rose confidently to address the jury. It was Van Benschoten, a graduate of Syracuse University, who had represented Roosevelt two years earlier in his suit against the *Iron Ore*. The *New York Times* reported colorfully that he had "assisted memorably in dragging that hoary and disreputable slander about the Colonel's overindulgence in alcohol into the light of day and squeezing the reprehensible life out of it."

In contrast to Ivins's more scholarly presentation, Van Benschoten adopted a more homespun approach. Rather than a teacher, he was the next-door neighbor awed by the impressive presentation they had all just seen together. "You have just listened to one of New York's best," he began. "I shall not attempt to instruct you as to the law nor go into the complicated questions of pleadings." Why Bowers had chosen Van Benschoten to open the case immediately became obvious. As Ivins had made a point of praising the "embattled farmer," perhaps noting the presence of three farmers on the jury, Van Benschoten began by reminding the jury that he was one of them. "My early training was behind the tail of a plough in this part of the state," he continued, "and those early characteristics which developed in a lad under such circumstances are never entirely wiped away by life in the great metropolis. So, as I come before you at this time to represent to the best of my ability the defendant's cause and his defense, I shall talk to you in a simple, plain and businesslike way..."

As he began speaking, Barnes quietly stood and left the courtroom.

The attorney then began picking apart Ivins's remarks, pointing out that the reason those embattled farmers had risen up was to fight a corrupt government, then adding, "I say to you that I never expected to hear a citizen of this state...declare to a jury that a citizen of our great Empire State had no right or duty to his fellow citizens, to himself, to his children, to his manhood, to stand and declare and urge for good government..."

The difference between the two contestants in this case was obvious, he went on. "The plaintiff stands above all things else for...organization, machine and boss. The defendant stands for the rights of the citizens, the welfare of the people and honest, decent government."

The ability of an attorney to relate to members of the jury at the beginning of a trial often can make a significant difference at the end, and Van Benschoten made a blatant effort to bond with those twelve men. "You and I," he said, "and every other lad of this state were taught in schoolboy days to be proud of the fact we lived in the American Republic, where each citizen was a sovereign and where there was a constitution which provided for a government by the people...

"There is not one of you gentlemen, I know, who cannot in this instant recall the time when you cast your first ballot. I can see your shoulders going back just a little straighter, your chin a little higher, a gleam in your eye. Why? Because it was the identifying mark of the American citizen…

"If there is poison in the government, the people suffer and the citizens pay the penalty… There were some who held office, who coming into certain political control, dictated, controlled, government action to an improper degree, which action too frequently was opposed to the best interests of the people…"

Van Benschoten then began a review of known corruption or mismanagement in the state government in 1914 when Roosevelt published his article: $10,000,000 wasted or stolen in the State Highway affair. The Barge Canal project going $30,000,000 over budget. Scandals in Albany. Payroll padding. Riots taking place in the state prisons. Unfit food being served in the State Hospital. The creation of useless offices by the legislature for patronage purposes. And who might "get rid of this corrupt machine of the bosses, so that we can have efficient, decent government?"

Who else? Reading from an unidentified editorial he continued, "Theodore Roosevelt will return to private life tomorrow with a record of accomplishment unequalled, in time of peace, by any other president of the United States, and with not only the hearty approval of his work and the good will of the people of this country, but also with the respect and admiration of the civilized world."

Judge Andrews interrupted. He had given both Ivins and Van Benschoten considerable freedom to introduce their case. "I have been quite liberal," he explained, but finally he had heard enough, telling Van Benschoten that this was "not quite a summing-up of the case" and cautioned him to confine himself "to the fact." No one failed to understand the meaning of this interruption: in Judge Andrews's courtroom, both men would get a fair hearing. There would be no favors done for anyone, whether he be the former president or a powerful political boss. This trial would be conducted by the rule of law; nothing more and certainly nothing less.

The attorney went on to read the last sentence of the editorial, then revealed it had been published in the *Albany Evening Journal*—Barnes's own newspaper!

As he made his surprising statement, around him the courtroom was finding its own rhythm as all the participants, the lawyers, the reporters, bailiffs and guards, the clerks and messengers, all became familiar with each other and the circumstances. Other than the principals, few of them had ever been involved in a trial of this magnitude.

Van Benschoten went on as long and then longer than Ivins. He traced the backgrounds of Barnes and Roosevelt, seeking to show that Barnes had far more in common with power brokers like Roosevelt than he did the hard-raised and working gentlemen of the jury. In case anyone in the jury might feel sympathy for Barnes, the attorney told the story of an unnamed prominent citizen who had gone to see Barnes to request a political appointment for a wealthy friend, only to be told by Barnes, "I don't want any person who wears a high hat and has

ONONDAGA HISTORICAL ASSOCIATION

One hundred and fifty spectators were admitted daily to the third-floor courtroom, and for most of the trial not a seat was vacant. Ten patrolmen and their sergeant stood duty outside the ornate room to preserve order, with an estimated forty additional officers working crowd control and serving as bodyguards for Roosevelt and Barnes.

shoes blacked, and who obtain pretty nearly what he wants. I want a candidate for this office who is down and out, on his uppers, and has fringed clothes. Then I can hoist him into office and he will be mine."

Then, like Ivins, he brought forth those issues that had caused the conflict between the two men. There were two in particular that had driven them apart: Roosevelt's insistence on taxing public franchises—essentially a tax on large corporations from railroads to water and gas suppliers which had been granted rights and had become generous contributors to the political parties—and his refusal to reappoint a man named Lewis F. Payn to the position of superintendent of insurance. Seemingly small and solvable issues, yet symbolic of the gulf that existed between his client, who endeavored to do the people's business, and the plaintiff who had a much more sinister motive.

Barnes had joined the other bosses of both parties in opposing the Colonel's desire to impose a tax on corporations. New York did not have an individual income tax, and Roosevelt believed such a tax on businesses was necessary to provide sufficient revenue for state government. But, Van Benschoten argued, "such a policy would irritate the powerful financial men of both parties which would be a serious matter. That a political organization could not be managed without money and that therefore the alliance between the organization and certain big men in business, both Democrats and Republicans, was a political necessity."

Van Benschoten hinted at the volatile mix of money and power. And perhaps in this instance, it led to the type of corruption that the Colonel was referring to in his statement.

Van Benschoten told jurors that the reappointment of Payn "was demanded by not only the Republican machine but also by certain big monied men of both political parties, whose contributions in the past had been heavy…" But in both conflicts T.R. won, he continued, the Franchise Tax Bill was passed and Francis Hendricks became the superintendent of insurance. The unspoken suggestion was that these defeats had ignited Barnes's anger, which may have been the reason for the lawsuit that had brought them all together.

And finally the direct attack on Barnes began. Van Benschoten told a damning story illustrative of his power to influence Republican state politics. In 1908, a Republican named William Grattan represented Albany in the state senate. That year a bill was introduced in that body by another Republican state senator, George B. Agnew, that essentially prohibited gambling on horse races. The Republican Governor Charles Evans Hughes had supported the bill, but it was a controversial measure. It would pass or fail by a slim margin. Initially Senator Grattan, whose career had been pushed along by Barnes, told Senator Agnew he would support the legislation. The day before the vote Grattan confirmed that he would be voting for the ban. "So imagine the surprise of Senator Agnew," Van Benschoten said, "when Senator Grattan came to him before the session and said, 'Senator, I am very sorry but I shall have to take back my promise to vote for these measures… Mr. Barnes tells me I must vote against it… I urged him to let me vote for it, I feel that the sentiment in my district requires me to vote for these bills but I am under personal obligation to Mr. Barnes and he wishes me to vote that way and I will have to do it. I am sorry.'"

The final vote was a tie, meaning Senator Grattan's vote would have carried the bill.

Barnes next demonstrated his power in 1910, Van Benschoten argued, when Governor Hughes requested legislation that would allow party members to select candidates for office through primary elections rather than have them selected by party leaders as was the current practice. Naturally, this legislation was "bitterly opposed" by the leaders of both parties, as it would "have meant the destruction of bossism," so they worked together to defeat it. Coincidently, Colonel Roosevelt returned from his postpresidency sojourn to Africa while this fight was in progress and joined in with Hughes on the side of the people voting.

After laying a foundation to support Roosevelt's charges, Van Benschoten directly accused Barnes of profiting, personally, from his political position. The printing industry had been used to generate revenue by politicians since Boss Tweed ran New York City a half-century earlier. Tweed established this questionable tradition by purchasing the New York Printing Company, then ensuring it was designated the city's official printer and stationery supplier, and did the work at wildly inflated prices. Barnes had seemingly followed that same path. In addition to being the official Albany County printer, the presses of Barnes's *Albany Evening Journal* also were used for outside printing jobs. Perhaps not coincidently, the state government contracted for hundreds of jobs, many of them going to Barnes either through the newspaper or other printing companies in which he held an interest. In addition to those regular jobs, the attorney continued, "we will show you also how hundreds of thousands of dollars of taxpayers' money was paid out for wasteful useless printing at prices absolutely outrageous; we will show you gentlemen how during the last 15 years there has been about $3,000,000 paid by the state for printing," much of it for duplicate or completely unnecessary composition.

As Van Benschoten finished his presentation, Roosevelt sat silently in his seat at the defense table, staring steadily at the jury, appearing to listen intently to every word, on occasion nodding in agreement and once or twice stifling a yawn.

"We will ask you to render a verdict, which you twelve men, sitting as jurors and citizens of this state, a verdict fair as between these two men... upon the real issues in this case, and which will show to honest citizens to believe that they have a duty in behalf of honest government, that they will be protected to the full extent of the law, in efforts which they make to maintain and secure to the people of this state the kind of government to which we are entitled and are guaranteed by the constitution and the fundamental principles upon which this State and Nation are founded."

As the veteran lawyer returned to the defense table, T.R. leaned over and offered some supportive words in full view of the jury.

During a short break in the proceedings, messengers scurried back and forth carrying copy from the reporters to the telegraph room. The newsmen had been jammed so close together that when one of them briefly left his seat, he had to crawl under the long table to return to his place. Judge Andrews allowed newsboys inside the courtroom where they peddled extra editions of the local newspapers. And the noise level got so high it briefly drowned out the relentless pile driver.

The judge gaveled the trial back into session and asked Ivins to call his first witness for the plaintiff.

Twenty-four-year-old John McGrath was asked to take the stand. After perfunctory questions Ivins asked, "What is your business."

McGrath said clearly, "Private Secretary to the defendant in this case, Theodore Roosevelt."

The purpose of McGrath's appearance was to prove that Roosevelt had ordered the libelous statement circulated widely. "Did you hand this statement to the newspaper reporters at Oyster Bay?"

"I did."

"At whose direction?"

"At the direction of Theodore Roosevelt."

Ivins then proceeded to read the long list of the newspapers that had published the article, from Barnes's own *Albany Evening Journal* to the *New York World*, newspapers with an aggregate circulation of 2,678,479. To reinforce his point Ivins stood at the plaintiff's table and opened a bundle of newspapers two feet high, consisting of sixty different newspapers from different cities throughout the country that had circulated the libel.

The defense did not dispute that list nor those numbers. The Colonel's statement had been distributed far and wide, which was his precise intention. When his list was done, Ivins startled the courtroom by looking up at the judge and saying simply, "I rest my case."

It was an unexpected, audacious strategy, but typical of the courtroom surprises for which Ivins had become known. He had what he needed; Judge Andrews had ruled the article was defamatory or what the law characterized as "libel per se," and he had proved that it was written and caused to be distributed by Roosevelt. The burden of proving it to be true was now laid squarely on the defense.

And with that, Judge Andrews closed the morning session.

In the corridors during the break for lunch, there was high praise for Van Benschoten's strong opening; people were heard to say that he had "scored points" and even more impressive, "was a good match for Ivins."

When the trial resumed, Barnes, who had absented himself for the defense opening, retook his seat only a few feet away from Roosevelt, but the short distance belied the vast gulf between them.

Bowers immediately made a motion for dismissal, raising two technical points: first claiming Ivins had failed to present any evidence of malicious intent and second that the article never referred specifically to Barnes. Ivins quickly topped him. "I will call the defendant and let him say so."

Ivins calling the defendant himself at this point in a trial was unorthodox if not downright risky. By calling McGrath as his first witness, Ivins had elicited the critical testimony that the statements at issue were made at the direction of Roosevelt. No pushback, no disputes and no cross-examination of the witness. But to call Roosevelt was to also effectively abandon Ivins's mostly theatrical effort to end the trial at this point.

In a civil case, the person suing—the plaintiff—typically would call witnesses that support his arguments but not the defendant himself. When it happens, the defendant would be considered a hostile witness thereby allowing the plaintiff's lawyer to ask the types of aggressive, pointed questions that would typically be permitted only on cross-examination. For now, however, Ivins only wanted to make a limited point.

This was what the spectators had come to see; Teddy Roosevelt rose calmly, walked the few steps to the wooden witness chair and sat down to be sworn in. Only two years earlier the moving picture shows had begun showing brief coming attractions to the audience, especially Chaplin's comic gems, hints of the delights to come. If such a concept might be extended to a courtroom, a legal tease, this was it.

"You are the defendant in this action?" Ivins asked.

"I am."

"Have you read the statement complained of in the complaint?"

The Colonel had no interest in cleverness or equivocation, snapping, "I wrote it."

Ivins stood only a few feet away and to the side, so when T.R. responded he would have to look at him rather than the jury. "You wrote it?"

"Yes, sir."

"Did you write it of and concerning the plaintiff, William Barnes?"

"I did," Roosevelt replied so quickly and emphatically that a ripple of laughter flowed through the courtroom. Even the normally placid Judge Andrews smiled at that.

Having his answer, Ivins rested. "That is all." It

was a daring strategic maneuver; the plaintiff's direct case had taken only seven minutes to present. The point was made: the article was legally libelous and Roosevelt had written it and circulated it. Refuting those facts would consume weeks.

No one was surprised when John Bowers, rather than Van Benschoten, rose to begin questioning the Colonel. Now the issues in dispute would be displayed for the world to see.

Bowers made his point with his first question. "The writing of the article in connection with Mr. Barnes was in connection with the other persons and the other principles that you attacked?"

"It was."

Bowers led Roosevelt through a series of questions intended to introduce him to the jury and demonstrate that he was a man of substantial character, although those facts were well-known: He was Theodore Roosevelt of Oyster Bay, fifty-six years old and a man of family, with a wife, six children and three grandchildren. He had studied the law at Harvard, but had become a writer and a state assemblyman, then went west and "spent much of my time on a ranch on the Little Missouri in western North Dakota for the next half dozen years."

The recitation continued; he had returned and filled several governmental positions until "going into the Spanish War," being appointed "Lieutenant Colonel of the First Volunteer Cavalry Regiment, ordinarily called the Rough Riders."

If this were a show, Bowers was setting the stage;

the Rough Riders had stirred American passions, and this was the man who had led the charge. Ivins objected, calling all of this entirely immaterial, but while there was little he could do to limit this testimony, Bowers was responsive, agreeing to rephrase his question "because I don't care to get into trouble with brother Ivins yet." Turning to the defendant, he asked him to explain what he did in the war.

"We marched on Guisimas where we fought the Spanish… We went forward to Santiago and fought there…"

Ivins tried again, suggesting it did not "bear on the question of character."

Judge Andrews disagreed. "He may state whether his regiment was in any fighting."

"My regiment was in the Santiago fight and lost in killed and wounded over a third…"

"I object…" Ivins began implementing his strategy, doing everything possible to confine Roosevelt's testimony to the charges in his statement, and clearly his wartime exploits had nothing at all to do with that. "…the number lost or killed is immaterial in this case."

While the court agreed, Bowers did not, stating, "I think I have the right to prove that he was in actual fighting and the loss of life in his immediate vicinity and the result of the fighting as bearing on the life work of this gentlemen and upon his character…" And just in case the jury did not get his point, that the man sitting in front of them had risked his life for America, Bowers lamented, "I don't think I have been able, with the objections that have been made, to show the men killed and wounded to the right and left of him."

After establishing his client's bravery, Bowers moved to his political success, leading him through his career as governor of New York, and President McKinley's vice president. And finally ascending to the presidency. "Where were you at the time President McKinley was assassinated?"

While asking his questions Bowers stood at the side of the jury box, which required Roosevelt to face the jury as he spoke. The Colonel appeared quite chipper as he responded to Bowers's questions. There was no question he was enjoying himself. At times, to emphasize the seriousness of his answers, he would tap his fingers together, or stretch his arms over the back of his chair, cross then recross his legs and adjust his glasses. "When he was shot I was in Vermont," he recalled. "I stayed there until we thought danger was past and that he would undoubtedly recover, and I then joined my family in the Adirondacks, at Mount Takawa, and was there when I was notified that he had taken a turn for the worse and that I must come at once to Buffalo."

And after serving as president for almost two terms "I sailed as head of the Smithsonian African Expedition..."

Slowly Bowers eased his client into the matter at hand, asking if he remembered his first meeting with Barnes. Oddly, given T.R.'s supposedly almost infallible memory, he did not; in fact he remembered very little of their early relationship until after his election as governor. After that, he explained, "I saw him very often, meeting in various places but especially in the Executive Chamber at the Capitol, at the Executive Mansion and communicated with him by writing also…

"I had a larger number of conferences with him than with any other organizational leaders, except Mr. Platt and Mr. Odell and certain members of the legislature… They were political discussions; for the most part about matters arising in connection with myself and Senator Platt…the leader or boss of the organization."

Barnes, it was established, helped resolve difficulties between Roosevelt and former state Republican Party chairman and United States senator Thomas Platt. "Boss" Platt had ruled the party for two decades, ending in 1902; it was Platt who had reluctantly agreed to give the returning hero T.R. the Republican nomination for New York governor, but then when he refused to accede to various party requests, had coerced him into the vice presidency, which Platt had expected would be a powerless and largely symbolic position. But when Bowers asked for specifics, suggesting one of those disagreements involved "canal matters," Ivins objected to that "not being pleaded in justification or mitigation, not covered by any bill of particulars. That is taking us by surprise as being irrelevant, immaterial and incompetent. Entirely out of the relation of the matter complained of in the article." If it wasn't specifically mentioned in the article, he insisted, it should not be entered in this trial. This was a key issue that would affect the way the trial proceeded, and it became clear that the judge had not yet established the boundaries.

Judge Andrews responded: "Now, this article charges, as you claim, and as I have held so far, that the article constitutes a libel because of the charges generally, a corrupt alliance between Mr. Barnes and Mr. Murphy with regard to the government of the state." After mentioning some of the issues that would fit under that umbrella if they could be proved, he concluded, "As I understand it, they intend to prove by this evidence that while they were discussing this franchise tax law Mr. Barnes...was receiving for the Republican Organization a contribution from both the Democrats and Republicans... with the understanding that the contributors should be protected by the State Government. Now I do not quite see why proof that that was so, was the fact...why the proof is not at least partial justification of this libel."

Judge Andrews had opened a door, just slightly, that would allow issues not specifically mentioned in the article to be used to support the broadest charges; in this instance Roosevelt's claim that Barnes colluded with Democratic leaders in ways that deprived New Yorkers of their expected options and opportunities.

With each question Bowers asked, Ivins's strategy became even more transparent: object and then object again. An objection is a formal protest that a question was improper under the rules of evidence or procedural law. There are numerous reasons to object; historically, it appears, objections first came into common courtroom usage in British criminal courts in the mid-1700s and eventually migrated to America. Generally, it's a defensive weapon, an effort to keep out information that would be legally improper and, of course, harmful to that side's case. But Ivins clearly intended to use it differently here. He began objecting to almost every question, both to prevent Roosevelt from wandering too far from the facts of the case as well as to make sure the Colonel could not get up a head of steam and develop a rhythm or rapport with the jury. "I object to that. I object to that. I object to that" became a common refrain. If a conversation was cited, he insisted that T.R. must remember exactly where it took place and repeat the precise words rather than simply relating the gist of it. If Bowers reached back to Roosevelt's time as governor, he objected that it had nothing to do with the present. He objected to the phrasing and the content of questions. It was risky, of course, as it might seem overly defensive or just irritate the jurors. It certainly frustrated Bowers. After Ivins had objected to the form in which a question had been asked, Bowers turned to him and asked politely, "In what form would you like the question put?"

Ivins's acerbic wit asserted itself as he replied, "In some intelligent form, if you please."

Bowers proved himself no slouch, responding politely, "I will take your form and then it certainly will be intelligent to the average man!"

Even T.R. was confused by Ivins's strategy, once asking Bowers, "Am I answering you or Mr. Ivins?"

"You are answering Mr. Ivins," Bowers admitted. "I have lost you."

The strategy was wearing through the whole afternoon of the Colonel's first day on the stand. After having one of his rulings challenged, Judge Andrews explained, "That is my suggestion to Mr. Ivins that (his objection) is not important."

"It may become material on cross-examination," Ivins said.

"Well, it is not important now," Judge Andrews snapped.

Bowers tried his own humor, telling Ivins of his interruptions, "I do not mind you cross-examining now, even…"

Like a weary schoolteacher, Judge Andrews admonished, "Now, gentlemen…"

After Ivins's next objection, an exasperated Bowers asked the court, "Is that proper for me to say or not?"

"Never mind that," Andrews replied. "Just give the conversation with Mr. Barnes."

When Ivins continued to object, in one instance claiming there existed no statute with regard to political contributions, Judge Andrews's patience was stretched too far and he said, "It does not need any statute to allow the jury to believe that a contribution made by persons sympathizing with each political party, to the organization of one of those parties with the understanding that the business interests of the contributor shall be guarded and protected by reason of their contribution, was improper."

Still, Ivins got the last word. "If that were the conversation."

The afternoon rolled on, and the Colonel did not disappoint his audience. Weaving his way through Ivins's objections, he found several ways of revealing that the Republican leaders Platt and his protégé Barnes had told him that prominent men willingly made large contributions to both parties in expectation that their business interests would be protected. Barnes had informed him, for example, that one Democratic businessman had contributed to the Republicans "not as a matter of politics but as a matter of business, because he could not have the great interests he represented exposed to attacks by demagogues and scoundrels in the legislature. I believe that the expression he used was that it would be unfair to widows and orphans who had invested in the concerns of which he was head."

In subsequent testimony he continued, "I answered that I certainly would not willingly do any injustice to any corporation; but that if any corporation made a contribution with the expectation that it would receive consideration which… I regarded as improper, that corporation was in error. I think the expression I used was that it would get left…"

If there was any doubt he was accusing Barnes of accepting a bribe—without calling it that—he settled it by adding, "I believe that at least on two or three occasions we went over in substance the question of the contributions by men of one political party to the other political party…and Mr. Barnes justified it on the ground I have given."

Roosevelt spoke in his familiar staccato, cutting his words short, sometimes so sharp it was possible to hear the clicking of his teeth—except when he named Barnes. Then he drew out that name and seemed to stamp down hard on it. The *Times* reporter wrote that each time he mentioned Barnes, spectators "were reminded of the noise made by a pebble dropping into a pool of water."

Ivins's continuing attempts to stop Roosevelt before he could respond were also based on a simple fact: while the judge can strike out testimony from the record, a jury cannot unhear something and those words might well get stuck in their memory. No attorney ever forgets that. So at one point, when Ivins interrupted the Colonel and Bowers requested he allow the witness to finish and then, if necessary, the answer could be struck from the record, Ivins refused. "I don't want it to get to the jury. If you get it before the jury and I move to strike it out, it is there, and I am left, as you said..."

Roosevelt again interrupted to wonder, "Then can I say..."

"No, you can't answer," his own attorney instructed him.

The toll taken by Ivins's strategy finally wore Roosevelt down, to the point where he finally turned to the judge and asked, perhaps as more of a summation than a question, "May I not be permitted to show that there was this boss system, that there was a system of complete control by bosses of politics?"

Judge Andrews's response was a reminder that

this was a trial, and had to be conducted by the established rules of procedure rather than what might be interesting or even what was logical, pointing out, "That is entirely immaterial so far as this libel is concerned." But what he would allow, he explained: "Assume that any information which the defendant received prior to the utterance of this alleged libel which tends to justify that libel in his own mind, that he believes in other words is competent if it is pleaded… It bears on the good faith of the defendant in making the charge."

When Ivins objected to that, a long conference ensued; this was a vitally important point and the full teams from both sides gathered around the bench, some of them leaning on it with their elbows. It was a lively discussion, and clerks were sent to bring back books and papers to support arguments. As it went on for some time, Judge Andrews finally suggested the jury might retire until it ended. While this was going on Roosevelt conferred privately with each of his attorneys, sometimes waving his hands through the air to make his point.

When the session finally resumed, Roosevelt interrupted Judge Andrews's explanation to remind him, with a display of his great toothy smile that warmed the cold marble courtroom, "I haven't yet answered the last question."

To which Ivins reminded him, accompanied by laughter from the entire courtroom, "That is what we are trying to prevent you from doing." Even Barnes nodded and smiled at that.

Finally though, the Colonel was allowed to have his say, and he took hold of the opportunity to recount a harsh and crucial statement. “Mr. Barnes stated that it was essential to protect the big business interests, because unless they were protected they would not make contributions to the party failing to protect them; that without such contributions it was impossible to carry on the organization, and without the organization, without bosses—he used specifically the word bosses—party government was impossible. And he used this phrase,” Roosevelt continued, looking directly at the jury until he held the attention of each one of them then firmly accented each word so its importance could not be overlooked or later forgotten, “‘The people are not fit to govern themselves. They have got to be governed by the party organization, and you cannot run an organization, you cannot have leaders, unless you have money.’” Roosevelt had clearly been preparing for that moment when he could tell the courtroom, and the world, the precise contemptuous words he claimed that Barnes had uttered.

As the first day of testimony began winding down, Bowers had his client recall the early days of his relationship with Barnes, who was, T.R. recalled, “a Harvard man, as I was. I was a great admirer of his grandfather, Thurlow Weed. I regarded Mr. Barnes as a very able man and I looked forward to his developing into exactly the same kind of leader that Mr. Weed had been. All my prepossessions were strongly in Mr. Barnes' favor. They were entirely friendly and continued so during the time I was president. I wrote him continually… I reappointed him twice to office (in the Treasury Department)… Mr. Barnes visited me in the White House. My relations with him were most cordial and pleasant."

Bowers then introduced correspondence between the Colonel and Barnes, all of it cordial and mostly complimentary, respectfully discussing positions Roosevelt would take on proposed legislation. That marked the end of the day on the stand for T.R.

There were several other items that needed to be tidied up, among them the defense request for thousands of pages of State printing records. After Judge Andrews signed such an order, he ruled that the long day had ended.

But for Roosevelt it was just the beginning, with many more days ahead to tell his spirited story to the twelve jurors, and many more days of withering cross-examination that would seek to put into question the man, and leader, Theodore Roosevelt had long claimed to be.

CHAPTER FOUR

As was traditional, the newspapers carried no by-lines. But in the *Herald* the otherwise anonymous "WGM" wrote of the proceedings, "Theodore Roosevelt who was sat in a witness chair in the Supreme Court Chamber is no more like the Theodore Roosevelt of presidential days than a bronco broken to the bit and saddled is similar to the steed raised on the prairie as a wild horse. That is the impression of a study of him at close range in a position the like of which he has never before occupied, a defendant in a damage suit…

"I wonder if he realizes that with all he has done he never did exactly what he was proving himself fully capable of doing, holding his own against skilled lawyers in a position where he must listen to their aggravations at times that must have seemed to him without an end. To me, there was something so pathetic about the spectacle of that man, who for years dominated government through his own will being compelled to look pleasant under the grilling of attorneys who were trying to pry $50,000 out of his pockets."

Columns across the nation were filled with subjective descriptions of Roosevelt, which ranged from "seemingly depressed" to "visibly enthusiastic." But for many people all that mattered was that T.R. was back on the nation's front pages.

Since Lincoln, no man had dominated the American landscape as thoroughly as Theodore Roosevelt. His story was well-known; he had overcome debilitating childhood asthma to become widely admired for his rough and ready lifestyle. Educated at home before attending Harvard University, he had become an ardent conservationist, seeking to protect, and make accessible to the public, vast tracts of land. In 1882, he had entered politics as a Progressive Republican, bringing his commitment to reform to the New York State Assembly. After the untimely deaths of his wife and his mother within twenty-four hours of one another in 1884, he retreated to the solitude of a Dakota cattle ranch, living the hard life of a cowboy. He returned to New York City to become president of the Board of Police Commissioners in 1895, leaving that position two years later to serve President McKinley as the assistant secretary of the navy. He resigned in 1898 to volunteer for action in the field, leading American soldiers into battles in the Spanish-American War.

Returning a red-blooded hero, he was rewarded

with election as governor of New York. By then he had become a national figure, a man of robust charm and boundless energy who had distinguished himself as an outspoken defender of the average man—and woman. After finally being convinced to accept the vice presidency, at forty-two he became the youngest president in American history when McKinley was assassinated in 1901. During his almost eight years in the White House, he had made conservation and reining in corporate interests top priorities domestically, and extending American prestige, power and ideals top priorities internationally.

After deciding not to run for a third term, he had led a Smithsonian expedition to Eastern Africa to gather specimens for the new Museum of Natural History, which had been established and partially funded by his father. On that journey, he had captured or killed more than eleven thousand animals and birds for the museum. Throughout this period he was a prolific writer, publishing several bestselling books. His continuous reinvention of himself, always boldly pushing forward, proved a perfect example of the new American spirit.

After splitting with the Republican party and failing to win the presidency in 1912, he once again began exploring, this time traveling to Brazil where he led a team down an uncharted tributary of the great Amazon, the mysterious River of Doubt. Warned of the potential dangers, he responded, perfectly in character, "If it is necessary for me to leave my bones in South America, I am quite ready to do so."

The trip into the dark jungles proved more arduous than anyone had imagined, and Roosevelt just barely survived; he lost about a quarter of his body weight. The fact that his son Kermit was traveling with him and helped save his life just added to his legend.

Now once again he was on the national stage, and most observers agreed that whatever he was feeling about the trial, he presented an air of confidence as he arrived at the courthouse to resume his testimony on the sweltering morning of April 21.

Judge Andrews had a pleasant surprise for the spectators. As usual, as he entered the courtroom, everyone rose in respect and he bowed a greeting to the jury and counsel. But then he turned and welcomed his father, the retired chief judge, Charles Andrews, who also was clad in a dark robe. The elder Judge Andrews then joined his son, taking a seat on the bench, which was brightly lit by the morning sun shafting through the cathedral windows. Both men had a great smile on his face.

In contrast, Roosevelt and Barnes looked quite serious as they resumed ignoring each other from only a few feet away.

The judge began the session by announcing his decision on the sticky question of what range of evidence he would allow to be submitted. "I am going to hold that while under the general denial of malice in the answer the defendant may give evidence as to his own state of mind, may state,

ONONDAGA HISTORICAL ASSOCIATION

Arriving at the courtroom accompanied by his private secretary and team of lawyers (Stewart Hancock is to his left) on April 21, Roosevelt proved the New York Sun *correct when it chimed, "To Syracuse led avenues, from far and wide. The big Bull Moose again is loose, and in his stride."*

for instance, that when the article was published by him he did it without malice, with no ill feeling or anything of that kind against the plaintiff, yet when it comes to proving independent facts which gave rise to the state of mind or which bear upon it, then those facts must be pleaded."

This was a small but important victory for the Barnes side; Judge Andrews would allow Roosevelt to testify about how he felt and maybe even why he made certain statements—but not allow the defense to try to prove Roosevelt was actually right about his conclusions or thoughts. Bowers objected, knowing this made his task more difficult, and while he lacked the courtroom showiness of Ivins, he was just as resourceful. He had a clever client who would inadvertently, or perhaps even intentionally, try to skirt this confining ruling.

Teddy Roosevelt did not seem the slightest bit deflated by the decision. Rather, he seemed infused with renewed vigor as he took the stand. No one was surprised when Ivins immediately resumed objecting to almost every question, so much so that Bowers drew laughter when he began, "Now I'm going to ask you, and you need not answer the question until Mr. Ivins can object if he wishes to, I'm going to ask you to state any conversation you had with Mr. Barnes in the summer of 1908…"

"I object to that on the same ground," Ivins said.

"The same ruling as before," Andrews said wearily, overruling the objection.

Ivins did as much as possible to control Roosevelt with the only weapon he had. When Roosevelt finally got around to answering the question, responding, "The conversation that I held with Mr. Barnes in 1908 on the question of the power of the boss and on his dominance in the party…" Ivins stopped him. "I object to that."

"Just give the conversation," the judge said.

Roosevelt continued, "Were continuations…"

"I want the conversations and not a definition or retrospective picture of these conversations," Ivins said.

"The witness may give the conversation," Judge Andrews said.

Ivins would have none of it. "I move to strike out…"

The Colonel held out his palms, complaining, "I haven't answered the question."

Even that did not deter Ivins, who said, "I move

to strike out the testimony which has just been given."

Eventually though, Roosevelt answered, and when he did he began filling the morning with stories of corruption and cooperation between the two parties in their quest to maintain absolute control of the government. In his conversation with Barnes, he said, "I raised the question of the dominance of the boss over the governorship...where I stated that the position that Mr. Barnes and Mr. Platt were taking inevitably led to corruption in government...

"I told him that (between the time I was elected governor and the time I assumed office) Mr. Platt had asked me to come see him at the Fifth Avenue Hotel... I told Mr. Barnes that Mr. Platt asked me if there were any friends I wished to receive special consideration on the committees in the legislature. I said no and expressed surprise at the fact that committees were appointed inasmuch they are supposed to be nominated by the speaker and the speaker had not been chosen... The answer of Mr. Platt was that no man would be appointed speaker who did not agree to carry out the wishes of the organization and Mr. Platt..."

The Colonel was animated as he told his stories, punctuating most remarks by rapping on the judge's bench with spread-out fingers, pounding the palm of his left hand with his right fist or thrusting out his chin at the jury box.

The jurors were riveted, their eyes locked tightly on him as he continued, "I then instanced the next conversation I had had with Mr. Platt...he had told me he was glad to say he had got the acceptance of the man whom he considered best qualified for the most important position under me, that of Superintendent of Public Works…and he handed me the telegram of acceptance by the gentleman in question…"

When Ivins objected, demanding to know the name of the man referenced by the witness, Bowers complained that he was doing so "to break up the continuity of the evidence which is being given."

Ivins responded, "I cannot break up the continuity."

To which Roosevelt agreed emphatically, pounding his hand on the bench and grinning broadly, "You surely can't!" Then he burst into his high falsetto laughter and the courtroom rocked with him.

After the laughter had subsided, Roosevelt identified the man as Francis Hendricks of Syracuse, for whom he had high regard, but "I didn't intend anybody to choose my appointee and accordingly I would not appoint Mr. Hendricks… Mr. Barnes answered that the Organization had to be dominant, and that he, and those who felt like him, were going to control the Organization…"

The questioning moved to 1907, when Roosevelt was in the White House and his ally, Charles Hughes, was governor of New York. That year, the Colonel remembered, "Mr. Barnes spoke with me generally on the subject of legislation… stating that Mr. Hughes was urging legislation outside of the Organization; that the Organization controlled the Legislature, and that the Democratic

Organization was in sympathy with the Republican Organization and would join with them in defeating any legislation to which they were opposed that Governor Hughes backed… The plaintiff said that he and his friends had control of the party. I don't recall that he said he, himself, controlled it…"

There was little Barnes could do but sit and absorb these blows. At one point as Roosevelt pulled back the curtain concealing manipulations in Albany, Barnes changed his seat and turned away, so his back was to Roosevelt. At times he grasped his chair with both hands and held on, as if squeezing the anger out of himself.

Ivins expressed it for him, angrily raising his voice and challenging the witness in a far more militant tone.

Bowers skipped between subjects, stopping in any one place only long enough to show through his client's testimony how completely the decisions of government were controlled by the bosses. Concerning the controversial subject of direct elections, Barnes wrote to T.R. in a letter Bowers read to the jury, "When nominations are made they should be final. If the people do not like them they can beat them at the polls, but the members of a party should have the chance prior to the primaries and convention to exercise their judgment and express their will."

The Colonel recalled that the battle over the Hart-Agnew racetrack bill, legislation that would have restricted gambling at state-operated racetracks, had been especially contentious. "They told me that the passage of the bill depended on one vote; that Senator Grattan had favored the bill and been for it very strongly, that he had then announced that he had to change because Mr. Barnes said he must change, and that he hated to do so but that he had to change because Mr. Barnes said he must change, and the change of that one vote for the time being beat the bill.

"It was Senator Davenport and Senator Newcomb that gave me in full the details of that transaction." Those many conversations, he testified pointedly, took place before the publication of his article; contending this knowledge was among the reasons he had written it.

Roosevelt said he first became aware of this proposed legislation in 1911 by reading an article in *McClure's Magazine*, which led to the discussions with the two senators and others. Bowers tried to enter the article as evidence. Ivins had spent more than forty years in courtrooms and knew how to vent his anger; in one great burst he thundered, "I object to the reception of this as being quotations from an article and not the article itself. I object to it as not being mitigatory; I object to it as immaterial, irrelevant and incompetent. I object to it because no foundation had been laid for its introduction, because no inquiry has been made of the defendant as to whether or not he believed it to be true and I further object that if he did not believe it to be true it is not mitigatory."

Despite the multitude of objections, Judge Andrews admitted the significant paragraphs in the article, several of which detailed the collusion between Republicans and Tammany Hall Democrats to defeat the bill, highlighting the comment, "Self-preservation is the first law of the gang."

Bowers then took up the shenanigans surrounding the attempt to pass the direct primary bill. By this time the Colonel was thoroughly enjoying himself; "Riding the witness chair," wrote the reporter for Tennessee's *Memphis Commercial Appeal*, "as if it were a fiery untamed steed." Each question from his attorney was the starting line for another story to be told, each providing more evidence that New York State was little more than a fiefdom ruled by the bosses. During the debate in the state senate about direct primary elections, for example, a temporary adjournment was called and, as T.R. told the jurors, "Republican State Senators went into that room which Mr. Barnes had gone and the Democratic State Senators with Senator Grady went into the adjacent room…"

Senator Davenport told Roosevelt he opened the door and saw his fellows meeting "with Mr. Barnes who was not a State Senator or a member of the Legislature…in conference with Republicans." Roosevelt did not remember the precise vote totals, "but I am clear as to the meeting of Republican Senators in one room in consultation with Mr. Barnes and the meeting of the Democratic Senators under the leading of Mr. Grady and coming out and voting successfully to beat the proposition."

This reliance on conversations with other people brought the Colonel perilously close to presenting hearsay evidence, and Ivins wanted to keep it out. Hearsay is testimony quoting a third party who was not in court and thus could not be questioned about that statement. Generally, it is not permitted into evidence. The decisions Judge Andrews was making in his Syracuse courtroom about the admissibility of previous conversations could be traced back hundreds of years, before America was colonized. As late as the 1400s, jurors were also the investigators of a legal claim; they were usually people who had personal knowledge of the events. But by the end of the Middle Ages that had changed, and jurors had become neutral parties whose task was to judge evidence presented to them; in most cases eyewitness testimony being considered the best evidence. As John H. Wigmore wrote in the *Harvard Law Review* in 1904, "By the early 1600s the jury's function as judges of fact, who depended largely on other persons' testimony presented to them in court, had become a prominent one, perhaps a chief one." Hearsay was permitted, but it was referred to as "a tale of a tale" or "a story out of another man's mouth" and given a different weight by jurors.

The admission of hearsay was called into question in the 1603 trial of Sir Walter Raleigh for treason. The most significant evidence against him was the sworn confession of his alleged coconspirator, Lord Cobham. Although Cobham was readily available to testify, the chief justice refused to call him, explaining in this situation "so many circumstances agreeing and confirming the accusation... the accuser is not to be produced." After Raleigh was convicted and executed, the evident unfairness of basing a verdict on statements of someone who did not appear in court, and could not be cross-examined, led to the exclusion of hearsay in future cases. Although there were numerous exceptions to that rule, the core principle that hearsay evidence may not generally be admitted remained.

Judge Andrews allowed Roosevelt to testify about these conversations he'd had with other political leaders, but only with the understanding that at some point later in the trial his counsel would tie them to other evidence.

When Roosevelt resumed his testimony, he asked the judge, "Am I at liberty to say what Senator Newcomb told me as the reason of his voting for Senator Allds?" This was in reference to Allds being elected president of the state senate.

"No," Judge Andrews responded, "that is not important."

But the inimitable T.R. plowed on anyway, gradually taking control of the entire proceeding. "Senator Newcomb informed me…in 1910 that it was necessary to elect a president of the Senate and official leader of the Republican Party." Roosevelt was trying to show that the bosses in the Republican Party worked with the Democratic bosses to maintain the political power structure rather than pursuing what was best for their respective parties.

"Senator Newcomb told me," Roosevelt continued, "that the machine Senators chose State Senator Allds for that position. That a section of the independent or anti-machine Republican Senators would not support Allds, leaving the machine men unable to elect Allds by their votes… Senator Newcomb then informed me that Senator Grady and a number of the Tammany (Democratic) Senators voted for Mr. Allds…a sufficient number, using his words, of the machine Democrats joining with the machine Republicans, I think he said the Barnes Republicans but it may have been the machine Republicans to elect Allds President of the Senate… with enough machine Democrats voting to offset the number of Independent Republicans that refused to support Allds…

"…so that Allds was made leader of the Republican Party in the Senate by Tammany votes under the lead of Senator Grattan."

Underscoring the Colonel's testimony was the common knowledge that Jotham P. Allds was corrupt. After being elected he had been impeached for accepting a $1000 bribe to vote down a bill and had resigned from the state senate rather than be expelled. When Roosevelt said later that Allds had been thrown out of the Senate, Ivins objected, pointing out he resigned. Judge Andrews told him that the exact cause didn't matter. "This is merely what he told the witness."

"Suppose he put in the first chapter of Genesis?" Ivins wondered, his noted sarcasm on display.

"If it was material," the Judge explained, "as I hold this to be, I would admit it."

Not surprisingly, T.R. made sure he got the last word, remarking with practiced incredulity, "And that after almost all the other members of the combination had abandoned the effort to defend Mr. Allds Senator Grady still made a speech on his behalf."

Teddy Roosevelt long ago had mastered the incredibly difficult skill of speaking to an entire room, and making each person in that space believe he was talking directly to them. So as he answered each question, he grinned at the jury and sometimes lowered his voice a bit so they would have to lean forward to hear him over the increasingly insufferable th-th-thumping of the pile driver outside, and in that way he held them in the thrall of that infectious grin.

Bowers had methodically brought Roosevelt through most of the claims he'd made in his article. More than just trying to show the context behind the statements, Roosevelt, in his own way, was trying to convince jurors that he was right and just in what he had written. He turned his attention to the Bayne Committee Report, a document that reported widespread corruption in the state legislature. Roosevelt had been handed a copy of that report by both his nephew, Douglas Robinson, then a member of the legislature, and his cousin, Franklin Roosevelt, then a state senator. While Ivins objected to this questioning, Bowers contended he would justify the article by showing "Mr. Roosevelt not only believed those different matters that came to his attention to be true, not only that he relied upon them, but that he acted as a reasonably patient man would in accepting them."

T.R. testified that he believed the charges made

in the report because both Robinson and his cousin Franklin supported the findings of the committee: "I asked specifically my cousin, Franklin Roosevelt, who was himself a Democrat, not of my political faith, not a supporter of mine, he also spoke highly of the other Senators..."

Bowers then asked, to make it clear to the jury, "And they, in company with other matters...of which you knew, you relied upon in writing the article in the suit."

"I did."

While the Bayne Committee Report found instances of corruption in several areas of government, Judge Andrews decided to admit evidence only pertaining to those subjects included in Bowers's pretrial filings, in particular the lucrative state printing business from which it appeared that Barnes had profited handsomely.

But the Colonel once again found ways around that limitation, telling the jury that his aide, William J. Loeb, "informed me...that the combination of crooked business and crooked politics, as to which I had spoken as being shown to exist by the Bayne report in Albany, extended not only to a business like printing, but to business of the worst type..."

Ivins was on his feet, objecting vehemently.

The witness replied to him, quite innocently, "I am giving what Mr. Loeb told me."

"You are giving what you said is the worst type..."

"I am not."

"Wait a moment," Judge Andrews interrupted,

attempting to regain control of his courtroom. To Ivins he said, "When an objection is taken it will be taken with me." And then to Roosevelt he said, "When an objection is taken the witness will stop answering until I have ruled on it."

Roosevelt was not deterred. As he began telling the jury about the fight to prevent the Democratic machine candidate William F. Sheehan from being handed the vacant seat in the United States Senate, his voice rose. Roosevelt wanted to make sure the jurors of both parties understood that this wasn't about Republicans versus Democrats, but rather about bosses of both parties entering into an unscrupulous pact to retain their power. With terrific force he lambasted his accuser, letting loose his anger at Barnes. The newspapers reported that the Colonel sat on the edge of his chair, his body taut with emotion as he pounded out the words, "I am not allowed to say that. Mr. Loeb informed me…that he went to see Mr. Barnes to ask Mr. Barnes if the Republicans in the legislature would not support an anti-Machine Democrat for Senator and that Mr. Barnes answered him, saying that he could not do so because his arrangement with Murphy was that Mr. Murphy had to have a free hand in the election of the United States senator."

That agreement, he continued in a torrent, was upset by Independent Democrats, among them his cousin Franklin, who told him, "that in his judgement material progress had been made in upsetting conditions that had so long existed in Albany, by which legislators were only figure heads or pawns, who moved exactly as the boss behind them pulled the strings…

"…he felt that the improvement was mainly due by the agitation by the little group of independent Democrats who stood out against Mr. Murphy, he called him 'Boss Murphy.' And…in the conversation once or twice he spoke of beating the combined forces of Mr. Murphy and Mr. Barnes."

Having shown Roosevelt had numerous reasons to believe and write that there was widespread corruption rotting both political parties, Bowers then set out to prove that his comments were not directed personally at Barnes but rather at his role as a boss. The Colonel readily admitted that he'd had many conversations with Barnes, including after he was elected chairman of the State Republican Party. "I said to him…that as a result of the election I and the people whom I represent were out…that I hoped that in that position he would act towards the Republican Party as a whole as his grandfather, Thurlow Weed, as shown in a letter I had just been reading to Abraham Lincoln…

"I earnestly hoped he would succeed in his leadership…but that in my judgement the time had passed when the Republican Party would submit to a revival of the boss system as practiced by Mr. Platt… That if that effort were made I believe there would be a revolt in the party; that the men like myself would revolt; whereas we would be delighted to support him if he would act in the spirit shown in that letter.

"Mr. Barnes said that he must act as he deemed

best, and the conversation ended." That was, he admitted, the last time he had spoken with Mr. Barnes.

Bowers then entered three additional magazine articles critical of the way business was being done in state government into the record, and Roosevelt acknowledged he knew, respected and had spoken with two of the men who had written them; and as a result he believed the statements contained in them to be true and claimed he relied upon them when preparing his own piece.

Throughout the day, reporters would regularly wave their small American flags to signal a dispatch was ready to go to the telegraph room. At times, following an interesting byplay, several flags would be waving frantically, suggesting, noted the *Times*, "a patriotic mass meeting that fascinated the spectators and, as old fashioned descriptive writers say, 'added a touch of color to the scene.'"

The trial in some ways had been a tour through the recent political history of New York State, and finally Bowers reached the controversial impeachment and removal from office of Governor William "Plain Bill" Sulzer. Governor Sulzer was a populist Democrat who had been elected in 1912 when T.R.'s Progressives had split the Republican Party. Once in office he had supported major reforms, including direct primaries, and refused to accede to the demands of Tammany Hall. As a result, the bosses went after him; among those charges was the use of campaign funds for personal expenses and a salacious claim made by a Philadelphia model that he reneged on his promise to marry her. A frame-up, he called it, and the night he left the Executive Mansion a crowd of ten thousand people turned out to support him. Roosevelt had met him "a great many times," and after his election remembered two conversations about state affairs. "Mr. Sulzer told me that he had discovered that the government of the state was rotten he said, either throughout or almost throughout… That he was being attacked by Mr. Murphy and the Murphy machine, which was aided by the Barnes machine…"

After Sulzer had been removed from office, Mr. Hennessy met with the Colonel "and told me that the condition of rottenness in the State government defied belief, that he could not have imagined, without having made the official investigation that there could exist such corruption and mismanagement in the State government… That there was frightful corruption in the prisons…" T.R. was on a roll, and he ticked off a list on his fingers and held them up for the jury to see. "…frightful corruption in the canal and the State Architect's office, instancing case after case when he would give me names of the padding of rolls where the men did not exist although the salaries were drawn by somebody else, of the charging for rock for roads when it was not rock at all but just stone picked up right beside the road, of the collecting of assessments on the salaries…"

Ivins made an attempt to interrupt him; Judge Andrews overruled and the Colonel just kept going.

"Mr. Hennessy stated that as regards masses of

employees a regular deduction had been taken out of their pay envelope often before they were paid and turned over to local bosses… He informed me that his object in telling it to me was so that we might get up a non-partisan citizens movement… to throw out both the old party machines because he said we could not get rid of the corruption that was eating into the state government until we got out both the old party machines."

"Did you believe his statements?"

"I did."

"Believed them to be true?"

"I believed them to be true."

"And you acted upon them?"

"I acted upon them."

"And you acted upon them—"

"In connection with the other statements that I have received."

"And as bearing upon the article that you have now been sued upon?"

The Colonel said distinctly, emphasizing each word, "Bearing directly upon the article that I published and for which I have now been sued."

After spending most of his two days on the stand defending his own motives, the Colonel was led by Bowers into a discussion about Barnes's motives. What created the bad blood between the two men. Several other politicians were identified and attacked equally harshly in the article, yet only Barnes took action. Also, when Roosevelt beat Barnes's chosen candidate to become the temporary chairman of the New York State Republican

Party in 1910, he immediately attacked the "powerful corrupt boss" clearly referring to Barnes. Yet Barnes took no action at that time. Part of the reason for the change may have been that now Barnes was intent on running for elective office.

As the afternoon wore down, Bowers began wrapping up the Colonel's direct testimony by producing a letter he had received from Barnes while serving as governor in 1899. "Dear Governor," it began. "It is rumored that you contemplate in your message the establishing of a State Printing House. I write you this letter because I presume your message will be a matter discussed between you and our friends tomorrow. It is not my desire to intrude my personal matters upon you but I wish merely to state that the establishing of a state printing house here will be a serious if not a fatal blow to me financially." Signed William Barnes, Jr.

Roosevelt's response also was put into the record, the key sentence in his rejection of Barnes's plea being, "There is a perfect consensus of opinion here that there should be a State printing office."

And in his message to the legislature, the Colonel said as proudly as he had recollected his charge up the hill, "I advocated the establishment of a State printing office." There it was, the first spark of animosity between the two men. Barnes had pleaded his case, and Roosevelt had responded that he did not intend to do politics the old way. It had become personal.

Bowers, finally, began drawing together all of

the disparate subjects he had broached. Still standing by the jury box, as if he were one of them, he set up the pins to be knocked down. "Now in writing this article were you doing it to gratify any personal feeling or were you doing it for what reason?"

The answer was obvious, of course. How could anyone doubt it? "I was doing it in pursuance of what I regarded as the highest duty of citizenship, without any personal feeling whatever, without any malice whatever or any idea of getting any benefit myself from it."

"Did you intend in that article to make any charge of corruption against Mr. Barnes?"

"No," the Colonel insisted in a tone that made it clear no reasonable man would ever believe such a thing. "I intended to state that there was corruption and rottenness in the State Government and that it was due to the dominance of the methods in political life typified and represented by Mr. Barnes and Mr. Murphy and by the way in which the two machines...had worked together at certain points where their interests were in common and adverse to the interests of the public as a whole."

It was 4:00 p.m. With that, Bowers looked at the judge and said, "We will drop the direct examination here..."

There was a stirring in the courtroom as Roosevelt returned to his seat at the defense table, as if a strong tide was going out. Bowers had done a professional job presenting the Colonel's testimony, giving to the men on the jury predisposed toward his client sufficient evidence to reach and defend the conclusion they wished. For his part, Roosevelt had given his audience all the shades of his renowned character they had read about for so many years and had come to see in person; at various times he had been forceful or vulnerable, he had been defiant or funny, and while his memory evinced an occasional lapse, he had never wavered in telling his story. That story included specific explanations for his words that implicated Barnes in some contemptible political bullying and deal making.

There was considerably more work to be done, but so far Teddy Roosevelt had come onto the stage and delivered a bravura performance.

There was a common vaudeville expression known as "Playing to the haircuts." That referred to the last act of the evening, generally considered a "chaser," who performed as the theater emptied so they saw mostly the back of patrons' heads, the haircuts. William Lyon, the treasurer of the J. B. Lyon printing company, was called to the stand to fill that role in the day. Bowers knew no one could follow Roosevelt, so he filled the rest of the afternoon with tedious testimony about the printing business.

Ivins undoubtedly would wage a fierce attack on the Colonel's testimony in his cross-examination, questioning his honesty and his integrity. But before that happened, Bowers intended to further muddy Barnes's reputation. It was not enough to simply defend his client; he also had to destroy Barnes's credibility. Barnes was most vulnerable, he had decided, in his other business activities.

Bowers established that Barnes owned 750

shares of stock in the Lyon printing company, but finally admitted, "I am only wasting the time of the court by keeping this man here." It would be far more productive, he explained, to examine the concern's ledgers.

It was a bit of a cliffhanger; it wasn't quite up to the level of the Saturday morning serials, but it was curious. The courtroom was left with the impression that Bowers had knowledge of some misdeeds that would be revealed later.

It was after 5:00 p.m. when Judge Andrews thanked everyone and sent them home for the evening.

CHAPTER FIVE

On Thursday, April 22, British naval expert Fred T. Jane revealed in Liverpool that the Germans had attempted to land an expeditionary force in England and been beaten back by the Royal Navy. In Detroit, Michigan, the Ford Motor Company announced an increase in the minimum wage for its Canadian workers to 50 cents an hour or $4 a day, while reducing working hours to 48 hours weekly, bringing them closer to the $5 daily minimum wage for American workers. While New York City sweltered under record-setting temperatures, more than 1,200,000 shares traded on the Stock Exchange, with the Dow Jones Industrial Average closing at 71.26.

In the city of Syracuse, business went on as usual. More than a thousand employees turned out seventy-five luxury Franklin automobiles with its unique air-cooled engine. In factories scattered throughout the city, workers assembled the various brands of typewriters that had established Syracuse as "The Typewriter Capital of the World," proudly producing more than half the standard typing machines in use in America. For five cents patrons could see Chaplin in a rip-roaring comedy as well as European war pictures in the "delightfully cool" Hippodrome theater. But the attention of the city remained focused on the courthouse, where William Ivins would begin his cross-examination of Theodore Roosevelt.

Thus far, Ivins had been on the defensive, limited to being a disrupter; but now he would have his opportunity to go at the Colonel with all of the skills in his kit bag. Roosevelt had made his case. Ivins's task was to rip it to shreds, and the only way possible to accomplish that was to prove the Colonel was a hollow man.

One minor change had been made in the courtroom: the small American flags reporters had been waving to attract a messenger had been disappearing, having become desirable souvenirs, and push buttons that flashed a light had been installed in front of each chair overnight.

When Judge Andrews opened the proceedings at precisely 10:00 a.m., the only empty seat in the otherwise packed courtroom was the front row chair reserved exclusively for Francis Hendricks, the revered Syracuse octogenarian, former mayor and state legislator. Guards turned away several spectators who sought to fill it.

Trial days almost always begin with legal bookkeeping; exhibits are entered into evidence, motions are made, procedural problems are discussed. On this morning the defense submitted the articles and reports previously proposed as evidence, to which Ivins objected and mostly was overruled. When all that was done, Bowers recalled Roosevelt to the stand to ask two questions he admittedly had neglected to ask. Most important was the Colonel's personal response to Barnes's plea not to open a State printing house.

Roosevelt retook the stand and smiled toothily at the jury. When he was ready, he jutted his jaw at Bowers, as if giving him permission to ask his question. Yes, he said, he had met personally with Barnes to talk about the fear he had expressed in his letter, but rather than Barnes complaining about the possibility of financial disaster or ruin, the man had argued that "the establishment of a State printing office would be in the line of a populistic or socialistic propaganda that would interfere with private initiative in business, and ought not to be done."

And second, T.R. admitted readily that he had wanted his article spread throughout the state, admitting, "I wrote it out carefully so that it should be carried in full…

"I believed that it would receive some publication outside the state, but as to that I was entirely indifferent…my aim was solely the publication in New York State, so it might be read by the voters of the state."

His questions done, Bowers sat down, and the

much anticipated Ivins cross-examination of Teddy Roosevelt began.

The courtroom was silent as Ivins moved into the spotlight, carefully placing his chair a few feet in front of the Colonel, forcing the witness to look at him rather than the jury, and speaking in a normal, almost conciliatory voice, a tone that suggested no rancor at all, that this was simply a conversation intended to clear up some pesky disagreements. His carefully tailored dark suit was set off by his silk skullcap and dapper white spats.

Roosevelt waited; crossing his right leg over his left, and perhaps displaying some element of nervousness as his right foot began wiggling. In preparation for this encounter, he had given his counsel one specific instruction: they were not to object at all during this phase; he needed no assistance, he would take on Ivins himself.

It was a significant pairing, two men who had reached the top of their professions, bringing their decades of experience to this moment. As pugilists might begin an epic fight, there was some feeling each other out. Like Bowers, Ivins led the Colonel through his personal history: He had graduated from Harvard in 1880. He had studied a year at Columbia Law School but was never admitted to the bar. He was a ranchman on the Little Missouri River. And had spent his life following three vocations or avocations: "An author and a ranchman and a naturalist or explorer." And, when prompted by Ivins, "I have also been an office holder," beginning in 1881 when he was elected to the lower house of the state legislature.

During your years in the legislature, Ivins wondered aloud, "(Did you) familiarize yourself with the Constitution of the state?" For example, he followed up, "Did you…have to consider the constitutionality of provisions with regard to the eligibility of the Governor?"

His initial foray had begun.

"No," the Colonel answered. "Never heard of it."

As Ivins had the witness recount the several governmental investigative committees on which he had served, the inevitable clash of two such massive personalities began. Ivins was attempting to show that rather than adhering piously to the law, when it suited his needs Roosevelt had been a lawless rogue. During an investigation of the sheriff's office, Ivins queried, "Did you see any representative of Sheriff Davidson, permit him to appear before you or call your attention to any of the facts of his administration or that office?"

"Why, our senior counsel was Wheeler H. Peckham…"

Ivins interrupted and demanded loudly, "You can answer my question yes or no, can't you?"

Roosevelt smiled as he responded, "I can answer to this extent, it is a great many years ago."

"Just as many for me as it is for you?" Ivins responded with a bit of sarcasm dripping into his voice.

"Just as many for you as it is for me," the Colonel agreed, as the spectators laughed loudly at this exchange, "and I can only say I employed Mr. Peckham because I believed him to be incapable of doing injustice to any man."

During these investigations, Ivins asked, "Did you as Chairman regard in any way the rules of law with regard to the competency or relevancy or materiality of testimony?"

Roosevelt responded that he took the advice of his counsel, because "I was not a lawyer!"

"Then," Ivins suggested, "you have no recollection whatever at this present time as to whether or not any of the rules of law were applied in the reception of testimony in the matter of this investigation?"

The art of being an effective witness requires not only answering each question to your own benefit, it also means not leaving opposing counsel any openings or falling into any traps. Roosevelt, perhaps not certain where Ivins was heading, was wary. "I have not," he responded, "because I trusted Messrs. Peckham and Miller as to that. I know that substantial justice was done."

Ivins smiled pleasantly. "How do you know that substantial justice was done?"

The Colonel literally yelled out his answer with delight, "Because I did it!" The courtroom rocked in appreciation of this repartee as the witness added, "Because I was conducting the investigation and doing my best..."

The battle was joined; Ivins was a ready match for him, turning his words back on him, "You mean thereby to say that when you do a thing that you thereby know that substantial justice is done?"

"I do. And when I do a thing I do it to do substantial justice; I mean just that."

For an attorney the art of being an effective interrogator requires listening to words rather than sentences, and instantly being able to infer their meaning and slip them seamlessly into your strategy. "You didn't say that you did it to do substantial justice; you said you knew substantial justice was done."

"I said I knew in that case that substantial justice was done."

Ivins moved on to Roosevelt's unsuccessful campaign for mayor of New York, ironically, something these two had in common. Ivins attempted to show that the Colonel had worked with the Republican machine in that effort, asking, "Isn't it a fact that the only nomination which you received was the Republican nomination, Mr. Roosevelt, isn't that a fact?"

"I think not!" T.R. responded, adding, "There was an independent citizen's movement of me and it was prior to the Republican nomination to office."

"Your memory is good," Ivins complimented.

Compliments, of course, are a fine weapon during an examination. "It is pretty good," the Colonel agreed.

"It has been especially good with reference to certain matters you have testified to, has it not?"

"It has."

"Can you make it more specifically good

as regards to the so-called Independents who nominated or supported you in that campaign?"

"I cannot," he conceded, then naming only two of the many men involved in the citizens movement.

Ivins pressed him on his reluctance to admit he was dependent on the Republican Party, asking, "Isn't it a fact that your speeches were made as a Republican?"

"My speeches were made as a Citizens and Republican candidate; I could not be more specific than that."

Eventually Ivins got to the result. "That was one of the campaigns in which you were not successful, isn't it?"

"I was beaten."

Ivins began playing his man as he might a fine instrument, bridging his strongest movements with seemingly pleasant interludes. He allowed the Colonel to talk about his ranch, where he had spent "a great part of the time" for almost six years writing there. "I think I wrote *The Winning of the West* in the year 1887; now I cannot be definite about that Mr. Ivins because many of the books I have written chapters and parts that would appeal to me and then I would put them aside and take them up years afterwards."

"Just like the rest of us authors," Ivins agreed. Ivins was the author of several books and articles, among them the 1887 book *Machine Politics & Money in Elections in New York City*, as well as coauthoring the article "Rosicrucianism," which was published in the *Spiritual Scientist* and led to his professional and personal relationship with the Mother of the Occult, Madame Helena Blavatsky.

After a pleasant sounding exchange, Ivins made his first direct assault on Roosevelt's character by suggesting this prominent man may have been a tax dodger: "From the Spring of 1889 until your retirement from the Civil Service Commissionership where did you live?"

"I lived the summer at Oyster Bay and in the winter and part of the summer at Washington."

"Your residence was at Oyster Bay?"

The Colonel steeled himself for the charge that was coming, his face turning serious, grim even as he replied, "My residence (was) at Oyster Bay."

Ivins asked evenly, "Did you pay taxes in Oyster Bay?"

Roosevelt was firm in his response, "I paid taxes in Oyster Bay. It may have been that for a year or two I paid taxes in New York."

Ivins established that the Colonel did not own real estate in New York City, and wondered, "If you lived in Oyster Bay or in Washington or at the Ranch, why did you pay any taxes in New York City?"

For the first time T.R. faltered, realizing Ivins was scoring points. "I don't think I did; but I can't be sure, Mr. Ivins."

The federal income tax had been instituted by a constitutional amendment in 1913, and after years of debate remained a very sensitive subject. The possibility that a former president had avoided taxes would be scandalous and seriously damage

Roosevelt's reputation for honesty. "Did you during these years pay any personal taxes in Oyster Bay?"

"My memory is that I did."

"Do you remember if there was a time came in which you did not pay personal taxes in Oyster Bay?"

"When I was Police Commissioner I resided in New York City and I believe I paid personal taxes in New York City."

From there Ivins launched a second attack on Roosevelt's credibility. "You testified that the purpose of your residence in the city of Washington in 1898 was in preparation for your war service in the army?"

"No sir," the Colonel responded firmly. The easy banter that marked the beginning of this testimony was gone now. "The purpose of my residence there was because I was to carry on my duties as assistant Secretary of the Navy."

"When did you receive your commission to organize the regiment as Lieutenant Colonel?"

"About May 1, 1898."

"So that your residence in Washington covered a period of about a year?"

Roosevelt agreed.

"Did you pay any taxes in Oyster Bay in the year 1897 other than real estate taxes?"

The courtroom was silent. Now Roosevelt was on the defensive. "That I can't tell you," T.R. responded.

"Do you remember having made an affidavit in 1897?"

"No, I don't remember." Having testified previously with great confidence about the strength of his memory, his failure to recall these things seemed curious.

"With the authorities at Oyster Bay to the effect that you were a resident of the City of New York?"

"No, I don't remember."

Ivins pressed his advantage but did so calmly, which made it even more effective. "Are you prepared to swear affirmatively that you did pay taxes on your personal property as a resident of Oyster Bay in 1897?"

The spectators shifted uneasily in their seats. "I am not."

"Are you prepared to swear that you did pay taxes as a resident of the City of New York on your personal property in 1897?"

Again, "I am not; I don't remember anything about it."

"Do you remember having received notice of assessment on personal property for purposes of taxation in the City of New York at any time in 1898?"

"Yes, I remember having received a notice." He sent it on to his lawyers, he added. And no, he did not remember appearing before the tax commissioners concerning this assessment.

Roosevelt had held sway in the courtroom, but now Ivins had turned it round on him. "Do you remember having made an affidavit on the 21st of March, 1898 in regard to your residence and the question as to whether or not you were subject to taxation in the City of New York."

The confident timbre was gone from Roosevelt's voice as he admitted, with a resigned calmness, "I do… I think it was made in Washington."

Ivins produced a copy of that affidavit and read it for the court. The key elements of it read, "Since 1897 I have not had any domicile or residence in New York City and have not or do not own or lease any dwelling house there whatsoever… In October last my family came on here from Oyster Bay, Long Island and since then I have been and now am a resident of Washington." It was then entered as evidence.

The attorney then sprung the trap he had so carefully prepared. This was about much more than just possible tax dodging; it was about Roosevelt's eligibility for office. In the same carefully modulated tone, Ivins asked, "Mr. Roosevelt, I call your attention to Section 2 of Article 4 of the Constitution of this State: 'No person shall be eligible to the office of Governor…except a citizen of the United States of the age of not less than thirty years, who shall have been five years next preceding a resident of this State.'

"When did you first become acquainted with that qualification on the eligibility for Governorship?"

"On my return from the Spanish War; after I came back and the Regiment was disbanded at Wyckoff."

In complete control now, Ivins made his point; Roosevelt had not been eligible to run for the governorship. By doing so, Ivins inferred, he was no different than those politicians he had called dishonest.

"So that when you made this affidavit you had no knowledge whatever that the Constitution of the State of New York required a previous five-year residence in the State for eligibility for the Governorship?"

Roosevelt maintained his calm demeanor, although there was a little fight in his response. "I don't believe I did; I may have, but my attention hadn't been called to it."

Ivins then put into evidence several certificates from the War Department dated May 1898 stating that Lieutenant Colonel Theodore Roosevelt was a resident of Washington.

In slightly more than two hours, William Ivins had proved his mettle, demonstrating beyond any doubt why he was so widely acclaimed. He had brought together great preparation, incisive questioning and a calm courtroom manner to shake the underpinnings of one of the most respected and admired men in the world. It had been the star turn the people had anticipated. "His reputation for sagacity is nationwide," reported the *Syracuse Journal*, "and he lives up to his reputation. His tongue is quick, his accents are vitriolic, he is a master of the art of retort."

And it was only the beginning. But to the relief of Teddy Roosevelt's supporters, Judge Andrews recessed the court for lunch.

The instant court resumed, Roosevelt launched his counterattack. He had been busy during the break, arming himself with the documents he needed to refute Ivins's claims. Rather than taking his seat in the witness box, the Colonel stood defiantly. "Mr. Ivins," he began in a booming voice, "you asked me about my paying the taxes at Oyster Bay in 1897. I told you I could not answer. Since then I have found—I have been handed the tax receipts. I did pay them in Oyster Bay for that and the preceding years on real and personal property."

Then he took a broad step forward and literally shoved the pile of documents into Ivins's hands. With that he took his seat on the stand, turned to face the jury to share this victory with the men, and smiled broadly.

Ivins was seated; he seemed barely ruffled by the Colonel's display. As he glanced at the papers he said, "You have handed me papers which apparently show that you drew a check to the Town of Oyster Bay for $412.57 on the 19th of January, 1898. That does not indicate, does it, whether it was for real or personal property?"

Roosevelt had regained some of his lost prestige; he responded so there could be no mistaking his submission, "I believe that that was for real and personal property precisely like the preceding receipts. I had receipts which said it was for real and personal property for 1897, 1896, 1895 and 1894, but in 1898 there is only a check, but for a larger sum than any of the preceding payments."

After a brief discussion Ivins regained his footing. "The endorsement shows where it was endorsed by the collector of taxes. Now Mr. Roosevelt had produced tax receipts for the years

1896, 1895, 1894 and 1893. The matter I asked about was the taxes in Oyster Bay for the year 1897."

"I have nothing," Roosevelt responded. "I have only that check showing that taxes were paid in 1897."

The two men went back and forth for several minutes, each of them playing far more to the jury than each other, until Ivins took a different tack, wondering, "When did you first hear of the discussion of your name as a possible candidate for the Governorship?"

"As well as I remember, beyond anything but the merest gossip, it was at Camp Wyckoff after I returned from the Santiago campaign… I don't remember who first spoke to me about it, but the first man of any prominence in politics whom I remember having spoken to me about it was Mr. Quigg." Lemuel Quigg was a Republican member of Congress from New York, or in Ivins's words, "A local Republican boss of New York City."

Ivins then introduced correspondence between Quigg and Roosevelt into the record, letters that were read to the jury. In his letter to the Colonel, Quigg informed him that Senator Thomas C. Platt, the so-called "easy boss" of the state, wanted to meet with him. He then wrote that the current governor, Frank Black, had angrily complained that Roosevelt "was not fit to be nominated because you are impulsive and erratic, that your military record, however it may attest to your personal bravery, displays your characteristic rashness and impetuosity and foolishness, and that as Governor you would play the devil with the organization and get the party into all tangles and ridiculous positions."

Platt had responded, Quigg wrote, that "he would prevent your nomination if he could see any fair reason your administration would be injurious to the organization." After explaining that party delegates were committed to supporting Platt's choice, Quigg related his recent conversation with the senator in which he had pledged "that you were not the sort of man who would accept a nomination directly out of the hands of the organization without realization of the obligation thereby assumed. To sustain the organization and promote and uphold it and you were prepared to meet the obligation and discharge it justly...you would take the office intending in good faith to act the part of his friend both personally and politically...that you would consult with the Senator freely and fully on all important matters, that you would adopt no line of policy and agree to no important matter or nomination without previous consultation...

"I told him," Quigg wrote to Roosevelt, "that you said you did not mean by this that you would do everything as it was wanted precisely as it was originally suggested, but you did mean in good faith and honest friendship to enter with him upon the consideration of all manners proposed without prejudice and with the intention to reach a conclusion which the Senator, no less than yourself would deem wisest and best."

As it was being read to the jury the Colonel listened intently, a hard scowl on his face, occasionally shaking his head apparently in disbelief, but of what no spectator could be certain.

The next letter from Quigg was even more shocking. "It was agreed that the 'hero of San Juan hill and the idol of the country' was to be the Republican nominee for governor, but there were other considerations. Far be it from Senator Platt to expect of Colonel Roosevelt any action that would trouble the conscience of an honest man or any promise binding him to acquiesce in any or all demands that the organization might make or deliver to hand over the reins of government to the senator, but if Colonel Roosevelt wants to be governor he must be governor and nothing more..."

Roosevelt scowled and bobbed his head as this letter was read, not looking at the jury.

"...without the endorsement and support of Senator Pratt he could not be governor. And that as a matter of fact he was a handmade governor and Senator Pratt was the artisan and that at all times the interest of the organization of the whole Republican Party and of the people, in that order, were to be concerned."

In addition to being potentially devastating to Roosevelt's reputation, these letters, read aloud, appeared to confirm the public's worst held opinions of politicians. They said flatly that the interests of the party were superior to the good of the people. It was exactly what the Colonel had railed about in his article, but now implicated him as someone who, rather than standing up against this corruption had embraced it for personal gain. The *Herald* characterized these letters "to be among the most sensational political documents that have come to light in the history of New York State."

The letters appeared to strip Roosevelt of his heroic aura and reveal a hard truth to those who idolized him. The impression left by the reading of them was still hanging in the air when Roosevelt's response was delivered. "I know that you did not in any way wish to represent me as willing to consent to act otherwise than in accordance with my conscience…

"I want to make it clear that there was no question of pledges or promises least of all a question of bargaining for the nomination… I was not making any agreement as to what I would do on consideration that I would receive the nomination."

Ivins established that in addition to conferring with Quigg, Roosevelt had met with other party leaders, among them the leader of the New York Republican Party, Senator Platt. When Roosevelt met with Platt, Ivins asked, were you aware of his position as leader of the party? Yes, Roosevelt was. Then, the attorney continued, "You deliberately, by agreement, met him for the purpose of discussing your nomination by the Republican Party?" Yes.

A subsequent meeting with Platt, where the question of Roosevelt's eligibility to become governor was discussed at length also had been attended by Elihu Root, a party leader who later would become President Roosevelt's Nobel Peace Prize–winning secretary of state and a US senator. The overall consensus in the meeting was that he was not eligible, and the question would be raised before the election. To counter that challenge, Roosevelt admitted, "When I got back from the war I tried to pay (my taxes) in Oyster Bay and found that the books were closed and found that they were to have been paid by my uncle, James A. Roosevelt, who had died just prior to the time of paying them and in consequence they had not been paid… they were then paid in New York."

This discussion continued for some time, and Roosevelt insisted, "I was residing in Washington but I did not intend the fact that I was residing in Washington should be used by my lawyers to get me out of paying or cause me to lose my vote… I did not know the legal technicalities of the question, but I was not going to be put in a position of seeming to escape paying my taxes."

When confronted by Ivins with forms he had signed that listed his residence as Washington, DC, the Colonel insisted that someone else had filled out that portion of the form and he had never seen it, but ended firmly, "I don't believe I ever saw that blank until this morning when you showed it to me. I knew nothing about it. My only part of that was my oath of allegiance to the United States."

The goal of every lawyer or witness in a courtroom is to connect on an emotional basis with members of the jury. Ivins had successfully raised a real but legalistic concern about Roosevelt's eligibility for a position he had held more than fifteen years prior. He had paid his taxes; the only issue was where and when. Regardless, he had been away from home, serving the country, risking his life. That was something every juryman might understand. This whole question of his residence, where he lived while fighting for America, fulfilling that oath to serve and protect the United States, might be seen as little more than a nuisance. Roosevelt hoped that any honest man would understand the situation. But the other question of how he actually got the position for which he may have been ineligible, went more directly to the heart of the case.

Ivins came back to the nomination, asking, "You know what a boss is?"

"I do."

"Is it not a fact they dictated those nominations?"

"Unquestionably."

Roosevelt's libelous article had raged against boss-control of the political process, claiming that system robbed citizens of a fair opportunity to participate in the political process; and Ivins was determined to prove that T.R. had knowingly and willingly been part of it. After showing that the Colonel had turned down the Independent Party's offer of its nomination for governor to accept the Republican nomination—without knowing who would be sharing the ticket with him—he wondered, "You did not know who you were going to stand by when you said you were going to stand by them?" *In other words, Colonel,* he inferred, *you are no different than any other ambitious politician?*

Roosevelt jutted his jaw and told him, "I did not know who I was going to stand by—excepting that they knew perfectly well if I thought a man was a dishonest man I would not stand by him."

Ivins appealed to Judge Andrews. "I move to strike that out." He wanted it out of the official record. The judge agreed it was not responsive. "It may go out."

But the reality of the courtroom was that it could not be unheard. If a man believed that Roosevelt was honest, this would strike him as true, that was the Teddy they knew; but if he had found him boorish, this would have little impact. In or out of the record, the point was made.

Ivins resorted to his noted sarcasm, pointing out, "You don't know what they knew perfectly well." His tone of voice suggested to the jury that he found Roosevelt's statement less than convincing. "You took for granted that they (the bosses Platt and Odell) would go straight, did you not?"

"At the time they showed every symptom of it," T.R. responded, and mild laughter rippled through the courtroom.

Ivins wouldn't let him get away with that. "Did you during that campaign in any way in any of your speeches attack machine politics or boss rule?"

"Not at all."

"Not at all?"

"It was not an issue."

Ivins was skilled at coloring his questions with multiple meanings. "Why was it not an issue if there was a machine and there was boss rule?"

"Because there was no feeling against it at that time."

"Then you do not attack anything unless there is a feeling against it, is that what you mean to say?"

"I attack!" Roosevelt said, reinforcing that by slapping down his hand on the bench in a by-golly punctuation. This was the Teddy of his best fighting days: "I attack iniquities, I attack wrong doing. I try to choose the time for an attack when I can get the bulk of the people to accept the principles for which I stand!"

"I think you have answered the question. You stand by righteousness, do you not?"

"I do… I stand by righteousness always."

Ivins made his doubt clear. "With due regard to opportunism."

"No, Sir! Not when it comes to righteousness… But you must, for righteousness you must stand, whether you are going to be supported or not." Adding confidently, "Just exactly as I did while I was Governor."

Ivins was now prepared to turn up the heat on the Colonel with a philosophical musing, wondering, "Did that rule apply to Mr. Barnes in 1912… with regard to righteousness and the opportunities for its expression as well as it does to you?…

"Has not every man an equal right to determine his own rule of righteousness and his own time of applying it?"

It was becoming clear to observers that Roosevelt was again enjoying this interplay. Rather than shrinking from the question and finding an acceptable answer, Roosevelt brought forth his principles: "He has if he has got the root of righteousness in him. If he is a wrong doer, he has not."

"Who is the judge, you or he?"

Throwing his arms up high, as if to proclaim the obviousness of it, he said, "It may be that I have to be the judge, of him. If I had to be the judge… I will give you an exact example, Senator Burton…"

Ivins stopped him. "You need not…"

Bowers stood. "Why not?"

Ivins turned to him. "Mr. Bowers, I do not object to his answering. I object to his manner."

Even Bowers smiled at that.

"I do not want to be eaten up right here now," Ivins added.

The Colonel objected to the objection, saying firmly, "I will gesticulate to the jury."

Ivins suggested, "You can say it to the jury without being so emphatic."

Even that caused titters in the courtroom, which became outright laughter as the chastised Colonel said, "I feel emphatic about it but I will try not to be emphatic. For example, two of my earliest associates and supporters when I became president…"

An increasingly frustrated Ivins again objected.

Roosevelt was on a roll and not about to be stopped. "It is, sir, if you will let me answer about the ruling of righteousness."

And the debate resumed with Ivins quoting him, "It may be that I have to be the judge, of him."

"No," T.R. snapped, "I have…yes! I have to be the judge of misconduct."

ONONDAGA HISTORICAL ASSOCIATION

Although seemingly relaxed on the stand as Ivins began his cross-examination on April 22, the Post-Standard *reported he spent most of the day sitting "canted over an angle of forty-five degrees, which enabled him to get a look at each juror, and when he caught the eyes of the talesman he looked fixedly at them with the old gaze" that had captured audiences.*

Ivins was no shrinking violet (a phrase that first had been used in America to describe the notorious nineteenth-century political legend, Boss Tweed), and he snapped right back at the witness, "Is it not possible that somebody else may have to be the judge of your misconduct?"

"It is possible."

"It is not impossible that you should be guilty of misconduct beyond criticism or comment, is it?"

The Colonel found a clever path. "It is not impossible that I should be guilty of conduct that would cause criticism and comment."

Ivins then returned to a discussion of the bosses with whom the Colonel had worked, Platt being the ultimate or "easy boss" followed by Benjamin Odell and then Barnes, endeavoring to demonstrate that the defendant had cooperated with the bosses throughout his career. Roosevelt didn't deny it, admitting, "I conferred and consulted with Mr. Platt with a genuine purpose to what he wished whenever I honorably could with regard to the interest of the party, with a genuine desire to keep the Republican Party together and minimize the centrifugal influences within the Republican Party to prevent it from flying asunder."

"I congratulate you upon you…" Ivins began, his trademark sarcasm springing up, but before he might complete his thought Bowers objected. Ivins then asked if Roosevelt had any differences with Platt.

"You congratulate me?" the Colonel came back with his own disdain. He used the word *centrifugal*, he explained, because it was an expression he had used in a letter to a colleague.

That too intrigued Ivins, who offered, "As a matter of fact you have used phrases, built them up, formulated them, finally got them into ultimate shape which was satisfactory to you, have you not?"

Like seasoned duelists, they thrust and parried, searching for an opening to exploit, while fending off the bothersome probes. "Sometimes," the Colonel agreed, a finger to his lips, his eyes raised to the ceiling in thought, and then added, "sometimes I have struck them off by accident."

Late in the afternoon the battering in the street became so loud that it became almost impossible to hear the testimony. Judge Andrews finally paused the proceedings and pleaded with Sheriff Mathews to do whatever was necessary to stop it. The burly sheriff nodded and said he would do his best.

Ivins eventually continued in his effort to paint Roosevelt as a different kind of political boss, but still a boss, wondering if in all his dealings with the bosses the defendant had any differences with them at all? Indeed he had, Roosevelt said. "I can't tell you all of them but for instance they wanted to pass the Astoria Gas Bill and I wouldn't consent save under conditions that made them abandon it. They wanted me to pass a bi-partisan State Constabulary Bill…but I became convinced that the people as a whole were against it so I declined to put it through… I had a disagreement with Mr. Platt about the appointment of a Superintendent of Public Works…

"I regarded the appointment of a Superintendent of Public Works who had charge of the canal as being the most important appointment that I had to make." Additionally, as governor he had to appoint the legal counsel for the canals, and as there was some question about the conduct of the canal management, that also was an extremely sensitive appointment. "Mr. Platt wished me to make the senior counsel a Republican and I declined to; I said I wished to appoint both of them Democrats so that there would be no question of party influence preventing the prosecution of any man who had done wrong…

"I had my own way on a number of those things. The point where I had to ask (Mr. Platt) to use his influence, where he of his own accord used his influence and where I thanked him for it, it would not have gotten through without his influence, was the passage of the Civil Service Reform. I remember that because I got one Democrat to vote for it and there were 25 Republicans and a good number of those 25 would not have voted for it if Mr. Platt had not asked them to do so."

Circling back once again Mr. Ivins chided, "You did not have an attack of righteousness…for his influence with the legislature?"

Heaven forbid, was the Colonel's attitude, who responded as if he were taken aback. "On the contrary I praised him for his righteousness in passing the bill. Mr. Ivins, I did my best to get on with Mr. Platt and all the other members of the organization; I in good faith endeavored to keep the organization intact and to make it the responsive servant of the rank and file of the party and of the people as a whole, and I never broke with Mr. Platt or Mr. Barnes until I could not help doing so in order to serve decency as I regarded it. I regarded myself as an organization man."

Hearing the echo of a self-serving political speech, Ivins dismissed it, telling him, "You need not treat me as a mass meeting because I am not."

Bowers felt a need to interrupt. "No," he said, "he is doing you good."

Ivins said drolly, "He is not getting me very much excited."

Bowers agreed with that, as the Colonel grinned. "No, you are sleeping." And once again the courtroom burst into appreciative laughter.

Persisting in finding those issues on which the defendant had disagreed with the bosses, Ivins asked if the Colonel recalled correspondence about a series of proposed bills or appointments. Roosevelt responded that he did not, explaining that "since 1898 I have answered in writing from one hundred to one hundred and fifty thousand letters."

This was an amazing claim, causing Ivins to note with a bit of dramatic awe, "Since then you have probably written more than any other man in the United States, haven't you?"

Roosevelt supported his claim, "I don't know," he said. "But I have written from one hundred to one hundred and fifty thousand letters. I have had to deal as Governor and President with thousands of bills. I remember many of them and there are many of those that I don't remember."

After a spirited and detailed discussion of several of those bills without either side making much gain, Ivins entered four letters into the record. Written in 1900, they concerned the search for Roosevelt's successor as governor. The Colonel and the boss had very different views on this; Roosevelt suggested an Independent would fit the bill, Platt insisted on a Republican. T.R. responded that the right Republican would be satisfactory to him and suggested either Root or former chief judge Charles

Andrews, the father of the presiding judge who had just been in court yesterday. In what clearly was an uncomfortable few moments, this letter challenged Platt's statement that either of those men would lower the standard; rather, Roosevelt wrote, they would raise that standard. Roosevelt was positively giddy as that letter was read to its end. "The organization should strive to give wise and upright government to the State."

The afternoon session closed with Ivins reading a telegram the defendant had sent to Platt after the Republican Party's watered down version of the Franchise Tax Bill, which Roosevelt had fought strongly against, had been passed. "Three cheers," the telegram read. Asked if he remembered sending it, he replied that he did not, but admitted with a booming laugh that resonated from wall-to-wall, "It is a characteristic telegram," then added in his truly characteristic high falsetto voice, "I have no doubt I sent it."

As the *Times* reported, "Court adjourned for the day in a gale of laughter."

CHAPTER SIX

Crimes and trials sold newspapers, and in return those papers increased public interest in the trials. It was a fine marriage that could be traced back to 1674 England, when publication of *An Exact and True Accompt of the Most Remarkable Tryals of Several Notorious Malefactors in the Old Bailey* began. Initially the popular *Proceedings*, as it became known, was published after each of eight annual sessions and provided only brief summaries of trials, but by the early 1700s grew to include details, transcriptions and interviews from the most entertaining and salacious trials. By the end of the eighteenth century, about a third of the news printed by most London papers consisted of stories concerning crimes, justice and the law.

In America, reporting on trials didn't become common until the early 1800s, when newspapers won the right to print that news without fear of prosecution. In 1836, publisher James Gordon Bennett practically tripled the circulation of his daily penny paper, the *New York Herald*, by personally reporting the murder of twenty-three-year-old prostitute Helen Jewett. "The body looked as white—as full—as polished as the pure Parian marble," he wrote. "The perfect figure—the exquisite limbs—the fine face—the full arms—the beautiful bust—all—all surpassing in every respect the Venus de Medicis."

Within a week the *Herald* was selling an astonishing fifteen thousand copies daily. A nineteen-year-old dandy named Richard Robinson was accused of committing the murder by chopping at the beautiful young woman with a hatchet. On the first day of his trial, six thousand people pushed into city hall to witness it. Throughout the six-day trial, New York newspapers covered every possible angle and sold out numerous editions. Bennett was even accused of paying someone $50 to forge a letter supposedly written by Helen's "real killer" in an effort to win this new circulation war. By the time Robinson was acquitted, newspaper publishers already were on the watch for the next big crime and trial.

The first great media frenzy of the twentieth century was the sensational 1906 trial of railroad heir Harry K. Thaw, who was accused of killing renowned architect Stanford White for seducing sixteen-year-old Evelyn Nesbit, the woman who later became Thaw's wife. Interest in this crime of passion was so great that Thomas Edison produced a short film about the murder only a week after it had been committed.

The second "trial of the century" took place only a year later, when radical miners' union leader William "Big Bill" Haywood was tried for murder. Haywood supposedly hired hit man Harry Orchard, who later confessed to at least seventeen murders, to plant the explosive device that killed former Idaho governor Frank Steuneberg. The trial made a young defense lawyer named Clarence Darrow nationally famous after he was able to raise sufficient doubt to win an acquittal.

While the Roosevelt trial lacked the sex and violence of those earlier cases, the presence of the outspoken former president on the witness stand made for hot copy. Readers swept up the newspapers, which filled endless column inches with news from the trial, reporting even the most mundane details. In addition to disclosing that Teddy Roosevelt drank a gallon of coffee a day and would usually add five to seven lumps of sugar, the *Journal* reported in a sidebar, "There were all kinds of glasses, surmounting all kinds of noses in the Barnes-Roosevelt courtroom. The Colonel wears his gold-trimmed spectacles when on the witness stand. When he sits with his counsel the spectacles disappear. In replace the Colonel pops out a pair of rimless eyeglasses with their black string attached. Justice Andrews wears rimless glasses, gold-framed. John H. Halperin is the only one of the thousands of attorneys hired in the case that effects the festive tortoise shell. Mr. Bowers wears small glasses minus rims and strings. Mr. Barnum modeled rimless spectacles patterned something after Judge Andrews…"

The daily columns noted which politicians or local celebrities sat in the gallery, and what everyone wore. For example, the *Herald* wrote, "Mr. Ivins has affected a black cutaway coat and vest with dark-striped trouser for the last two days." And attorney Bowers's wife "has brought some extremely charming costumes with her and is most smartly and becomingly…carrying out her part of the much-photographed sartorial elegance of the visitors connected with the trial."

Even newspaper advertising exploited the excitement in the city, one department store declaring, "The verdict! Will he pay $50,000? Syracusans are immensely interested… A jury of 12 couldn't render any other verdict than our clothes are worth the money!"

Interest was so great, in fact, that like the Thaw trial, this one was filmed and scenes from the trial were shown at the Strand. Roosevelt had been planning to attend but had to cancel to participate in a meeting with Bowers. But several other participants did attend and "for the first time, they saw themselves as others see them."

And like those other trials that held the attention of the nation, even without the salacious background this one continued to make headlines in every corner of the country. As Ohio's *Toledo Blade* reported, "Colonel Roosevelt is a good witness for the news associations."

The principals became familiar to readers: "The Colonel hasn't missed a trick yet," wrote the *Sault Ste Marie News* of Michigan. "No disparagement of Mr. Ivins is intended, but the Colonel is toying with this famous lawyer—in the merriest sort of mood—as the cat does with the mouse… Bless you, sir, you are merely a victim of the worst 'bonehead' Barnes has been credited with in his entire political career, and in the meantime one T. Roosevelt is giving to the public a clever movie of how to enjoy life even at someone else's expense."

As a result of all the excitement the *Post-Standard* lamented that the city had made a mistake in "not staging the Barnes-Roosevelt trial in the arena instead of the courthouse."

So on the morning of April 23, when Roosevelt and Barnes once again took their seats facing each other, separated only by a few feet, America was watching them through the eyes of the gathered newsmen.

It quickly became clear that Ivins's intention for this day was to pore through Roosevelt's career, highlighting all those instances when political necessity outweighed the Colonel's oft-proclaimed rectitude. Roosevelt bobbed and weaved, responding many times that he didn't know of some fact, that he didn't remember certain details, that he wasn't sure of an answer, and that he "thought" rather than knew his response to a question was accurate.

The day began getting testy when Ivins read from Roosevelt's autobiography published in 1913, wondering why the Colonel wrote at length about

ONONDAGA HISTORICAL ASSOCIATION

Republican Party leader William Barnes (center), here arriving at the courthouse, had been fighting the progressive policies of Roosevelt for a decade, claiming, "I accepted the position of chairman and retained it to contend against certain policies fathered by Mr. Roosevelt."

other politicians but made no reference to Barnes, who only two years later became the focus of his scorn. The answer was obvious, the Colonel retorted, "Because I particularly wished not to make any wanton or malicious attack upon him. If my autobiography had been written as an appeal to the voters of New York to get rid—"

Ivins cut him off, objecting to that.

"But you asked him why," Judge Andrews interceded. "That allows him to answer."

"I think he has answered," said Ivins, quickly realizing he had made a tactical error by asking such an open-ended question of Roosevelt.

"I have not," T.R. said firmly, sensing an opportunity, "I have only begun." Allowed to continue he explained, "I never mentioned Mr. Barnes in any unkind way if I could avoid doing it, and scrupulously in the autobiography refrained from making any attack upon any man unless it was impossible to avoid doing so, and then I made it as mild as facts would permit."

Ivins pointed out that "you used the word just now that you did not in your autobiography make any *wanton* attack upon Mr. Barnes or upon any one."

"Or upon any one," the Colonel agreed, adding confidently, "When I attacked Mr. Barnes it was not wanton."

The lawyer then took a short diversion, wondering if the witness had used some of the same phrases found in his autobiography in his testimony because he had relied on it to refresh his mind or simply due to excellent memory.

Roosevelt said he didn't know, but when Ivins persisted Bowers finally appealed to Judge Andrews. "The witness says he does not know that he has."

Ivins snapped at him, "You need not help your witness out."

"I do not need to help him, he does not need help," Bowers agreed, then for the first time questioned Ivins cross-examination. "But what is the object of putting questions which are perfectly useless?"

Ivins promised, somewhat mysteriously, "The utility or the uselessness of these questions will be discovered later on."

Referring again to the autobiography, Ivins wondered why he had not railed against secret campaign contributions in the book but had attacked Barnes for accepting them. Roosevelt responded that several times, beginning in 1908, "I advocated the enactment of a law making campaign contributions public," but had not made it a significant part of his proposals as president "because the publicity of campaign expenses was only one feature, and a small feature, of the evils against which I was warring."

Throughout the morning, Ivins's frustration had been building as the Colonel had squeezed out of his carefully built traps, often by speaking through objections to offer a complete explanation. Finally Ivins began questioning him about the battle to replace superintendent of insurance Lewis F. Payn, which Roosevelt had claimed was an example of the bosses at work trying to impose their will on elected officials. Senator Platt essentially had placed Payn in the position before Roosevelt became governor. So the Colonel could not remove him, but when his three-year term ended Roosevelt named Francis Hendricks to the post. The machine refused to confirm that appointment, ensuring that Payn would be kept in office as a "holdover" until a new man was approved—which they were not going to allow. Barnes had warned him, Roosevelt testified, that he "would be beaten in the effort to remove Mr. Payn," by a coalition of both the Republican and Democratic machines. The political battle got national publicity—until Platt finally relented. "You spoke of the removal of Mr. Payn," Ivins asked. "Mr. Payn was not removed, was he?"

"In place of saying the 'removal,' I will say the getting out of office of Mr. Payn."

Ignoring the controversy, Ivins framed his question artfully, "Is it not a fact that Mr. Payn's term of office expired and you appointed his successor?"

"Yes sir; but, Mr. Ivins..."

Ivins snapped angrily him, "That answers my question."

As far as the Colonel was concerned it did not. "Do you object to my stating to the jury..."

Ivins interrupted him again—and in turn Bowers rose from his seat to complain, "The witness should be allowed to complete his answer."

Ivins had had just about enough of Roosevelt riding roughshod over his objections. "Instead of having you tell the jury things, I would like to ask you questions and have you answer my questions. If the rules of law are to prevail when this witness is on the stand like any other ordinary witness..."

As the adversaries argued, the Colonel sat quietly in the witness chair, leaning forward and clenching and unclenching his fist as if he would like to jump in but knew better.

Judge Andrews gaveled for quiet, warning the lawyer sternly, "Mr. Ivins. This witness will be treated as any other ordinary witness. I cannot have any discussion of that kind in my courtroom."

Ivins apologized, then pleaded for the judge to harness the witness. "What I wished to insist on is that this witness answer my questions categorically, yes or no, when he can do so; that when he is asked for a statement of facts...he shall not go beyond them or outside of them. That is the rule of evidence which I shall have to insist on in respect to this witness."

Judge Andrews agreed, cautioning Roosevelt, "The witness will answer the questions," then to Ivins, "and if he goes beyond that you may stop him at any time."

When the room finally settled down, he made his point. "Did you consult with Mr. Platt in regard to the appointment of that successor?"

"I did."

And, Ivins showed, he did it privately and without the newspapers reporting this story or learning about these meetings. The inference was clear: while making a public show of his independence from the machine, Roosevelt was privately meeting with Platt, sometimes at the home of his own brother-in-law, to reach a deal.

While this exchange between Ivins and the Colonel was captivating the courtroom, Barnes sat quietly at the plaintiff's table; overshadowed as he had been throughout his political career, by Theodore Roosevelt. At times he shifted in his chair, sometimes seemingly distracted. He had brought Ivins into this trial, but as a great attorney might, Ivins had made it more between Roosevelt and himself rather than simply representing Barnes. Ivins had not only taken on the case, he had burdened himself with the emotion attached to it, and at times appeared personally affronted by the Colonel's conduct. The *New York Times* described it as "a battle between two master minds, one trained in the intricacies of the law and the other in large human affairs, and those privileged to listen to it followed every word."

Ivins focused on the long relationship between

Roosevelt and Barnes, which stretched back to his time in the governor's mansion. The advocate wondered why Roosevelt continued to associate with him if he did not consider him "a man of high character?"

This was a question the jury could easily understand: *If you felt about him the way you wrote in the article, why did you continue to meet with him through so many years?* The Colonel had to navigate through these murky waters very carefully. "Because I thought he was above the average of the ordinary political leaders, I thought that his morality was at least level with the common political and business morality as I found it expressed at the time. I believe that he had it in him, if he would abandon these standards, to become a useful public servant..."

Ivins was not about to let him off his hook. "So that while you were Governor you were acting as monitor of Mr. Barnes in the effort to develop his political character, make a good and (useful) citizen of him, is that what I understand?"

Roosevelt grabbed hold of the arm of his chair and swung around to face the jury directly, then gave a response perfect for the headlines: "Only to this extent, Mr. Ivins. That with all these men whom I met, I found they had two characters, a good character and a bad character, a Dr. Jekyll and Mr. Hyde, and there were a few of them that were absolutely straight and upright and disinterested, a few of them that were hopelessly vile and most of them had mixed character, and my constant effort was to appeal to the side that was decent and get the man to act rightly and if he would act rightly I would not bring up his past against him at all; I would only be too glad to hail him as a decent man…and I never broke with him, with any man, until I became convinced that it was hopeless to get the good side out of him."

"And then you regarded Mr. Barnes as, in a measure, a Dr. Jekyll and Mr. Hyde?" Robert Louis Stevenson's novel of a diabolical split personality, *The Strange Case of Dr. Jekyll and Mr. Hyde*, had been published three decades earlier and remained a sensation.

The Colonel shouted his answer so there could be no doubt as to his belief: "I do, as most of them were." When Ivins pointed out that Roosevelt had appointed Barnes to two different offices, the Colonel defended himself, "I thought there were both sides in him; I did not know which was uppermost. I was trying to do the best to get the Dr. Jekyll side uppermost…"

"This question of severing the ligaments between these Siamese twins, Jekyll and Hyde, did not arise, did it, until you had ceased to agree?"

"Oh, no, sir! There was no question of severing the ligaments—it is absorbing one by the other!"

Ivins seemed to mock him, asking, "You mean absorbing Mr. Barnes by you or Mr. Barnes absorbing you?"

But the Colonel was dead serious about it. "I am not speaking of the absorbing of either of us. I am speaking of the absorption in the man of the good character or the bad. That is all."

"According to your testimony you were endeavoring to reconstruct Mr. Barnes and in the meantime keeping him in office?"

The answer to that seemed obvious to Roosevelt. "I was endeavoring to appeal to what was best in him and in that sense to reconstruct him."

Ivins returned to the autobiography, referring to it somewhat derisively as "your opus major," asking once again if he had referred to it in preparation for this testimony. When Roosevelt answered that he hadn't looked at it in months, the lawyer suggested, "Then if there is a similarity of phrases it is because of the phraseological persistence in your mind, is it not?"

The Colonel clearly was amused by the use of that term, grinning broadly as he answered with a hint of disbelief, "Phraseological persistence in my mind? Did you ask me to answer that?"

There was a snarl in the lawyer's return. "I certainly do, if you are capable of understanding my question. Maybe I am not intelligible to you?"

Roosevelt clasped his hands in his lap, his elbows resting on the arms of the chair as he fumbled for an answer. "Well, if you mean, by that, that I..." He gave up. "I'm trying to state just exactly what you mean."

"You are trying to ask me now what I mean?"

"So that I may answer your question."

"Yes, that is right."

"Intelligently and properly."

"Go ahead." Ivins's point was that Roosevelt so

often used the same words and phrases that it might be considered a formula.

This time it was the Colonel who objected, claiming, "Nothing that I say ever assumes a form of a formula... As I understand, a formula is something formed on rote, which you do not believe; whereas, for such phrases as I write, it is something that I believe and have tried to translate into action whenever it occurred."

Ivins would not let go, and his questioning became more confrontational. "Now, we will take your very definition. Formula is something represented by rote 'which you do not believe.'"

"Which you do not believe," Roosevelt repeated.

"You believe that two and two make four?"

Gritting his teeth, the Colonel agreed, "I believe that two and two make four."

"Is that not a formula?"

"I do not know," he retorted.

As they battled, an amazing thing happened: the drill press across the street was shut down. Everyone had become so accustomed to that endless din that for just a moment the complete silence from outside was almost jarring; but suddenly it was possible to hear every word spoken clearly. It seemed to calm the entire courtroom, and Ivins finished the morning session by reading numerous polite letters from Roosevelt to Barnes, reinforcing the testimony that once they had worked together in harmony.

In the afternoon session Roosevelt immediately took charge. In earlier testimony he had claimed to have fought the infusion of corporate money into politics for his entire career, but had fallen short of showing that. During the lunch break, he explained, he had found evidence, citing a message he'd sent to Congress in December 1906 in which he had written, "I can recommend a law prohibiting corporations from contributing to the campaign expense of any party… Let individuals contribute as they desire, but let us prohibit in effective fashion all corporations from making contributions for any political purpose directly or indirectly."

As Roosevelt kept going with this, Ivins protested he hadn't asked that question about campaign financing and didn't need this answer. But Roosevelt was committed to sharing his views on this important topic with the jurors.

America had been long wrestling to find a way to fund politicians without that money buying influence. The problem went back to before the founding of the Republic, to 1757 when George Washington, a candidate for the Virginia House of Burgesses, bought a goodly portion of punch and hard cider for supporters. The new legislature reacted to that by passing legislation prohibiting candidates or people acting on their behalf from giving voters "money, meat, drink, entertainment or provision or…any present, gift, reward or entertainment" to aid in his election.

It was a restriction that did not hold very long, and since then money and politics had become bedfellows. It had been an important issue to Roosevelt throughout his career. He even campaigned on the issue in his 1904 presidential bid, proposing that corporations be prohibited from funding politicians or campaigns and urged public funding of candidates for office. And in 1907 Congress passed the *Tillman Act*, which prohibited corporate contributions in federal elections, but included no real way to enforce it.

When Ivins asked him if he had worked with political bosses to secure his nomination that year he replied, "I had not. I never moved my little finger to get the nomination excepting by my public acts as President."

"Is it not a fact," Ivins continued, "that during that election…a discussion, more or less heated arose with regard to the contribution of funds to the respective parties for political purposes?"

It was, the Colonel agreed, and admitted that after that election he had been charged by a senate committee of "extorting contributions from corporations and in my answer I explicitly stated the fact that contributions had been given to both parties…"

Ivins then began asking the witness if he knew that merchant banker Isaac Seligman had contributed $10,000, that Jacob Schiff, a backer of railroads, had contributed $10,000, that the Wall Street banker James Speer had given $25,000, that Frick and Carnegie, and Perkins and Hyde had made substantial donations. He knew they had contributed, he admitted, though not always the amount. He chuckled as he remembered that the twenty-eight-year-old Equitable Insurance executive James Hyde "was afterwards urged on me for appointment as

Ambassador to France and I did not think it was a proper appointment and I would not make it, and offered to make him Minister to Venezuela and he would not accept it...

"I did not consider the question that he had contributed as establishing a claim on his part or disqualification, either one, but I felt it entirely improper to appoint a man as young as that, with as little experience to such a great position. That he should win his spurs."

Ivins named man after man after man who had contributed thousands of dollars to the 1904 campaign; the Colonel knew some, but not all of them, and claimed to have no knowledge of the size of their donations. These men were bankers and oilmen, lawyers and financiers, miners and those who ran insurance concerns; it was Standard Oil and Pierpont Morgan and the Sugar Association; it was the Missouri and Southern Pacific Railroad, Prudential Life Insurance and City Bank. The long, long list made his attacks on corporate contributions seem quite toothless. Ivins droned on and on for more than an hour, quoting figures of $5000, $10,000, and $100,000, name after name, company after company. In his defense the Colonel said that when he learned the Standard Oil people had contributed, he told his campaign finance chairman to return that money and it was done. He told them, he said, and had received assurance "that no gifts of money would be accepted with any implication that anything whatever was to be done in the way of legislative or executive action or political action of any kind in return for their gifts of money...and that I would take office free from any obligation of any kind."

He added that his campaign specifically refused to accept contributions from any interest that had business pending with the government, citing a donation returned to a tobacco company that had a question before Treasury, or from any person who "stated he would like to have his name considered in connection with a diplomatic mission."

"Do you mean to tell this jury," Ivins asked, speaking slowly to make sure that everyone understood his doubt about this, "that you never knew the names of the parties who contributed to your election in 1904, and you never had the curiosity to inquire into the contributions whether they were private or corporate or for what purpose they were given?" By the time he was finished he was shouting, "Why didn't you find out who passed the hat for you?"

"Because I knew who was collecting the money... they were men of stainless probity on whose word I could absolutely rely...

"I had their guarantee that not a dollar was taken improperly... I restricted them to get money only from people who had contributed with the explicit knowledge that whether they gave it or withheld it their position would be in no way affected as regards to any public action which I controlled."

Ivins remained dubious, asking Roosevelt if he saw "any connection whatever between business and politics in contributions of $100,000, $50,000, $20,000."

"No more connection than there is when those same men contribute to the YMCA." And then he put those donations in context. "The contribution from Mr. Perkins of $25,000 might be considerably less (to him) than a contribution of $25 from the station agent at Oyster Bay and I should feel as grateful to the one man for the $25 as to the other man for $25,000 and I should be incapable of acting for either in any way because of that contribution."

"We don't know about your capability," Ivins said. "You have answered the question which I asked and I shall have to ask you to confine your answers to my questions and if you don't I shall have to ask the court to interfere." Then he pressed down even harder, asking if the Colonel really believed $3,000,000 contributed to a political campaign could be considered in the same class as donations to the YMCA?

He did.

Then, Ivins asked, waving a finger at the witness, did he not see the possibility of evil in those large contributions?

"When they become too large," T.R. said, "I think there is a real evil."

Despite Ivins's efforts, Roosevelt appeared to be succeeding in turning the trial into a referendum on his political philosophy. Who couldn't agree with the Colonel that moneyed interests had too much political power? Ivins set out once again to show that Roosevelt's noble words were not always matched by his actions in office. While he said, "I hope it will be worked out…for the nation at large so that there shall be a limit as to what amount of money shall be spent on a national campaign," he did admit to Ivins that during his almost eight years in office he made no such suggestion.

Ivins threw his own words back at him, asking, "If it is all done sincerely and in an honest political belief that it is being contributed to the welfare of the nation why should there be any limitation?"

Roosevelt had always been a student of human nature and a realist; his candor was a great part of his appeal to ordinary Americans. And it was experience and behavior he relied on to answer, "Because I think that after a certain amount of contribution has been reached then it is impossible legitimately to use it for that purposes..."

Ivins had the ability to move seamlessly between subjects, knowing that he would eventually find a thread to tie it all together. He began a discussion of the presidential election of 1908, trying to show how T.R. acted as a power broker, a boss to pick his successor. Roosevelt admitted he had suggested and recommended William Taft, claiming that "I found that if I didn't suggest or recommend the nomination of somebody I would be nominated myself," which he did not want at all. "I had to fight it tooth and nail!" he said boldly.

Although during his term in office he had said numerous times that he unequivocally would not be a candidate for what was in essence a third term, there was great pressure on him to run again. He warned those people in his administration urging him to do so not to put his name in nomination. Hearing about

Roosevelt's self-proclaimed principled independence was of no interest to Ivins, who quickly pivoted to Roosevelt's actions before and during the convention to win the nomination for Taft. That line of questioning, while interesting to the political enthusiasts in the gallery, ended with a bit of a whimper and led into the conclusion of the first week of the trial.

While Barnes retreated to his Albany home for the weekend, Roosevelt spent the weekend being his irrepressible self. After meeting with his lawyers Saturday morning, he went horseback riding, accompanied by a few reporters, in whom he confided that he was thoroughly enjoying himself and looked forward to spending another full week on the stand.

Despite the acrimony between them inside the courtroom, for the lawyers, this was still a noble battle in an honorable profession where the combatants could put down their rhetorical gloves and socialize together. And on Sunday, attorneys for both sides accompanied by their wives, all now in Syracuse just for this trial, visited Judge Andrews's country home for afternoon tea at the invitation of Mrs. William S. Andrews.

The Colonel attended morning services at the First Reformed Church, where he happily greeted parishioners. As he shook hands he was approached by a kindergarten teacher who told him about an elderly blind woman who professed to be his most loyal supporter. Eighty-five-year-old Susan McLane had written to him while he was in the

White House, and had received a return note from Mrs. Roosevelt signed by the president and the First Lady. "Why," the Colonel responded, "take me to her. I will go and see her."

Surrounded by several friends and reporters, they walked several blocks to her house and the Colonel surprised her. They spent fifteen minutes privately, and Miss McLane later gushed that she didn't even need her ear trumpet to hear him. "It hardly seems true. In all my life I've never had such a warm handshake."

The first week had generally been a good one for the Colonel, and not simply based on what had transpired inside the courtroom. As the *New York Times* described it: "One thing at least the trial has accomplished—it has put T.R back on the front page, where he delights to be…for the present at least he is the most prominent political figure in the country."

CHAPTER SEVEN

This was an unusually expensive trial. It was estimated that the libel suit was costing both Roosevelt and Barnes as much as $8000 a week for their attorneys and support staff. Jurors were paid $3 a day, witnesses received 50 cents a day plus 8 cents a mile for traveling expenses. Reporters' expenses averaged about $65 a week plus telegraph tolls. While the city had to pay a wide range of expenses, the revenue from visitors likely covered those costs and more.

But even at a cost of $8000 a week, it seemed like neither Roosevelt nor Barnes was in much of a hurry to end the trial. Courtroom observers estimated it might continue for another three or four weeks. The two sides had listed almost one hundred possible witnesses, and no one could even guess when the Colonel would finish his testimony. It seemed like he was having a grand old time on the stand.

After all, few civil trials in American history had received the nationwide attention that this one was receiving. Those few had generally involved interpretations of law that affected a great number of people—like the Zenger trial or the Dred Scott decision—rather than a simple dispute between two people. Civil trials, or torts, typically lacked the excitement of criminal trials. At stake was property or money rather than lives and freedom. But tort law was fundamental for a society to exist; most often when the common people looked to the law to settle disputes it was in the civil law. As long ago as 1765, Sir William Blackstone in his *Commentaries*, long considered the sourcebook for British law, referred to torts as "all actions for trespasses, nuisances, defamatory words and the like."

A century and a half earlier, juries in Virginia were already deciding civil cases, although it wasn't until the mid-nineteenth century that torts became a separate branch of the law in America. Law schools did not teach torts as a separate subject until 1870, and the first torts casebook was published four years later. Even then, lawyers were supposed to be conversant in all aspects of the law, and on the same day might just as easily represent a man accused of murder as someone who had been injured when a horse ran him down. Ivins was one such attorney. Only a few years before this trial, he had represented the American Tobacco Company in front of the Supreme Court when it was sued by the government for operating a monopoly, while also maintaining an active criminal law practice.

* * *

Picking up the previous week's testimony, in which he had established that Roosevelt and Barnes once worked in harmony, Ivins asked the Colonel about a meeting that took place at his home in Oyster Bay that Barnes and several others attended. The purpose of that meeting was to discuss the candidacy of Charles Hughes for governor. The Colonel supported him; the others did not. Roosevelt admitted, "I was in greater sympathy with Mr. Barnes and the other gentlemen than I was to Hughes… (but I supported Hughes because) I believed the people wanted him to be governor."

In response, Ivins wondered, "Did you regard it as any evidence of wrong, immorality, corruption or unrighteousness on the part of Mr. Barnes and Mr. Hendricks that they favored another candidate?"

Roosevelt tried to avoid a direct response, but Ivins cut him off. "No. Answer the question." When the Colonel continued to equivocate, Ivins appealed to Judge Andrews "to direct the witness to give a categorical answer…"

Judge Andrews told the witness that he must answer the question yes or no, but still the Colonel resisted. "I can't answer it collectively for all?"

Ivins was adamant; his voice rising as he asked again, "Did you at the time regard it as evidence of corruption, immorality or unrighteousness on the part of Mr. Barnes?"

There was no way for Roosevelt to avoid answering. "I did not," he finally said.

Ivins then introduced what was undoubtedly his strongest evidence that even if Roosevelt, when he was Governor, did not always work hand-in-hand with the previous New York boss Thomas Platt, he certainly was in league with him. He entered into the record a pile of handwritten letters estimated to be a foot high, detailing numerous incidents of the two men working together on almost every appointment or decision Roosevelt made. The letters revealed that Platt had substantial input into these appointments and Governor Roosevelt never made an important decision without consulting him. The newsmen wrote that when Ivins produced these letters the Colonel looked unusually grim.

And for good reason. The letters undermined a fundamental tenet of Roosevelt's political identity that he had so carefully cultivated throughout his career—his independence.

Oddly though, rather than reading them himself, Ivins designated his co-counsel, the former Onondaga County district attorney William L. Barnum, to read the letters to the jury and then cross-examine the witness about them. When asked why after the session, Ivins explained, "Oh, we just decided that we had been letting the line run out long enough. Now we are going to keep our finger on the reel. Up to the present we have been letting the Colonel make an Exhibit A of himself. Now we are going at him in a different manner."

That different manner quickly became apparent. Unlike Ivins, who had mostly let Roosevelt have his say, Barnum was going to try to force him to answer his questions.

The Syracuse lawyer read a letter about the appointment of a Buffalo judge, for example, in which Roosevelt concluded, "In any event, I would like to see you and consult with you about the matter."

Asked if that meant precisely what it appeared to mean, T.R. said, "I can't tell you in that specific case. I consulted..."

"Just answer the question," Barnum snapped.

"I do not remember. I consulted him; I presume I did, Sir, because I consulted him on all matters where he wished to be consulted." And then he added, trying to redeem himself, "And then I did what I thought was right."

Barnum demanded that last part be stricken from the record, which it was, and a few minutes later, after Roosevelt once again avoided answering a direct question, said curtly, "That answer was not responsive. And I would suggest that your honor instruct the witness to answer the questions and nothing else."

The Colonel grinned broadly at that complaint, and before the judge could respond replied, "I do not remember."

Gone was the courteous duel of wit between Roosevelt and Ivins, replaced by the curt Barnum. The whole mood of the courtroom changed. "There were burrs under Barnum's tongue," the *Herald* wrote. "He lacks the suavity, the soft-voiced courtesy and the Chesterfielden manner of his seniors. There were times when his roughness in style and his lack of

William Barnum, who assisted Ivins, was described by his hometown Rochester Herald *as lacking "the suavity, the soft-voiced courtesy and the Chesterfielden manner of his seniors. At times his roughness in style...displeased a great many persons who did not like to see an ex-president of the United States addressed like a police court offender."*

respect for Roosevelt displeased a great many persons, who did not like to see an ex-president of the United States addressed like a police court offender."

But it was the letters that did the real damage. These were letters the public clearly was never intended to see. For example, in one T.R. wrote, "Locke has refused to act as counsel, I am at a loss who to suggest. I wish to get some man whose good name would be a guarantee of the good faith in which we are acting. What do you advise?"

Referring to Roosevelt's libel about an invisible government, Barnum wondered, "Did you make it known to the public at large at that time that you were consulting with Senator Platt..."

"That I could not say," the Colonel replied. "You will have to look at the newspapers to see."

Barnum had him and did not let loose. Roosevelt's swagger was muted as he tried his best to explain away a correspondence that detailed a relationship few members of the public were aware existed. Even the progressive magazine *The Nation* wrote harshly, "Colonel Roosevelt did not come into court with clean hands…when governor he practiced with gusto all the arts that he afterwards came to call black." The letters describe Roosevelt in 1898 "not as the apostle of righteousness and social justice that he was said to have become in 1912, but as a vigorous young man, not too fastidious, intensely ambitious, consumed with desire for high office, who had deliberately made up his mind that the road to success for him lay with the party organization and the party boss."

Letter after letter after letter, the cumulative effect was damning. "I am inclined to agree with your view of Beckett and the inadvisability of appointing him. What do you think of Jessup?"

"All right, I'll change the whole board of tax assessors."

"If Cohen would take it, of course I should only be too delighted to appoint him. Shall I try?"

Roosevelt twisted in his seat as these letters were read. Often, when asked about this fact or that, he professed not to remember. "I do not know."

"I do not remember." Over and over. Once, in frustration, Roosevelt blurted out, "I've made 40,000 appointments to office…"

But Barnum held up a warning hand, and the Colonel stopped his complaint. The lawyer did his best to keep the witness off-balance. Once Roosevelt blurted, "Yes, I remember it perfectly now. Assemblyman Hill…"

Barnum stopped him. "I have not asked you…"

"I was only going to correct my previous answer."

"But I did not ask you, you know."

After being chastised several times, Roosevelt asked simply in frustration, "What is their exact question?"

Judge Andrews replied, "It is their right, Colonel Roosevelt, to have the questions answered without any explanation unless they desire it."

Barnum focused on the close relationship between Senator Platt, the Republican Party boss, and Roosevelt, suggesting about two appointments, "And you did not appoint either one of them until after you had received the endorsement of Mr. Platt, as I understand it. Is that so?"

"Until after he had said he would not oppose them, yes."

This evidence that Roosevelt worked closely with Barnes's mentor continued unabated into the afternoon session. It bore heavily on the Colonel's credibility. After reading another letter Barnum asked, "Do you remember sending a bill to Mr. Platt…providing for the expenditure of money in connection with the water front in New York City?"

"I do not. I have no doubt that I did."

"Do you remember what the amount of the appropriation finally was as passed the legislature, if any?"

"I do not."

Barnum picked up a bit of Ivins's sarcasm, suggesting, "A little matter of $12,000,000 wouldn't make any impression on you, wouldn't affect your memory at all?"

"After sixteen years," the Colonel responded angrily, practically pushing himself off his chair with indignation, "during which I have had to do with billions of expenditures, that item does not remain in my mind."

The realities of politics when exposed in a contentious courtroom can sound far harsher than in practice. Governing is always a collaborative effort, but Barnum's masterful use of the language made everyday decisions seem dark and nefarious. For example, he said quite accurately, "You had to take nobody's suggestion unless you cared to as to whom you nominated, did you?"

Roosevelt's response was equally accurate. "I did, if I wanted to have my nomination confirmed."

Barnum made his point. "That is, you had to be in an alliance with the 'invisible government,' so-called, to get your nominations confirmed?"

The Colonel held himself back, replying, "To get the nominations confirmed I had to have the support of the Senate and the Senate was responsive to Mr. Platt's wishes."

Reading still another letter, this one in which the Colonel wrote that he was "'more touched than I can say'" that Platt had helped pass important civil service legislation, Barnum asked pointedly, "At that time you didn't consider him a bad boss, did you?"

The best reply T.R. could muster was "I didn't consider that action bad."

Barnum pressed him. "Well, with Mr. Platt, whenever he was doing things which you requested, to aid you, those transactions were always righteous? Is that so?"

Sometimes, it seemed, the Colonel was a victim of his own hubris. "They always were when he aided me," he agreed.

Barnum wouldn't let go. "You never criticized Mr. Platt at any such time, did you?"

"I never criticized Mr. Platt at any such time."

The plaintiff's counsel then began attacking the pillars of the defense, laying the groundwork to go after Roosevelt's claim that Platt and Barnes opposed a franchise tax bill and he stood up to them on it. On the contrary, Ivins explained, "I expect to prove…that they did not oppose it, but that the franchise tax bill, as passed, was passed by their consent and approval and in consultation with the defendant…"

Barnum's questions were quite specific and hinted at some ulterior motive. The fact that Roosevelt replied numerous times that he didn't know or didn't remember or couldn't recall if, for example, certain people were at a breakfast meeting, created an impression that he was trying to avoid answering. It was a fine bit of lawyering from Barnum even when sometimes less than fair, as can be the case with cross-examination. Roosevelt had led one of the grand lives of the end of the nineteenth century and the beginning of the next. It was chock-full of extraordinary experiences, momentous decisions and significant events. So it was not surprising that when Barnum asked questions such as, "Do you remember what the duties of the Tax Commissioners of the State were at that time?" the best answer he could give was "No. Merely in general." The impression left though was not one of forgetfulness, but at least in some cases, intentional avoidance.

The Supreme Court justice Oliver Wendell Holmes, then in the midst of his second decade on the court, once observed, "Lawyers spend a great deal of their time shoveling smoke." Barnum had done as much in his examination and successfully had made it seem meaningful. In a criminal case a juror has to be convinced the defendant is guilty "beyond a reasonable doubt," but in a civil case jurors must simply decide if "the preponderance of evidence" favors the plaintiff. It's a less rigid test; the burden of proof rests on the plaintiff, who attempts to show through evidence that what he or she contends is more likely to be true than not. Lacking the proverbial "smoking gun," Barnum had to resort, at least in part, to Justice Holmes's smoke. The Colonel had pretty much had his way through the first week of the trial, but Barnum's pile of letters made an impressive display, and Roosevelt's halting testimony had stopped whatever momentum he had developed.

Barnum persisted, making sure there could be no lingering doubts about Roosevelt's respect for the boss. "Is it not a fact," he asked, "that on all matters where you appointed judges, district attorneys, that before doing so you talked with Senator Platt about it?"

"I should say that on most of the times it was," the Colonel agreed, "whether on all I could not answer."

"Do you ever remember now an occasion when you had the appointment of a judge to any court, that you did not talk to Senator Platt about it prior to the time you made the appointment?"

"I cannot tell you," although minutes later he testified that he had not conferred with Platt when appointing judges "in every instance," and on occasion had even declined to appoint a candidate recommended by him.

After this long and sometimes repetitious reading of these letters, the courtroom had settled into a general malaise, but the spectators were brought to attention by the final letter from the defendant to Platt. Written in 1900, it showed the Colonel musing about accepting the Republican nomination for the vice presidency, a letter that demonstrated the closeness of their relationship. But it also revealed the behind-the-scenes negotiations for the country's second highest office. There had been rumors that the organization nominated Roosevelt for the job because they wanted to replace him with a more loyal and cooperative Republican governor. Among politicians, the vice presidency was considered a dead-end job, little more than a ceremonial post. In fact, Roosevelt himself had written to Platt, "I would a great deal rather be anything, say professor of history, than vice president." But to the American people it remained a very prestigious position, and the concept of someone being forced to take it was surprising. The Colonel had written, "I have, of course, done a great deal of thinking about the Vice Presidency since the talk I had with you… I have been reserving the matter to talk over with you, but in view of the publication in *The Sun* this morning, I would like to begin the conversation…with just a line or two.

"I can't help feeling more and more that the Vice Presidency is not an honor in which I could do anything, and not an office in which a man who is still vigorous and not past middle life has much chance of doing anything. As you know, I am of an active nature… In spite of all the work I have thoroughly enjoyed being governor. I have kept every promise, expressed or implied I made on the stump, and I feel like the Republican party is stronger before the state because of my incumbency.

"Now, I should like to be Governor for another term…but as Vice President I don't see that there is anything I can do. I should simply be a presiding officer and that I should find a bore. As you know I am a man of moderate means and I should have to live very simply in Washington…"

In the very human terms that had enabled him to connect so well to average Americans, the letter continued, "My children are growing up and I find the burden of their education constantly heavier, so that I am in no means sure that I should go on in public life at all… The only reason I should like to go on is that, as I have not been a moneymaker, I feel rather in honor bound to leave my children the equivalent in the way of a substantial sum in actual achievement in politics or letters… The more I look at it the less I feel as if the Vice Presidency offered anything to me that would warrant my taking it.

"Of course, I shall not say anything until I hear from you, and possibly not until I see you. But I did want you to know how I felt."

With those words, the thought that the defendant would not respond to this offer "until I hear from you" was the last bit of testimony jurors heard before recessing for the night. Measured against the Colonel's words attacking the boss system, it did make him sound disingenuous.

After listening to the Colonel's testimony, the reporter for the *New York World* had created a satirical Rooseveltian dictionary. Among the highlights were *Boss*, a political leader opposed to Roosevelt; *Leader*, a political boss in favor of Roosevelt; *Jekyll-Hyde*, a duel character, Jekyll supporting Roosevelt, Hyde opposing him; *Testimony*, a stump speech by Roosevelt addressed to a jury; *Liar*, a person who says anything in contradiction to Roosevelt; *Barnes*, an incorrigible person beyond the means of salvation.

When questioning resumed the following morning, Barnum focused on that last letter, asking Roosevelt if he took Platt's advice about the nomination. "I did not," the Colonel said firmly, but when pushed admitted, "He advised its acceptance at the time." Barnum intentionally left unasked and unanswered the question of what eventually led Roosevelt to take the position of vice president, leaving jurors with the impression that Platt eventually won out.

The Colonel sat somberly through the morning as Barnum continued reading the letters. An especially ominous exchange concerned the Franchise Tax Bill; Platt wrote, "Our friends of New York Central are very anxious to have you sign Senate bill 763 exempting from the franchise tax bill grade crossings of steam railroads. I hope you can consistently do so. Senator Depew is very anxious."

"I received your telegram yesterday," the Colonel had replied. "It was too late for me to act as I had already published a memorandum… I am exceedingly sorry if any damage has been caused to the New York Central or the Long Island Railroad, but it was a matter where I really had to act in accordance with the advice of the commission unless it could be shown they were wrong."

As these letters were read to the otherwise silent courtroom, the Colonel sat stoically in the witness box, no doubt aware that jurors were watching him carefully for any reaction. At times he would shift in the wooden chair, or cross and recross his legs, but mostly he kept his eyes focused on Barnum and gave away no hint of emotion as these occasionally embarrassing details were revealed. If the jurors were looking to him to determine the impact, they got none. One letter that drew considerable attention was Roosevelt's response to a wire from Platt demanding he attend a meeting in Washington. "All right. Of course, in view of your second telegram. I will come but you are not an easy boss."

The reporters picked up that phrase, "easy boss," and pinned it to both Roosevelt and Platt.

Barnum had been matter-of-fact throughout his cross-examination, and for the most part Roosevelt had managed to maintain his composure, even when some of those revealing letters were being read. But glimpses of anger still managed to surface; for example Barnum asked if the correspondence he was reading covered practically all of the important "acts or measures" that took place while Roosevelt was governor. When the Colonel said it did not, Barnum asked what percentage it did cover. When T.R. began mentioning some of the issues left out, Barnum stopped him. Roosevelt shrugged. "I am only trying to help you."

To which Barnum retorted coldly, "I appreciate it, but I have not asked for your help and do not need it."

With that, Ivins resumed the questioning. He continued with the readings, although now he began reading the exceedingly friendly correspondence between Roosevelt and Barnes. Among those first letters was a note the Colonel had sent to Barnes in Albany following the 1904 election. "Pray let me thank you most cordially and warmly for what you have done in this election. I appreciate it to the full. With regards to Mrs. Barnes, believe me..."

Jurors have been known to reach their verdict for almost any conceivable reason, but at times it just comes down to a feeling: Who did they like better?

Who did they believe? It's why attorneys try to form some sort of ethereal bond with jurors, and walk a tightrope when questioning a witness between seeming too lax or too tough. The jury listened dispassionately, but the impression left by these letters certainly could hardly have supported the claims of corruption and dishonesty that came later.

At one point Ivins stopped and wondered, "At this time you had not yet discovered that Mr. Barnes was Mr. Hyde, had you?"

"Wasn't my testimony that I thought that element was in him from the beginning?"

"I don't think it was."

"I think it was;" the Colonel corrected. "I think you are in error."

Suddenly, without laying any preparation, Ivins set off on an entirely new path, seeking to show that Roosevelt was an active participant in the "invisible government," this alliance between corrupt business and corrupt politicians that he had railed against. He did so by tying together campaign contributions and actions either taken or not taken during his administration. One of the most significant controversies during his administration was the 1907 purchase of the Tennessee Coal and Iron Company by the Steel Corporation. Critics tried to stop that merger, claiming it gave the Steel Corporation a monopoly over the industry. Roosevelt himself had so often taken action against these large corporations, or trusts, that he had become known as the Trust Buster. But during the financial panic of 1907, he assured the president of the Steel Corporation that he would not invoke provisions of the Sherman Anti-Trust Act to prevent his merger of two industrial giants. Many people wondered why he had stepped back, and Ivins offered a suggestion. "Was Mr. Frick one of the contributors to your campaign?"

Henry Frick was a coal baron, a founder of U.S. Steel and one of the wealthiest men in America.

"He was."

"Was he interested in the Steel Corporation?"

"He was."

"Was Judge Gary one of the contributors to your campaign, interested in the steel corporation?"

Elbert Gary also was a founder of the Steel Corporation.

"He was."

"Was Mr. Perkins one of the contributors to your campaign interested in the steel corporation?"

J.P. Morgan banker George Perkins had helped put together the steel corporation.

"He was."

Ivins asked if the Colonel had considered prosecuting Perkins Harvester Company for violations of antitrust legislation. Roosevelt said he did not remember such a step being discussed, causing Ivins to ask, his words dripping with sarcasm, if contributions figured in the decision not to go after that company.

The inference was obvious: in exchange for real or promised campaign contributions, the Colonel had allowed a merger to take place that furthered a monopoly and ignored other potential violations. This was the ultimate affront to Roosevelt, and the anger showed on his face. He gritted his teeth and with his hands grasping the arms of his chair pushed forward, as if ready to burst out of his seat and pounce.

The defendant's counsel, Bowers, finally showed spunk, objecting vehemently. "Now they seek to show that contributions were made by certain persons who were interested in the steel corporation. Nothing is suggested that there was any prosecution that ought to have been brought against the steel corporation. Nothing is suggested that any favor was sought for by anybody whatsoever concerning the steel corporation. Not a word is given to indicate any reason why any action should have been brought against the steel corporation. I object to going on with such questions as that leave the assumption of very serious and substantial matters."

Ivins responded, thumping his table and declaring, "That is not material here."

"Yes!" Roosevelt shot back, slamming his hand on the bench with equal fury. "It is material."

It created a dilemma for the judge, who admitted, "The trouble with a good deal of evidence in this case is that I cannot tell at the outset whether it is to be connected to it... Mr. Ivins says he is going to try to. If he does not make it material, I shall strike it out."

Ivins's response was modest; with a bow he said, "I suffer from some human limitations, that is that I can only ask one question at a time."

Bowers countered, "You have only asked one question at a time, but I am inclined to think that the course I have taken in permitting the introduction of evidence of almost every kind and character here has resulted in your having used a great deal of time for a great deal of unnecessary matter."

After some legal bickering, Judge Andrews accepted Ivins's plea that he intended to connect all his points in forthcoming testimony, pointing out correctly, "I cannot introduce evidence of that kind in my cross-examination of this witness."

Bowers was finally unleashed. After another question he deemed pointless, he pleaded, "Now stop please with that. We will be here all summer trying this case."

"We may," Ivins said, not the slightest bit deterred. "I cannot tell. We did not start this game."

"Yes, you did."

"Yes, *you* did, Mr. Roosevelt made the first publication."

The entire courtroom was laughing lightly at the sight of these accomplished lawyers exchanging playground insults. But eventually Ivins got back to his point: Did Roosevelt accept campaign contributions from Perkins who was interested in the American Harvester Company? Was Pierre du Pont of the chemical concern a contributor to his 1904 campaign?

Roosevelt had staked his reputation on being independent, that his influence or power was not for sale, but now Ivins seemed to be promising to produce evidence that the Colonel was duplicitous. If he was successful, Roosevelt's reputation would be greatly damaged.

Ivins moved from there to relations between his

client and the Colonel, which Roosevelt asserted was "entirely pleasant until sometime after February, 1911," or when Roosevelt decided to run against President Taft. "I opposed him strongly in 1910," T.R. testified. "But my relations personally were perfectly pleasant."

Ivins then handed him a speech and asked if he remembered having said anything of this kind? Roosevelt read it and handed it back to him, explaining, "Mr. Ivins, you showed me a speech made by Mr. Barnes and asked if I said it. Of course I didn't." The courtroom responded with great laughter.

It got worse. Ivins gave Roosevelt an article from a 1910 edition of the *New York Times* and asked, "whether you noticed a reported or alleged statement by Mr. Barnes..."

Bowers explained that Ivins wanted to know "whether you see that there now?"

"No, not at all," Ivins said. "I am not an idiot. I know he sees it now." Once again, laughter filled the courtroom.

Judge Andrews continued to tread very lightly, explaining to the jury that he was allowing a series of newspaper and magazine articles to be entered as evidence only about the "feeling of the defendant toward the plaintiff" and not to prove the truth of it.

Perhaps the most difficult challenge facing Ivins in order to win any real damages was showing malice, proving that Roosevelt's libelous words were written with the intent to do harm to Barnes. Doing that in this case required showing the history of the dispute between the two men and the source of Roosevelt's anger. To begin that task Ivins read an article from the *Times* in 1912, when the two men were battling over the Republican nomination at the Chicago convention. This was the tipping point that turned what had been a friendship or at least an alliance into an irreconcilable political and personal rivalry. In the article, Teddy Roosevelt, the candidate fighting for the party's nomination, was introduced to the courtroom and the jurors. And as had usually been the case, he held nothing in reserve: "There are many honest men who have not agreed with me in this contest," the Colonel was quoted as saying, "and who do not believe that the people are fit to govern themselves. But surely these men must agree with us when we come down to a question of making right and wrong such as it is involved in the effort of Mr. Barnes and his associates on behalf of Mr. Taft to reverse the popular verdict and to nominate at Chicago some man whom the rank and file of the Republican party have declared they do not desire to see nominated..."

The battle to appoint a temporary chairman was significant, as that person would control the convention floor. Roosevelt was adamant that "no man should be chosen as temporary chairman who is put forward by Mr. Barnes and by those men who represent the principles and practices of Mr. Barnes."

"Did you say that?" Ivins asked his witness.

Roosevelt agreed, "I said that."

Days later he was again quoted by the newspapers, "The (party) platform and the speeches expounding it...show that it was designed in defense and advocacy of the twin principles for which Mr. Barnes stands—the bosses to rule the people and the supremacy of privilege over the right of humanity."

"I said that."

Still later, "Mr. Barnes stands as the representative of the very worst forms of bossism and politics. No progressive delegate can afford to vote for any man supported by Mr. Barnes and his allies, for any such vote is a vote against popular rule and against the basic principles not merely of the Republican party but of decent American citizens.

"Mr. Barnes...states that the doctrines which I have advocated are subversive to our form of government. The doctrines that I have advocated are, first, the right of the people to rule, and second, their duty so to rule as to bring about not merely political but also social and industrial justice... Mr. Barnes thoroughly distrusts the people and says so. He disbelieves in democracy. In his preaching and in practice he embodies boss rule in its most effective form."

Harsh words. "He distrusts the people and says so."

"He disbelieves in democracy." As they were being read, Roosevelt sat upright, paying close attention, occasionally glancing at the jury to make sure they were hearing every word. These articles were much easier for him to absorb than the private letters.

In still another article the Colonel accused Barnes of stealing convention delegates to obtain the nomination for Taft. If there was any concern that jurors were not paying attention or were confused, it was allayed when talesman Walter Zuill suddenly spoke out from the jury box, asking the judge, "Are we to understand that these last three articles are received with the same privilege as the other two?"

It served as a reminder that jurors throughout history had been active participants in trials, permitted to ask questions.

Judge Andrews said his same ruling applied to this article as the others. The intent, he reiterated was to show "the state of mind of the defendant towards the plaintiff prior to the alleged libel."

Roosevelt's bitter attacks on the evils of the boss system continued after the election. In a speech in Pittsburgh he said, "They stole from the rank and file Republican party the right to govern themselves, to nominate their own candidates and promulgate their own platform… They are foes of decent citizenship. Their political lives depend upon their keeping politics in such condition that decent men cannot succeed them and the ordinary citizen cannot get control of their own government."

"I said that," the witness admitted, and court was adjourned.

CHAPTER EIGHT

While the trial continued to dominate the front page of hundreds of newspapers throughout the country, the war in Europe was always lurking in the background. The *New York Times* headlines read, "Hit at Roosevelt as Trusts Friend;" "Ivins Intimates Campaign Gifts Held Back Steel, Harvester and Other Prosecutions;" "How Colonel Worked Hand in Glove with Platt and Barnes Is Emphasized." But it was the other stories that seemed more ominous: "Allies at Ypres Take Offensive," "Allies Battle for A Foothold at Dardanelles" and a small sidebar near the bottom of the page that warned, "Says Poison Gas Killed Canadians."

The Great War had been raging in Europe for almost a year. In America, a sizable number of immigrants from countries on both sides of the conflict lobbied for support for their nations, but President Wilson pursued the narrow path of neutrality. Roosevelt had spoken out repeatedly and forcefully for America to intervene on the side of England and France. Two months before the trial began he had written, "More and more I come to the view that in a really tremendous world struggle, with a great moral issue involved, neutrality does not serve righteousness; to be neutral between right and wrong is to serve wrong."

On numerous occasions Roosevelt urged Wilson to begin preparing for war by training soldiers and refitting the navy. But the president had refused, believing there was protection in neutrality.

As the participants entered the Syracuse courtroom on April 28, 1915, news was arriving that a French cruiser, the *Léon Gambetta*, had been torpedoed by an Austrian submarine and its 529-man crew had perished. The German government also was refusing to compensate the owners of the American sailing ship *William Frye*, which had been boarded off the coast of Brazil by the crew of the *SMS Prinz Eitel Friedrich* and subsequently destroyed. The highest profile trial in the country was taking place against the backdrop of increasingly ominous signs that the United States could be dragged into a truly world war.

Ivins resumed his attack by asking Roosevelt if he recalled making a speech *after* the publication of the statements at issue in a town named Hudson Falls. The Colonel did not, and asked Ivins where Hudson Falls was. The tone of the day was set when the lawyer replied sarcastically, "I have never been Governor and I have not been all over the State and

I have not made many speeches. I am not a good geographer of the State." When the witness suggested he had no doubt he'd made the speech but didn't remember the place, Ivins asked, "If I were to tell you that it was north of Saratoga would that help?"

Roosevelt cut to the chase: "If you would show me the speech I think I could remember it."

Ivins quoted a line from the speech, then demanded the Colonel, "Just answer yes or no. Did you make that speech?"

And with that the Colonel threw back at the lawyer his continued demands on precision. "You ask me if I made it at Hudson Falls. I cannot answer that yes or no."

The essence of the material Ivins wanted in the record was Roosevelt's belief, as stated in this speech, that the Republican and Democratic bosses often worked together for the good of the political boss system rather than the people. And that his deliberate repetition of this charge both before and after publication of the allegedly libelous article, even after the action against him had been filed and his attention had been brought to it, supports the charge that his intentions were malicious. Instead of rectifying or modifying his statements, he continued to speak out, using words and phrases such as, "What I object to is their going through the form of being in different parties when on the great issues that must concern our whole people they stand together."

Ivins quoted from the speech: "The principles and practices of politics in which one of them believes are just exactly the principles and practices which the other believes... It is the same type of government that they have been responsible for..."

When that was read to the jury, Roosevelt objected that several sentences had been omitted. From memory, he added, "Such as this, 'If there were real party distinctions in this state Mr. Barnes and Mr. Murphy would be in the same party and I would not object to that.'"

"It is a sorry jest," Ivins quoted from another Roosevelt speech. "It is brazen effrontery and hypocrisy for them to assume that they are against Tammany. They are against Tammany before the election if it will help them. They are for Tammany after the election if anything can be put through..."

Roosevelt made similar speeches throughout the state; in Utica and Gloversville and Amsterdam and Norwich and Oneonta and Syracuse and other places, all of them attacking party bosses. "I won't say their principles are the same because I am not ready to admit myself as to whether they have any principle but their practices are the same. When either is in control of the State government at Albany we get just the same results out of that government..."

Ivins read portions of another stirring speech, this one reprinted in *Putnam's* magazine: "There are in the body politic, economic and social, many and grave evils and there is urgent necessity for the sternest war upon them... I hail as a benefactor every writer or speaker, every man who, on the platform or in book, magazine or newspaper, with merciless severity makes such attack, provided always that he in his turn remembers that the attack is of use only if it is absolutely truthful. The liar is no whit better than the thief, and if his mendacity takes the form of slander he may be worse than most thieves. It puts a premium upon knavery untruthfully to attack an honest man, or even with hysterical exaggeration to assail a bad man with untruth…

"…The effort to make financial or political profit out of their destruction of character can only result in public calamity. Gross and reckless assaults on character, whether on the stump or in newspaper or magazine or book, create a morbid and vicious public sentiment, and at the same time act as a profound deterrent to able men of normal sensitiveness and tend to prevent them from entering the public service at any price."

When Ivins finished he asked, "Do you remember saying that?"

"I do."

All of these speeches, Ivins emphasized, repeated the alleged libel. "He took it upon himself… to repeat the very matter which under the law of libel…which was his duty to have investigated and seen or else take the consequences of the repetition so far as it bears upon the question of malice."

And with that thought reverberating through the courtroom, Ivins ended his cross-examination.

The duel between the two men was hardly done; there would be several more confrontations before the trial was through, but both of them had staked out territory and defended it well. Now it was the

ONONDAGA HISTORICAL ASSOCIATION

This sketch from the Syracuse Journal *tried to capture the extraordinary testimony of Roosevelt, "who used all the gestures and expressions that have become so famous" to "hypnotize the jury with his personality" while his courtly attorney, Bowers, and the dapper Ivins unsuccessfully tried to harness his energy.*

job of Bowers to clean up after Ivins, after which the next great confrontation would begin when William Barnes took the stand.

As Bowers began his redirect examination the Colonel seemed suddenly and completely reinvigorated. He leaned forward in his seat, a great smile on his face, his arms poised in front of him, ready to leap into action supporting whatever statement he made. Bowers began by reminding his witness, and the jury, that Ivins had asked about a series of campaign contributions, citing an "official report."

This was the long and telling list of industrial giants who had contributed to Roosevelt's presidential campaign. And then, piece by piece he demonstrated that the document was not official at all, that there was little evidence to support the numbers quoted by Ivins. As he did so, the generally civil tone between the attorneys grew hostile. "I had the same confidence in Mr. Ivins. I had not the slightest doubt he was reading from an official report. It was not until I read the report that evening I saw the real situation… We will not have the jury misinformed by reason of the complete confidence of my client in the gentleman that examined him."

This was far more damaging to the plaintiff than simply whether or not the figures were accurate or inflated. It went right to the credibility of their case. If Ivins knowingly slipped in bogus figures, what other deceptions might be part of his case? How could he, or his client for that matter, be trusted? Bowers persisted, demanding he be allowed to show "this inaccuracy to the fullest extent."

Ivins attempted to defend himself. "If your honor please," he objected, "my good faith has been directly put in question by my dear and devoted friend, Mr. Bowers."

"Well, sir," Bowers responded, "there are matters beyond our friendship."

Ivins then attempted to minimize the damage, claiming he simply was reading testimony given before a United States Senate committee and if anyone was at fault it was Roosevelt himself. "Instead of relying upon his memory he turned to me from time to time and put me on the stand, and I simply from time to time referred to the fact that had been reported."

Bowers reread from the testimony. "Then the witness, 'I assume you are reading from the official report?' Mr. Ivins, 'I am reading from the official report.' Mr. Ivins is a trained lawyer, an able lawyer, a man who has studied these things with much of care. He knew whether that was a report, whether it was testimony."

Judge Andrews agreed, informing the jury, "If as (Mr. Bowers) claims the witness was misled or mistaken into regarding this list of contributions as an official list and…he did make these admissions, they are swept away by the situation as you now reveal it."

It was here Ivins finally exploded, claiming once again all he did was read a report, and that, "I misled nobody. And I will not stand here, if the Judge will permit me, in the position of a man who has attempted to mislead, as to a witness, as this… Mr. Roosevelt said he knew more about it than the committee did…"

The Judge finally interrupted, calming things down and pointing out that the trial was moving away from the issues. He permitted Bowers to pursue it at some length, pointing out, "The cross examination was intended, I assume, to show that the contributions influenced the action of the witness subsequently," so he would allow the defense a good deal of latitude to correct that impression. Bowers then established that the real cost of Roosevelt's

1904 presidential campaign was about $1,800,000, or substantially less than the $3,000,000 Ivins had claimed. Bowers continued to draw out questioning on this subject as long as possible, while Ivins sat mostly silent.

Bowers then returned to his client's relationship with Boss Platt. Ivins had done a good job showing how often and well the two men had worked together to demonstrate that Roosevelt willingly participated in the boss-run system throughout his career, then wondering when he finally had developed his self-righteous conscience. Bowers asked Roosevelt to describe that relationship. The Colonel replied with what a newsman described as "a volley of words, pounding home his statements with his fist. Soon the old-times smiles were seen on the faces of the jurymen and several times the court attendants had to rap for order as the audience gave open expression to its enjoyment."

Roosevelt did not stint in his praise for Platt—when he claimed it was deserved, saying, "On certain points I found Mr. Platt's suggestions very valuable; on points where his wide knowledge of political conditions in the state obtained, gave weight and what he had to say, his advice was of real and sometimes of great value…

"It is a fact that I consulted with Mr. Platt on all the important matters that came up… My purpose was partly to take advantage of his experience, and largely to see if I could not come to an agreement with him as head of the organization, which would let me avoid a break with the organization, while at the same time, and primarily, doing what the interest of the state demanded…

"My purpose in not breaking with the organization was in the first place a large desire to avoid disrupting the Republican Party as long as I did no wrong…"

Few men understood and appreciated as well as Roosevelt did, the good and the bad done by the existence of partisan political parties. They collected the donations, selected candidates and supported them financially and in return, expected loyalty to the party's stated ideals. In the *Federalist Papers*, Alexander Hamilton and James Madison each wrote about the inherent dangers of partisan political organizations. The Democratic Party, which evolved from the Jeffersonian Republicans, became fully formed in the 1820s in support of Andrew Jackson. The party split over slavery in 1860, when northern and southern Democrats each nominated their own candidates for the presidency.

The Republican Party was born in the fight over slavery, when a coalition of antislavery groups came together in 1854. Both parties continued to gain power through the rest of the nineteenth century and eventually completely controlled the political process. Teddy Roosevelt's 1912 attempt to create a third Progressive Party based solely on the force of his own charisma had shaken the Republican organization and cost it the national election. That split with his party came after he had won nine of twelve primaries against the incumbent Taft and proved far more popular with rank-

and-file voters than the president, who had won only the Massachusetts primary. But the bosses, who had retained power on the state and local levels, maneuvered state delegations in the remaining thirty-six states to ensure Taft's nomination, causing Roosevelt and his Progressives to walk out of the convention and form their own party. The Colonel's bitterness at the system that had cost him a nomination he believed he deserved was embodied by Barnes. So it made sense that he could have worked with Platt years earlier, before the division.

Freed from the constraints put upon him by Ivins and Barnum, Roosevelt once again seemed to be having a grand time in the witness chair, his arms flying through the air for emphasis as he testified about his relationship with the bosses. "I could prevent wrong being done if I broke with them but I could not get affirmative right done if I broke with them."

Ivins protested Roosevelt's display of enthusiasm. "Now if your Honor please I ask that this witness be requested to testify without gesticulation, and in the ordinary and the usual way of a witness."

Bowers chuckled. "Well, he won't do that."

Ivins did not think it humorous. "I ask that this court compel him to do it."

Judge Andrews understood the folly of trying to restrain the man's natural exuberance, deciding, "This witness can testify in his ordinary manner. The court cannot of course regulate the precise manner in which the witness will testify to a jury or the precise emphasis which he shall give to certain words."

Ivins had watched Roosevelt play to the jury, smiling and pointing at them as if asking them to join in his crusade. He knew precisely what he was doing. That was the old Roosevelt, the Colonel on the stump, raising the roof with his words, carrying the audience with him on his dreams, and somehow Ivins had to prevent that. If Roosevelt could exercise his charisma, the case would be lost. The lawyer's frustration at being unable to prevent that boiled over, as he demanded the near impossible. "I object to the witness being permitted to testify to this jury, accompanying his testimony by gesticulation, which is not evidence. We cannot control his emphasis, vocally; and gesticulation is just as much a part of the testimony as the spoken word and I object to the gesticulation."

The judge added, "I should not attempt to regulate the ordinary manner of the witness with regard to language or emphasis or even gesticulation in giving his testimony."

The Colonel looked at Ivins with a great big grin, then turned and shared his amusement with the jurymen. He might have won them right then with a knowing wink. Instead, he continued his explanation for his long-term association with the party leaders. The reality was that "unless I got popular feeling tremendously aroused I could not get affirmative legislative action against their wishes through the legislature; and their control of the Senate would have prevented my getting any of my nominees confirmed...

"I became convinced in my own mind that the organization controlled the majority of the Senate and that if I wished to discuss questions of appointment...it was advisable for me to go to where the real power was, to talk with Mr. Platt and not talk with men who I had become convinced in my own mind would merely carry out the bidding of Mr. Platt and therefore I must consult with him if I wished to get affirmative action."

Bowers returned to the early correspondence between Roosevelt and Congressman Lemuel Quigg, then a major power broker in the party and the go-between carrying messages to and from Boss Platt and Roosevelt, in which Quigg had laid out what the organization expected of the Colonel in exchange for the gubernatorial nomination. He asked if it was a fact "that you took your nomination without being pledged in any way to Mr. Platt or to any organization?"

"Absolutely so!" the Colonel roared.

Roosevelt said he had responded to Quigg's letter in a unique way. "There was a trooper...in the regiment who could write on a typewriter, he got a typewriter, or I got a typewriter and I dictated some of those things to him; but he was not an expert typewriter and I had to interlineate things that he wrote..."

The letter concerned the controversial Franchise Tax Bill, which large party donors strongly opposed. Platt objected to any type of franchise tax bill; Governor Roosevelt supported it. To assist the jury in understanding a dispute that may have been confusing up to this point, Judge Andrews explained, "What the witness means by a Franchise Tax Bill is a bill for taxing the franchise held by public service corporations." At that time corporations were granted legal permission to operate a public utility, like a trolley system, or street railroads as they were known, or power companies, and until then had paid no taxes for that grant.

The redirect examination barreled through the morning into the afternoon, and Roosevelt lost none of his energy. Bowers read portions of a letter his client had written to Platt describing the situation with respect to the Franchise Tax Bill. The men of means who controlled these corporations "were perfectly willing to have a committee appointed because they would take care that committee made its report in such shape as to prevent franchises being interfered with, but that no substantial action recognizing their taxation should be taken. They also urged upon me that I personally could not afford to take this action for under no circumstances could I ever again be nominated for any public office, as no corporation would subscribe to a campaign fund if I was on the ticket and that they would subscribe most heavily to beat me, and when I asked if this was true of Republican corporations the cynical answer was made that the corporations that subscribed most heavily to campaign funds subscribed impartially to both party organizations..."

In other words, these corporations would be willing to participate in a public charade, the appointment of a toothless committee, so long as they controlled the outcome. Their threat was obvious; if Roosevelt dared fight them, they would end his political career. The Republican Party, they warned, was dependent on their money and had become, in essence, a mostly owned subsidiary to carry out their wishes. This brought to the courtroom an unpleasant truth about American politics: the moneyed interests used their money to protect their interests.

As Bowers brought out, following that letter, the Colonel and Platt had several conversations in which the party leader emphasized the importance of working with the corporations to meet their needs. Platt attempted to couch this threat in a most palatable fashion. "At one of those conversations," Roosevelt remembered, "Mr. Platt said to me that it was true that the big corporations which had very expensive interests and whose directors were morally bound to look after the interests of their investors, especially the widows and orphans, that those corporations did contribute to both parties. That they did it as a matter of self-defense; that it was not done as a matter of politics but of business, that they were not coerced into doing it but that their interests had to be taken care of by conservative men; that they had to be protected from the onslaughts of fanatics and dishonest men. I can't say that he used the words 'fanatics and dishonest men' but words equivalent to them. Fanatics and dishonest men. That the only way to protect their interests was to keep alive responsible party organizations…and he stated that it was a matter of honorable obligation on his part as having received those contributions to defend the corporations when they were unjustly attacked, as he believed them to be unjustly attacked in connection with the franchise tax bill that I was advocating."

Bowers was methodically tearing apart the case Ivins had painstakingly constructed. As for consulting Platt when making appointments, why, the answer was obvious. "Whether Democrats or Republicans I insisted upon getting the best for the position; if I could possibly do it I would accept the organization's recommendation of such a man, if he was a first-class man."

At the 1910 convention, at which Roosevelt bested Barnes, the Colonel said he made his fight on two issues: "Whether or not bosses should be perpetuated as a necessity in party government, and whether or not we should have direct primaries in the State of New York."

Ivins had, through his careful questioning, made it appear that Roosevelt's regular breakfasts with Platt were intended to be clandestine, that they took place in private homes so the public would not be aware of this association. Roosevelt refuted that, saying, "I insisted that there should be no possible concealment of the fact that I was meeting with Mr. Platt, that wherever it was…" his purpose in those meetings was "to get the benefit of any advice he might give me and find out if he had any objections, so I might meet them, if possible, and so, also, that he should know, fully and fairly, just what my position was going to be."

Bowers might have written a script and carefully rehearsed his witness, but instead he brought him along small step-by-step to paint a glowing portrait of a politician above reproach. Roosevelt's replies, which seemed like short speeches, buttressed his reputation for the Square Deal he had so forcefully advocated. He made decisions, he said, "that unless the people could be persuaded that it was advisable to have legislation then it was not well to have the legislation…no matter what my personal views of the point could be unless the people favored it or unless I could get them to favor it."

The day was spent with the defendant clarifying innuendo raised by Ivins and sweeping away any impression of wrongdoing on his part. Of course he never simply agreed to nominate a man he didn't know, even when recommended by the party. And he was steadfast in his determination not to cave to party pressure on removing insurance supervisor Payn or the franchise tax.

The difficulty through much of the afternoon for all sides was that so many letters and documents had already been entered in the record. Everyone, including the judge, had now lost track of his rulings and couldn't easily remember what was in the record and what had been rejected. At one point a confused Bowers said to Ivins, "You say it was put in in one breath and in another not?"

To which Ivins agreed, to the accompaniment of laughter from the gallery, "The gentleman says

I have to take two breaths. I frequently do, and having breathed twice, I do not object to his going on with it."

The letter at issue, Bowers recalled, was already in.

Much of the testimony seemed as repetitive as the letters, as when the Colonel remembered, "Mr. Platt insisted that Mr. Payn must be reappointed, dwelling…partly upon the fact that his relationship with big financiers, and the liking that they had for him, was such that it was necessary that Mr. Payn should be reappointed. And we had a good many conversations which became pretty acid… I had to say that I would fight him on it, showdown on it. Finally Mr. Platt accepted Mr. Hendricks."

With that the Colonel looked at the jury and asked, "I think I explained to the jury the other day about the question of confirmation, did I not?"

Barnum was on his feet, somewhat incredulous, "I object to the witness asking questions of the jury."

Even Bowers had to admit, "I agree with you."

They had delved into the minutiae of a governor's power: numerous appointees for positions few people even knew existed. But Roosevelt remembered many of the nominees, often with great glee as he explained that this man was one of the finest men in the state, an excellent man, or he had been warned off that man. This was Roosevelt the administrator, bringing into public service good men both Republican and Democrat while rejecting those with questionable motives that he could discern.

Eventually though, as the slanting rays of the sun grew longer in the afternoon, the conversation came back to the pressure on Roosevelt to accept the vice presidency of the United States in 1900, which was then-treated as little more than an undesirable burden. McKinley's vice president, Garrett Hobart, had died months earlier leaving the position open. While the powerful Republican leader Mark Hanna of Ohio thoroughly despised Roosevelt and offered his own slate of candidates to the Philadelphia convention, the majority of delegates strongly favored the new American hero. New York was certain to be a pivotal state in the forthcoming election, and Roosevelt's presence on the ticket would almost assuredly put it in the Republican column. Boss Platt had a simpler reason: he could not control Roosevelt and wanted him gone. The Colonel recalled several conversations with Platt and "toward the end he became insistent that I must take the place and stated that the New York delegation would put me in nomination…

"I stated in effect that I would not take it… It was at Philadelphia that the thing came to a head… Senator Platt had urged that it would be necessary for me to run on the ground that the party leaders… felt my nomination would strengthen the ticket and the party had a right to expect me to run, and I told him that to me it was a very unproductive place…

"I mentioned to him that two or three individuals who had a right to speak on the subject had spoken of my taking a professorship of history and that I thought I would rather take up (that position) rather than go into the vice-presidency."

In Philadelphia, he continued, Platt was mostly confined to his hotel room, suffering from a fractured rib that left him in great pain. It was an odd injury, which had occurred in his office several days earlier when he spun around too quickly in his office chair and was thrown hard against its right arm. Heavily bandaged he had gone to Philadelphia against the advice of physicians to make the case for Roosevelt, and when that was assured he returned to New York. "Mr. Platt informed me that I must accept the vice-presidential nomination and if I refused, I would not be renominated as governor, and I said, 'All right,' then we would fight… I would go downstairs where the New York delegates were assembled and inform them that if New York declared me for vice president, I would accept it as an assault on me by the organization in order to get me out of the governorship…and that we would have a flat out fight in the fall for the nomination…"

The Colonel had the room enthralled as he related this history. The bones of the story were widely known, but hearing Roosevelt's account in his own words was magical for the people in the room. They would remember this for years and tell it to others, how Teddy Roosevelt fought bitterly against taking the step that would lead him to the White House.

"…Mr. Platt said all right, then it would be a fight." But later, when it had become clear that Roosevelt was preparing to do just precisely what he had threatened, Platt relented. He asked the Colonel to return to his room and "said he had been in great pain and I must not mind what he had said; that in view of my opposition he would withdraw any idea of nominating me for vice president…"

And there the topic ended with the jurors and gallery of spectators left, once again, without a definitive account from Roosevelt himself, of what eventually changed his mind.

Roosevelt rolled on and on and on, seemingly inexhaustible on a variety of other subjects. His redirect testimony continued into the next morning. When he had entered the courtroom to begin the new session, a number of female spectators were so taken by his presence that they raised a hearty cheer for him. An entire section in the gallery had been reserved for women, but their numbers were greater than the allotted seats and they were sprinkled through the room. The applause "was taken up by the emotional women," reported the *Post-Standard*, growing into an ovation. The Colonel "sank in his chair" and did not acknowledge this break in decorum. Judge Andrews, still in his chambers, was furious and instructed the sheriff to warn the gallery that the courtroom would be cleared should another outburst occur.

Roosevelt did not appear to even need the support. He remained perched on the edge of his chair for an incredible eighth day of questioning. "When it comes to work," reported the *New York Press*, "the San Juan Hill charge was like child's play in comparison to the full day of mental stress he endured only to bob up…very much alive and wide awake. His energy is inexhaustible, instead of showing traces of fatigue he is still dominating the courtroom with that marvelous personality of his and has won more friends in Syracuse than he made at any particular time."

Roosevelt had been removed from the fray for several years, at first by choice and then by circumstances, and there could be no doubt he was savoring every minute of this return. Whether this was a beginning of the next part of his remarkable career or a victory lap was impossible to determine. But the Colonel had grabbed hold of the moment and was squeezing it tightly, reluctant to let go.

In the morning session Bowers continued to demonstrate that rather than being subservient to Platt, the Colonel was in every way his equal, usually considering the boss's position before making his own decision based on what would be best for the people. While lacking the dynamic courtroom presence of Ivins, Bowers had done a fine job painting an extremely flattering portrait of his man—or, in this instance, giving the Colonel free rein and allowing him to take the lead.

However, Bowers did struggle to complete the saga of how Roosevelt became vice president. When he tried to raise the issue, Ivins objected that it wasn't relevant and Judge Andrews sustained it. As a good lawyer, Bowers approached from different angles. "Did President McKinley send a communication to you upon that subject?"

Ivins objected, but the Colonel was allowed to respond, "Yes." Bowers came at it from a different place, "Did you accept the Vice Presidency after receiving your message?" Objection made and sustained, so the lawyer tried again, "Was your motive in accepting the Vice Presidency, of giving up your personal wishes, for what you felt your duty?"

"Yes, sir." Finally it became clear that it was McKinley, not Platt, who convinced him to change his mind. Roosevelt had been a strong supporter of the Republican president, who had rewarded him by appointing him an assistant secretary of the navy, a position he used to lobby for America's entry into the Spanish-American War. After considerable maneuvering at the convention Roosevelt had finally been convinced accepting the nomination for vice president was necessary for the good of the nation, which he believed should be governed by the Republican McKinley. In the final vote he received the vote of every delegate—except his own. During that campaign against William Jennings Bryan and Adlai E. Stevenson, the Colonel's whistle-stop tour covered twenty-one thousand miles in twenty-four states, helping lead the ticket to a landslide victory.

When Bowers asked the Colonel to respond to the plaintiff's suggestion that he had personally profited from donations to his 1904 presidential campaign fund, Barnum objected, attempting to limit the response to a yes or no. It was here the sometimes complex rules of courtroom procedure came into play, as Judge Andrews explained, "This is not cross examination. On a redirect examination if the defendant asks for explanations they have a right to have them in practically the form that they desire as long as they keep them within the bounds of evidence. You cannot require that their witness shall answer yes or no as you can in your own case."

Roosevelt took full advantage of that. "Until I left the presidency I never heard the names of most of those that were read the other day as having contributed. I knew that Mr. Frick had contributed, and Mr. George Perkins had contributed…then I knew of small contributions that were made where there would be some particular reason that attracted my attention. For instance, the widow of a veteran in the Soldiers Home sent me one dollar, I remember that more vividly than the big ones."

Barnes's newspaper, the *Albany Evening Journal*, had been especially harsh in its accusations, writing, "Mr. Roosevelt, a candidate for president in 1904, permitted his campaign managers to accept contributions from millionaires connected to the steel trust and failed to direct his attorney general to proceed against that corporation, as was done after he left the White House."

The Colonel was adamant in his rejection of that charge. During his presidency, he testified, he had directed legal proceedings be initiated against the very corporations whose owners had donated to his campaign: the New York, New Haven and Hartford Railroad, the Harvester Company, DuPont Powder Corporation. As for the specific charge, that he had permitted the Steel Company to merge with Tennessee Coal & Iron, the Colonel reported, "The Steel Corporation at that time had in the neighborhood of 60 percent of the total output; The Tennessee Coal & Iron corporation included about 1-9/10 per cent of the output... The action occurred at the very height of the panic of 1907; the whole financial structure of the country was tottering and swaying; and I think I am within bounds when I say that the prime necessities...was that some measure should be taken to stop the panic to restore confidence to prevent the frightful disaster impending over the ordinary men and women of this country. In New York the situation was trembling on a hair as to whether every institution would have to be shut up or business stopped; and as a result all business throughout the country stopped..."

Judge Andrews stopped this recital. In a trial with such loose boundaries, he had often struggled with precisely what evidence and how much of it to allow, or keeping track of what he had already ruled was either permissible or had to be stricken from the record. At times he had wavered, and so his rulings weren't quite clear. This ambiguity at times led the trial to become bogged down with procedural disputes and many sidebar conferences, during which attorneys for both sides stood around the bench and argued their points. This topic was another of those issues; how much should the jury hear? What reflected on the defendant or the plaintiff and in what way? The judge sometimes seemed to be forced into trying to thread a needle with a rope, but managed to persevere.

In the three-week-long banking crisis in October 1907, the stock market had lost almost 50 percent of its value, and small banks throughout the country became insolvent. The collapse was prevented personally by J.P. Morgan, who injected millions of dollars into the system to support banks, and convinced other financiers to do the same. A second crisis a month later took place when the stock of the Tennessee Coal, Iron and Mining Company dropped precipitously, threatening the existence of a major brokerage that had used that stock for collateral in large loans. That collapse would have disrupted all financial markets, perhaps igniting a depression. There was only one way to prevent that from happening.

Steel magnates Henry Frick and Elbert H. Gary, the chairman of U.S. Steel, had come to see him, the Colonel explained to the absolutely silent courtroom. These people had lived through those terrifying few days and the fear of complete economic collapse was still part of their emotional memory. The two men "represented to me that if the Steel Corporation, that is, if Mr. Pierpont Morgan's company, took possession that morning at once of the Tennessee Coal & Iron Company it would add such value to the stock, which was deposited as collateral in threatened banks and institutions in New York that they were sure the storm would be weathered and the panic stopped, and that this was the general sentiment in New York...

"They were only purchasing it as the only way of getting rid of the dangerous financial situation..."

Ivins interrupted. "If your Honor please."

Bowers snapped back, "Will you please not interrupt the witness."

"I will interrupt!" Ivins said sharply. "I am talking to the Court with as much voice as the Lord has left me. If this is to continue as part of the cross examination..."

"This is not a cross examination," Bowers pointed out.

"If this is to continue as part of the direct examination, I shall have to insist on going into the matter..."

The judge rebuked him. "Now, the difficulty about this evidence is merely this: You have asked the witness on cross examination, you have brought out certain contributions made to the witness' campaign fund by Mr. Frick and others. You have asked him if he knew that Mr. Frick was interested in the Steel Corporation. And then you have asked him about the connection between the Steel Corporation and the Tennessee Coal & Iron Company. Now, that, of course, obviously must have been done for the reason that you claim that there was something illegal or improper in the consolidation of the two companies which the witness knew about and which he should have prevented. Now, that being so, in re-direct the witness has the right to testify that this combination was made with his consent and that he acted in good faith. Now he can do that. Of course, the question is as to how much detail shall be given to it is another matter."

Eventually Roosevelt was permitted to conclude his story. "I asked them if I could not defer action… The answer was that the panic had reached such a crisis that if it was not stopped that morning they doubted if they could stop it at all without ruin to the country everywhere…that in order to do good the action must be…given the widest possible publicity so that it should be known before the (stock) market opened.

"Accordingly, I acted… It was published widely and the panic stopped."

Bowers was moving toward the end of his redirect examination, tying up threads that might have been left dangling. Roosevelt estimated since becoming governor he had written "over 190,000 letters, made 40,000 appointments where my signature has been affixed to the commission. I have signed over 20,000 laws and signed appropriation laws whose total items aggregated several billions of dollars; and have made several thousand speeches."

On several subjects Bowers struggled to get his question answered, but as was becoming clear that was not always his objective. There were questions that he asked with the certainty the plaintiff would object, but his actual purpose was as much to make certain the jury heard his thought as to actually get a response. Asking the witness about testimony given by Thomas Platt in front of a committee investigating campaign contributions given in return for political favors, Bowers wondered if

Roosevelt "believed (that testimony) to be true and relied upon" it when writing the alleged libelous article? The Colonel, as anticipated, was not permitted to answer. No matter though that the Colonel's response was not in the record; the thought was in the heads of the jurymen.

In this final phase of the redirect testimony, Bowers stepped back and William Van Benschoten handled the questioning for the defendant. The younger lawyer's objective was to show that there was widespread corruption in Albany that could be laid at Barnes's feet, and that was at least part of the basis for Roosevelt's article; but the plaintiff's attorneys successfully foiled almost every attempt to get evidence of that malfeasance into the record. Judge Andrews enforced the rule that if an issue was not raised on the initial direct or cross-examination, then it was not a proper line of questioning for the redirect.

One key piece of evidence that the defense desperately wanted to enter was a letter that had been written in 1914 by the very popular current governor, Charles Whitman, when he was serving as district attorney, to attorney Charles Duell, and subsequently published in the *Times*. In it, Whitman supported Roosevelt's call for less party dominance in politics. Ivins was taken by surprise when the defense presented it. Duell had been in the Syracuse courtroom for several days and might have been asked about it. Ivins was adamant it not be admitted, arguing that it was correspondence between two men not involved in the trial. "Mr. Whitman, as Governor of this state is not a party to this and this is not in any way relevant to the controversy or material as not naming Mr. Barnes, or as not referring to Mr. Barnes."

Judge Andrews struggled with it, finally deciding that if Roosevelt claimed he relied on this letter when making the charges, he would allow that portion of it bearing on the alleged libel.

Ivins sighed. "I am the most acquiescent person that ever lived."

The letter was read to the courtroom. "In line with our last talk, I agree with you that the time is ripe for an alliance between Progressive Republicans and members of the National Progressive Party, as well as of all good citizens sharing their opinion to rid the state of the kind of party control which, in my opinion, is mainly responsible for the corruption which has been clearly shown by the various investigations and examinations which have been had during this last year. These conditions are not localized and the men and policies responsible for them are not confined to any one party." It was signed Whitman.

While it was being read, Barnes scowled angrily and busied himself jotting down notes.

What made the letter even more potent was the well-known fact that Roosevelt and Whitman had been at odds, as the Colonel had refused to support Whitman's gubernatorial campaign. Van Benschoten asked Roosevelt if he believed the statements contained in the letter, which proposed an alliance to rid New York of bossism, to be true.

He did. Bowers then asked if he had relied on them in writing the article in question and giving similar speeches. "Yes, sir." He asked if the Colonel believed the letter referred to the plaintiff Barnes. "I did," then added in case the hammer blow was missed, "and I relied upon this so implicitly that it influenced me greatly in making the statements complained of."

Van Benschoten also got into evidence an article written by state senator Harvey Hinman, in which he announced his own candidacy for governor; he wrote, "I have no personal quarrel whatever with either Mr. Barnes or Mr. Murphy, but I believe they in their influence are alike hostile to decent and efficient government, and that the time has come for their overthrow..."

That article was published the day before Roosevelt's alleged libel appeared.

With that, the defense ended its redirect examination. After a few inconsequential formalities, the witness was excused. Colonel Roosevelt had been in the witness chair for eight consecutive days; he had been questioned for thirty-eight and a half hours, as long as anyone could remember a single witness on the stand. "He had been heckled for hours at a stretch," reported the *New York Times*, "and through it all he had come up smiling and happy and ready for more." And as he stepped down from the stand, he looked at the jury, and grinned broadly.

CHAPTER NINE

Now that the Colonel was finished testifying he faced a new and difficult challenge: trying to sit quietly and listen, one thing at which he had never been very good, and there were no signs of improvement.

The plaintiff's lawyers had technically rested their case at the outset, right after they were able to prove the libelous statement was made by Roosevelt and distributed at his direction. But Ivins and his team knew they would have a chance to present all of their witnesses to respond to, or rebut, the defense case and that would include Barnes himself. For now, however, it was Bowers and his defense team who began presenting witnesses to support Roosevelt's claims. As a legal matter, much of Roosevelt's testimony was intended to show that there wasn't any malice on Roosevelt's part, but if they wanted to win the case and not just minimize the damages, they had to justify the article by proving that the Colonel had been correct in his charges.

The defense began by calling former Republican state senator George Agnew to the stand whose testimony would later become the subject of a significant legal battle. Agnew was called to prove a critical point made in opening statements, that Barnes strong-armed legislators to protect certain special interests. At issue was legislation that would effectively end all organized betting at racetracks. This would be a blow to several large concerns that financially supported the Republican Party, and Barnes strongly opposed it. An extremely controversial measure, it had been proposed at three different legislative sessions. The point the defense wanted to make was that an Albany senator, William Grattan, had initially agreed to support it with the blessing of Barnes. But within days, Barnes had changed his mind and persuaded Grattan to change his vote. Senator Agnew, who had proposed the bill, testified that after learning Grattan intended to change his vote, he went to see Barnes at his home in Albany, and there "I said to Mr. Barnes that his Senator Grattan had come to me that morning to take back the message which he gave me on the previous day when he told me Mr. Barnes had told him he could vote for the anti-racetrack legislation, and that I had come up to his house to ask him if he understood the seriousness of his action in requiring Grattan to vote against these bills..."

Agnew testified in a loud yet composed voice,

which filled the courtroom to its farthest corners, although at odd times his voice cracked into an agreeable falsetto. Listening to him, Roosevelt sat steady at the defense table, an interested observer staring straight at the witness, occasionally making a note in response to the testimony and sliding it across the table to one of his attorneys. Roosevelt knew that this testimony went to the heart of his comments about Barnes.

"I asked him why he himself had changed his mind and he said he thought it was good politics to do so..." Agnew recalled. "I said to him that Senator Grattan had said to me that he was very sorry that he had been obliged to take back his word to me, but that Mr. Barnes had made such a point of it and he owed so much to Barnes that he felt it was a question of loyalty with him to carry out Mr. Barnes' request or demand."

"And Senator Grattan voted against that measure?"

"He did. The measures."

The final vote, Van Benschoten read, was twenty-five to twenty-five. "And I ask you how many votes did it take to pass the measure?"

"Twenty-six." The point was obvious. By strongarming Grattan to change his vote, Barnes had successfully defeated the bill.

During his redirect examination, Agnew recalled the rest of his conversation with Barnes, stating that "heretofore I had stood up for Barnes whenever I heard him rundown, on the ground that whatever other failings he had, still I believed him to be a man of his word; and that I stated to him that day that having taken back his word… I was through with him. He said that he was surprised that I took the matter so seriously and asked me to go in the other room to lunch with him." Senator Agnew refused the invitation.

Those words certainly were telling and powerful. Maybe too much so, since their legal value was questionable. Ivins demanded that Agnew's testimony be thrown out because it had "no bearing on the allegation of the relation of crooked politics to crooked business," and that Barnes had a right to ask Grattan to change his vote.

The judge pointed out that these allegations had to be proved step-by-step and he would allow it, at least for now.

William Loeb Jr. was called next. The stocky, square-jawed Loeb was quite famous in his own right, having been Governor Roosevelt's stenographer and then later President Roosevelt's personal secretary. Loeb had become the gateway between the Colonel and the media, in essence the nation's first press secretary. Maybe more importantly, he had served as the Colonel's trusted political and policy adviser. The two men were so close that when T.R. took jujitsu instruction in the White House, Loeb was his training partner. While some steam had gone out of the courtroom when the Colonel stepped down from the stand, Loeb brought enough celebrity to the moment to keep spectators excited.

Loeb was vitally important for the defense; he

was to testify that Barnes had worked with the opposing party boss, Democrat Charles Murphy, to completely control the city of Albany. Loeb testified that he had met Barnes "right after he returned to Albany after graduating from Harvard University."

"Did you have any conversation with Mr. Barnes as to his control of the city of Albany in 1907," asked Van Benschoten.

Ivins objected; here was a key turn in the case. The defense wanted to show the extent of Barnes's power, but Ivins complained that such information was not contained in the alleged libel and therefore was irrelevant, immaterial and incompetent—in the legal context, incompetent is effectively synonymous with inadmissible.

The purpose, Van Benschoten argued, "is to show that the plaintiff himself admitted that it lie within his powers to control the conditions and affairs as they were carried on in Albany, and there were certain combinations which he had with Democratic forces in the city of Albany to keep him and his organization in power there…

"It seems to me it is very pertinent to the issues in this case."

Judge Andrews seemed willing to be convinced. "Now that we have reached this point we may as well have it settled once and for all. Why is the local political condition in the city and county of Albany material here? How does it justify the alleged libel?"

"There is a statement contained in the article…

that the plaintiff and Mr. Murphy are of exactly the same type, the same moral and political type," Van Benschoten replied. "Now we find this plaintiff in Albany where he is in absolute control of the organization and has been for years, is making political combination with the Democrats in order to keep himself and his organization in power; and I submit that it comes pretty well under the terms of the article in justifying the meaning which the defendant intended to convey."

This legal debate continued for more than a half hour, both sides recognizing its potential import to the final outcome. The defense argued for the widest possible latitude to prove that Roosevelt's words were more broadly true; the plaintiff was insistent the court limit testimony to just the very specific allegations.

The judge wrestled with it, asking at one point, "Would it be competent for you then in justification of this article to show that Mr. Murphy was a forger and Mr. Barnes was a forger?"

Van Benschoten agreed that would not be competent.

Finally the judge decided. "The subject was the political government of the State. The subject was the corruption between Mr. Murphy and Mr. Barnes as leaders of the political government of the state. The subject was the alliance between corrupt business and corrupt politics in governing and controlling the State government. The subject was the crookedness of the State government throughout.

"Now, it seems to me that when you attempt

to justify it by showing other independent crimes, other independent violations which you allege Mr. Barnes was guilty of, or had permitted, that you are going beyond the justification which this article permits. In other words, it seems to me that the justification here must relate to a justification of the charges as affecting state government."

Van Benschoten refused to let go, pleading, "The discussion of the two men whose names are used in the article is discussed as to what kind of men they really are, what kind of leaders, bosses, they really were, what the character of those men were, and to a certain extent as political characters and figures in our political life."

Judge Andrews tried to give him some space. "I think if you're able to justify by showing an alliance between corrupt business and corrupt politics you may do so, whether it affects the state or whether it affects the municipality...but the mere fact that there was misgovernment in Albany, the mere fact that Mr. Barnes was familiar with the misgovernment, the mere fact that he could have prevented it if he wished to do so, if that is true, it seems to me is immaterial."

Van Benschoten insisted that it was vital for the defense to show that Albany was riddled with corruption that was permitted to exist by Barnes in concert with Murphy. That the bosses were aware that gambling and prostitution existed and did nothing to prevent it. But as the judge explained, "You have not alleged that in your answer. That is the trouble."

Ivins finally weighed in. "It is alleged that there has been a conspiracy between these two men. No evidence of that conspiracy has yet been offered."

And then Bowers shot back, claiming, "It matters little whether the charge refers to state government action or county government action. After all, Albany County is part of the state, the most important part of the state in the sense that it is the capital of the state... In deciding the question of corruption...it would be limiting the charge not to its real substance but to the place, that is state-wide instead of county-wide... It is almost impossible to separate the connection between the state and the county when you deal with a charge of corruption..." In this context, Bowers began discussing "the printing question," and Ivins asked that the jury be excused while the subject was argued. Judge Andrews dismissed the jurymen. This was simply too sensitive a topic for the jurors to hear unless the judge would be admitting it into evidence.

Bowers immediately pounced, making the sensational claim that Barnes was paid by both county and the state for the same printing jobs, and that in several ways he misused his position to profit personally. Ivins tried to deflect it, suggesting that rather than Barnes being named, any reference to this matter should refer to the Journal Company.

Bowers countered that Barnes owned the majority of the stock in the company.

"I want the real names," Ivins insisted.

"How much of the stock does he own?" Bowers responded.

The argument continued like this for some time. "We set forth facts," Bowers implored, "that is the only way we can justify. These facts are laid under the direction of the court before the jury to draw a conclusion as to whether or not they establish the charge... We have pleaded somewhat in detail which show a base use of power... Gambling of various forms was permitted in the city and the plaintiff did not oppose it, and many workers in the Republican organization were employed in connection with said gambling houses with the knowledge of the plaintiff..."

Failing to show that Roosevelt's original answer included actions taken in Albany, Bowers suggested that the fact his client did not specifically limit his charges to Barnes's actions taken to further his power in state government was enough to allow him to demonstrate Barnes's malfeasance in county government too. "It is limited to machine rule government, whether it be state, county or town!" Bowers went on and on, making point after point, probing for an acceptable angle. "This is a case of great importance to the people of the state; it is a case of great importance to the people all over the country...no technical rulings should deprive the defendant of his fullest opportunity to lay before the jury the full facts of the situation.

"...we are stopped because it is said that when we get down to the place where the plaintiff lives, where his life work is done, where he obtained the power to do the wrong, if any he has done, because that is the initial place of his power...you cannot show wrongdoing there because perchance the language in which you made that pleading was not sufficiently definite."

When the plaintiff's representative reminded the judge he had ruled earlier on this subject, quoting him saying, "I do not think the part of it relating to the local government of the City of Albany is competent," Bowers again tried to widen the scope, drawing the attention of the court to an organization called the Albany Lincoln League, whose "chief object is to secure funds by levying assessments on the salaries of public office holders in the city and county and to use the money thus secured (three per cent of their salaries) in a manner and for purposes unknown to the main body of the members of the League..."

Membership in this organization was not voluntary, Bowers contended. Anyone who held a politically appointed post in the city—clerks, policemen, firemen and other city employees—was forced to pay 3 percent, "and the conceded activities of the organization inevitably point to corrupt object and criminal practices which justify and require the impenetrable mask employed by the officers of the body."

William Ivins stood behind his table and wound his decades of experience and his vast knowledge into his response. "...you cannot, under any circumstances at law, justify a libel unless you are able to swear to the truth of the libel, and then prove the truth of that libel, and that must be specific; if any of these libelous matters be not sworn to and be not proved then so far as those not sworn to and not proved are concerned they are left entirely without justification... Now let us see, in the language of the gentleman from Virginia, 'Where we are at.' There is no reference to the city of Albany. There is no allegation of the rottenness in this vituperative argument or statement of anything in New York City, or anything in Syracuse, or anything in Buffalo or anything in Albany. The whole question is a question of state government; it was not confined to questions of vice. Some reference has been made about the fact that Mr. Barnes knew that vice existed in Albany. Well, since the time that Ecclesiastes was written and since the time of the Apostle to the Romans, everybody has known that there has been vice in the world, and that knowledge does not make him responsible for the vice. It does not connect him to the vice...

"Moreover Governor Roosevelt was Governor of this state for two years and as Governor, if there were vice...he is supposed to know as much about that vice as anybody else." With that Ivins whirled around and pointed an accusing finger at the Colonel, then yelled so the shades covering the windows shook, "And he was the one man in the world who had the power to have caused the investigation into vice conditions and put an end to it. At that time there was no rule of righteousness in him."

The English philosopher Jeremy Bentham wrote, "The power of the lawyer is in the uncertainty of the law." The uncertainty in the hands of Ivins and Bowers, and even Barnum and Van Benschoten, was to be used skillfully to shape and shift and finally sculpt the story they wanted to tell to the jury. But doing so required great knowledge of how to use the law, sometimes like a bludgeon, other times with the deft touch of a surgeon. Watching Ivins and Bowers spar was to see two men who greatly respected each other for their knowledge and, as much as that, savored the duel.

Ivins turned to his noted sarcasm, telling the judge, "Of course there was no malice in the mind of the defendant; of course he was gentle, kindly, considerate—fighting like a lamb, trying to do his utmost for the welfare of the public and without any intention to injure anyone. So the argument of the learned counsel follows: This again is a mere political argument. On the one side clean and popular rights, and on the other corrupt and machine government."

Finally Ivins went full circle, returning to his original objection that Loeb offered nothing relevant to this case. "The precise question here is to conversations between Mr. Loeb and Mr. Barnes held at Albany in 1906 or 1907 and my objection is that this has nothing to do with this libel."

The arguments done, it was time for Judge Andrews to make his determination. A judge sits higher than the participants to mark the fact that he is above the fray. According to legend, this tradition goes back more than one thousand years, when the British king conducted the court from his raised throne. As the court system spread throughout his realm, the king's chosen representatives served as judges, and to signify their importance they sat higher than anyone else. In addition to its practicality—the high seat enabled the judge to view the entire courtroom—it also became symbolic of the fact that the impartial keeper of the law was not a participant in the dispute. So Judge Andrews, in his soft, steady voice, decided, "I can agree with a great many of the propositions that both sides have laid down in this argument... You will all agree, I imagine, that where a libel for instance charges a man with being a thief it is not enough...to say that the charge that he is a thief is true. You have got to set forth facts from which the inference can be drawn at least that he is guilty of certain specific things... Now so far there is an utter failure to allege any facts which would justify the jury in imputing personal corruption to Mr. Barnes." Therefore, he continued, "I will sustain the question that was put to Mr. Loeb."

By sustaining the objection by Ivins, Bowers and Roosevelt immediately realized the trouble Andrews's ruling would cause for their case. The Colonel clearly appeared surprised and disturbed. He became animated, whispering urgently, even angrily, to his attorneys. His face reddened.

To some observers the decision might have seemed curious; if a man could be shown to be corrupt in Albany was that not sufficient evidence that he was a corrupt man? Then again, Judge Andrews was not going to allow the defense to impugn Barnes with every possible barb as if this were a political campaign rather than a court of law.

Widely respected Judge William Andrews was described by Outlook *magazine, where Roosevelt served as an associate editor, as "firm, strong and good-natured," as well as "patently honest and fair." But at times even he had difficulty controlling Roosevelt on the witness stand.*

After that long argument Van Benschoten resumed questioning Loeb. But before he could complete his question, Loeb pointed out the court had forgotten to bring back the jury! Judge Andrews called for them to take their seats. Van Benschoten then asked a seemingly innocuous question about a lunch Loeb had shared with Barnes. At that time it was impossible to know how large an issue this was to become. In response, Loeb recalled having a conversation with Barnes in the banking office of J. S. Bates and Company sometime in 1911. It was a coincidental meeting, Loeb testified; he had been doing business there and had been invited to stay for lunch. Barnes had arrived unexpectedly and joined them. During that meeting, "I said to him that some Independents, representatives of the Franklin Roosevelt Democrats in the legislature, had asked me to find out from Mr. Barnes whether he would not support an independent Democrat upon whom they could agree. Mr. Barnes said that he could not do it, because his arrangement with Mr. Murphy was that he was not to interfere in Mr. Murphy's plans about the Senate."

It was startling testimony, supporting the Colonel's claim that the two political leaders worked together in a sort of corrupt alliance to carry out the desires of the bosses rather than the will of the people.

Loeb testified further that on several occasions he had seen Teddy Roosevelt conversing with William Barnes. "Did you ever see them alone conversing?" Van Benschoten asked.

Ivins caused a cascade of titters in the courtroom when he pointed out, "He could not have seen them alone."

Minutes later Judge Andrews ended another day.

Despite his legal win on the scope of the testimony, Ivins had been forced into a defensive stance, fending off as much as possible from the Colonel's witnesses. The plaintiff's case had been dented but his attorneys continued to display confidence, one of them telling the *Post-Standard*, "We haven't begun to drive the nails in the Roosevelt coffin as of yet."

The next day, Friday the thirtieth, began quietly, but tension escalated throughout the morning as tempers began fraying. Republican state senator Harvey Hinman, who only a year earlier had been T.R.'s choice for governor, although he lost the Republican primary, was the first witness for the defense. He was called to testify about his efforts to enact direct primary legislation that would remove significant power from party bosses. In New York and many other states, United States senators were chosen by the state's legislators rather than directly by voters. Roosevelt's Progressives strongly supported a direct primary that would allow voters rather than entrenched politicians to choose their candidate; naturally the party leadership opposed it with equal strength, and Hinman had been in the middle of the battle. Van Benschoten wanted to show that Governor Hughes supported this legislation and Barnes "strenuously" objected to it. The problem with that, Ivins explained, was that "every man has the absolutely perfect right to oppose or support any legislation." He then proceeded to object to almost every question Van Benschoten asked. The judge appeared to agree with him, suggesting that the defense argument seemed to be that Governor Hughes was a man of sterling character and that whatever position he took on a bill was the right one, and those who opposed him must be wrong, which was nothing more than political opinion.

Ivins made short work of Hinman and his argument, asking, "During that eight years (in the Senate) is it not a fact that you frequently voted on the same side with Democrats?"

Hinman responded in a slow, even voice, and as

he did, he looked first to the plaintiff, then to the defendant. "That is correct."

"Did you regard it as evidence of corruption on your part that you voted on the same side with the Democrats?"

"I did not."

Young attorney Royal France, a member of the Brooklyn Young Republican Club, then testified that Barnes had told him direct elections were not practical, "because it exposed the candidates to too much publicity; that the double campaign for the same office threw too much limelight on the candidates and that he could ruin the reputation of any man living if he threw enough limelight on it." France had disagreed, he said, saying the kind of man who could stand any kind of limelight was the "kind of man we wanted to get into public office.

"He said that he could show the whole foolishness of the proposition in any event; that he could get the riff-raff of the Democratic Party to take them down…or that he could vote Republicans in the Democratic primaries and nominate such rotten candidates that he would disgust the voters with the entire proposition…"

Barnes sat at the plaintiff table, his eyes fixed on the witness, showing no response as France continued, "He said that the system of direct primaries was subversive of party organization and party organization was essential to the maintenance of our institutions."

Next up was Herbert Vreeland, president of the Metropolitan Securities Company, a company that held the stock of New York City Street Railroads. This was the beginning of the defense effort to demonstrate that corporations might purchase protection from legislation by donating to political parties, in this instance protection from the proposed franchise tax. Vreeland testified his company had dutifully contributed to both parties. And once again the judge legally shrugged, explaining contributions alone without evidence of some quid pro quo was evidence of making contributions, and nothing else. Also, as Ivins gleefully argued, neither Barnes nor Murphy were the leaders of their parties when these contributions were made.

Bowers leaped in to help, reminding the judge that Roosevelt had testified that "it was demanded of him that he should not oppose franchise legislation because of the obligations the leaders of the Republican party were under to men who had made contributions simply to protect their own monetary interests."

"If they gave it to one," Van Benschoten added, "it might be because of their party affiliation; but when trusts or corporations gave contributions to both political parties in the same campaign there can be but one fair inference drawn from it, that it was given for some purpose, of protection or something of that character."

The defense's problem was that it could not produce evidence that Barnes knew the corporation was donating to both the Republicans and the Democrats, nor was there evidence that any contributions were given for corrupt purposes, and Judge

Andrews said that proving the money was given simply wasn't sufficient to support their point.

Once again, Ivins dug through the jumble to get at the point. "Did you ever give any contribution of any kind, or pay any money of any kind directly or indirectly to Mr. Barnes?"

Vreeland had sat through this argument with a satisfied smile on his face, making it clear that he was testifying about this episode with considerable reluctance and appreciated the vigor with which Ivins was protecting him. When given the opportunity, finally, he responded, "I do not know Mr. Barnes. I never met him."

In the afternoon, newsman Henry C. McMillan took the stand. McMillan had been a reporter for thirty years, the last three with New York's *Evening Post*. He was called by the defense to show that Barnes had been meeting with state senators in the senate clerk's office on the day and night the direct primary bill was voted on, the inference being that he was managing the vote. While hardly a telling punch, it was the kind of jab that can add up when the jury had to make its decision.

State senator Frederick Davenport was next, a close friend of the Colonel's who had been the Bull Moose Party's gubernatorial candidate in 1914. Davenport recalled the events of May 1910, when the Senate was considering the direct primary bill. During a recess in that debate he testified, "I walked out into the corridor between the Senate Chamber and the room of the Clerk of the Senate… I saw Mr. Barnes go into the clerk's room.

Numbers of organization Senators and numbers of machine Senators followed him into the clerk's room. I went to the door of the clerk's room and saw Mr. Barnes there. (The Senators) kept coming in numbers of twos and threes into the room."

The purpose of this meeting, he believed, was to "bind the entire Republican vote as to certain action regarding this bill."

At a subsequent special session of the Senate, he vividly recalled Senator Grattan denouncing Governor Hughes, Roosevelt and other Republican leaders for trying to force this legislation upon them. It was here that Senator Davenport got his ire up; his voice got louder, his words were sharper and carried an accusatory tone. "I recall saying to Senator Grattan, 'You speak as the mouthpiece of a political Nero who fiddles just outside this chamber while Rome burns.'"

When his turn came, Ivins leaped on that remark, asking, "Your reference to Nero and the burning of Rome and fiddling, I suppose was a figure of speech, wasn't it?"

Davenport would not back down. "Not entirely."

A look of curiosity crossed Ivins's face. "Was Mr. Barnes fiddling?"

"Mr. Barnes is not a fiddler, I believe, but he is ruthless like Nero, I thought."

Ivins snapped angrily, "You think that history teaches that Nero was both ruthless and a fiddler?"

"I think that history teaches that Nero was both. That was pictorially intended to enforce certain things that I wanted to enforce."

Ivins literally shouted at the witness, "Did you believe at that time that Rome was burning?"

Davenport would have none of it. He would not be bullied. Shouting right back at the attorney he responded, "I believed at that time that the Republican party in the State and Country were in a great deal of danger as a result of what I saw going on, the setting up of an authority in the legislature in opposition to the Constitution, in opposition to representative government."

One of the spectators seated in the gallery only a few feet from the witness was the attorney Charles Duell, who had received that letter from Governor Whitman about ridding the state of corrupt party control. He had also served a brief stint as a judge on the prestigious court of appeals for the DC Circuit after being appointed by then President Roosevelt. Apparently, Duell could not restrain himself and began applauding. The claps echoed through the courtroom, and several spectators joined him. Judge Andrews banged his gavel for silence. His face flushed with anger, he ordered a court attendant. "I want the man who started that applause taken from the room. I am not going to have that sort of thing going on here." The room watched silently as the attendant escorted the former judge out to the corridor.

When decorum was restored the witness continued, "I believed that there was danger to the Republican party and the institutions because of what I saw going on in the Senate chamber."

Ivins was wary of this witness and during his

recross examination set out to discredit him, wondering if he substituted the wishes of the community "or have you a sense of right of your own."

Davenport remained feisty. "I hope I have a sense of right of my own, but I regard the community sense of right as paramount importance."

But Ivins wouldn't back down either, trading gibes with him. "You don't mean to say that you would take their instinctive feelings if demonstrated and illustrated by a mob action as being better than your own individual sense of right?"

"I will tell you just what I mean by it," the witness said, in essence describing the progressive movement that had gained traction throughout the nation. "There was coming across the United States of America this movement for the political control of nominations by the whole people. What you could easily study and find to be a community sense of democracy and right; it was a community sense of democracy and I acted in accord with it."

That was enough for Ivins, who recognized the danger and dismissed the witness.

Former state assemblyman and senator Josiah P. Newcomb took the stand next; Newcomb had been on the Senate floor when the direct primary bill was brought up for consideration. On that day he had angrily charged Republican Senator Grattan and Democrat Senator Grady with entering into an alliance to defeat it. "And Senator Grattan arose," he remembered, "and replied, 'That is all right. We admit it. But you are only sore because we put it across on you!'"

The parade of witnesses continued to march to the stand for a few questions. The former Democratic mayor of Kingston, New York, Roscoe Irwin was called to testify that Charles Murphy was the Democratic leader. When Ivins and Bowers got into a spat over his testimony, Judge Andrews wondered in frustration, "Who are we trying here?"

Ivins couldn't resist, offering, "If you want to try me, you can."

Mayor Irwin agreed, with some reluctance, that when Murphy wanted someone to receive an appointment to a position "the appointment was subsequently made."

Ivins declined to question the witness, deciding, "This witness is too good natured to be cross-examined."

The defense then launched its attack on what it believed was Barnes's most vulnerable area, his business career as a publisher and printer. Bowers called Michael V. Dolan, a man who had spent the last half-century engaged in printing and publishing in Albany as an employee of the Argus company. Bowers did not diminish the importance of this testimony, telling the court, "It is essential for me to have this evidence as bearing upon future evidence."

Judge Andrews understood what was at stake. The defense was going to go after Barnes's honesty and integrity. They were going to try to prove, just as Roosevelt had written, that he had used his political position for personal gain rather than the public's benefit. If Bowers and Van Benschoten could destroy Barnes's reputation, the jury would find it difficult to return a verdict in his favor. But there was a legal question to be answered: Was it a defense to the specific charges? "We may as well take that up now as any time," the judge decided, asking the jury to retire as he heard the arguments.

The plaintiff's libel expert, former United States congressman John J. Adams, a Democrat from Queens, New York, made the argument. He began by quoting from the defense brief, which said, "'There is no charge in the article at any point that Mr. Barnes profited in any manner by any matters that are made the subject of criticism.'" He then quoted the Colonel's testimony, in which he said specifically that he did not intend in the article to make any charge of personal corruption against Barnes. Returning to the article, Adams reminded the judge that it attributed the rottenness in government by reason of the two parties working together, so showing that one party was rotten does not justify the libel. He went on, telling the court, "Nowhere is it charged that the plaintiff was guilty of corruption or wrong-doing except in conjunction with Mr. Murphy; it is not charged he used his political influence for his own enrichment or profit…

"Evidence," he continued, "is only admitted to prove the truth of the charge and not something they may insert in their plea different from the charge which they make." Adams then went through the various charges connected to printing contracts, and suggested under the court's decision prohibiting testimony about alleged gambling and vice in Albany that any suggestion of wrongdoing in this matter must also be excluded.

Further complicating the situation, Ivins added, was precisely "how far an individual is liable for the acts of a corporation." The question of exactly how much control Barnes had and exerted in the operations of these printing companies had to be established before any potential corporate misdeeds could be allowed into the record.

After considering the plaintiff's plea, Judge Andrews decided that "both sides take a too technical view of this article… I do not believe this article… is to be construed as meaning that the actual corrupt alliance between business and politics made by Mr. Barnes and Mr. Murphy must be joined in by both… I am going to admit this evidence." But then he went further, cautioning Bowers that "even if Mr. Barnes was guilty of this, that or the other thing, it would not be enough unless you can also show that it was the result of an alliance between business and politics."

Here is the needle, he appeared to be telling the defendant, *see if you can thread it*.

The jury was brought back in and Bowers went to work. Dolan testified that the Argus printing company was a large concern that had often done printing for the state legislature. There were three other large printing companies in Albany, and at various times all had bid for government work. But under Bowers's questioning Dolan revealed that sometimes the winning bidder subcontracted parts or all of the work to a competitor.

Bowers had the difficult task of making complex industry practices fathomable to the jurymen, farmers and clerks who had little understanding of these sometimes-arcane business practices. He brought out the fact that some government reports, bills, calendars and documents were printed and then reprinted or slightly amended several times. Certain bills had been reprinted as many as four times with only minor changes or corrections made, yet each time at full cost. In other instances, type set for a specific report might be sold a year later to a competitor for as much as 50 percent of the value of the contract if the report was to be republished with only a few modifications as often was the case with legislative documents, or as Dolan explained it, "whatever dicker we can make for it."

As Bowers explored the letting of government contracts, it became clear that the decision was not simply a lowest bidder situation, although the particulars of it seemed byzantine. At one point Dolan said, "I bid sometimes to win, sometimes to lose. Once my bid was 1 cent a thousand and it cost 40-cents a thousand to do the work." It appeared that Barnes's Journal Company controlled the disposition of city printing and Dolan's Argus company found it necessary to pay that Journal Company a percentage of most of the city contracts it received.

The defense had dived headfirst into the printing issue. The fact that Dolan was a reluctant witness made drawing information from him even more difficult. He answered in short complete sentences, adding no flavor to his responses. He sat stern-faced until Bowers struggled to clarify some technical information, and then smiled smugly. When Bowers offered a number from the firm's account books and asked if it was accurate, Dolan replied sarcastically, "It must be correct because it is in the book." It seemed clear that somewhere in that fog of details about printing and reprinting; commissions, discounts and credit; buying, selling and trading, there was going to be clarity, and it would show Barnes profited improperly.

But before that could be reached, the clock struck four o'clock and Judge Andrews sent everyone home for the weekend, once again cautioning jurors to avoid reading anything about, or discussing the trial.

CHAPTER TEN

Sunday, May 2, 1915, was an atypically warm spring day in Syracuse, causing some men to remove their jackets. Theodore Roosevelt went to church in the morning, then spent part of the afternoon with his lawyers in their "war room" in the Onondaga Hotel. William Barnes raced back to Albany to take care of political business. For one day, at least, the trial was off the front pages. The *Times* featured a column reporting that the Cunard liner *Lusitania* had sailed from New York on Saturday morning. The 1,960 people had been undeterred by an odd advertisement placed by the German consulate that had appeared in the newspaper that morning, warning Americans against sailing on British flagships.

Among the last to board was Alfred Gwynne Vanderbilt, the revered businessman and sportsman, who told reporters he was traveling to London to inspect his stables there and look at some property.

No one aboard appeared to take the German threat especially seriously; Alexander Campbell, the general manager of John Dewar & Sons, dismissed it casually, calling it "a lot of tommy rot" then adding confidently, "The *Lusitania* can run away from any submarine the Germans have got and the British Admiralty will see that she is looked after when she arrives in striking distance of the Irish coast."

The local newspapers had covered the trial so completely they appeared to be running out of material. The *Post-Standard* featured Ed Hoffmeier, who operated the rear elevator that was reserved for the use of parties to the case and newsmen. "He has his hands full," the paper reported, "preventing the Colonel and Mr. Barnes from riding together on the same trip, a position that demands tact..." The *New York Times* presented a broad but ominous legal analysis of the trial, which included an assessment that the "Justice May Direct a Verdict" against Roosevelt. If that were to happen, the only issue for the jury to resolve would be how much he would have to pay in damages.

The fact that the Colonel would not be on the stand had taken some steam out of the trial. On Monday morning there was no line of spectators waiting in the corridor to be admitted, and when Judge Andrews opened the session there were empty seats in the gallery for the first time. There was a noticeable calmness in the courtroom, as if the parade had passed, when Dolan resumed his place in the witness box.

The printer was no more forthcoming than he had been the previous Friday, his answers short and sullen, and whenever possible he avoided a direct response. Bowers worked hard to pin him down, but it was like trying to bottle the mist. Dolan remained elusive, his answers confusing: commissions were paid on this; he didn't remember if they were paid on that; this was the price on this day but not another day; this job did not come under that contract; ems and folios are completely different. "Did I understand you to say that this one which you made was four different orders?" Bowers asked.

"No," Dolan responded. "One order delivered at four different times."

In another instance, for example, Dolan's Argus company printed a small police book that indicated it had been printed by "The Journal Company."

While this questioning was going on the Colonel appeared to be as bored as any spectator, and for a time sat at the defense table opening and reading his mail, while Barnes yawned and conversed with his attorney.

When Dolan's direct testimony concluded, Ivins asked permission to recall him at a later time for examination admitting, "I am as hopelessly lost in this situation as any one can be..."

Edward Platt, the tall silver-gray-haired son of the late senator and party boss Thomas Platt and the sole executor of his father's estate, took the witness seat. Platt had brought with him as many as three hundred handwritten letters, almost all of the correspondence between his father and Roosevelt and between his father and Barnes. Ivins and Bowers wrestled about the sheer number of letters, which seemed to be far greater than either of them had expected or, in fact, wanted. Neither of them knew what gems these letters contained, and were wary of simply allowing all of them to be entered as evidence. Ivins objected to allowing the defense to pick through a "dead man's records" without first knowing what issues they covered and what people they named. "I asked for production of all the letters," Ivins admitted, "and I did not know until today that my subpoena had been unwittingly obeyed."

It was agreed that both sides would have someone read through the letters, picking out those that had some bearing on the case.

As the pace of the trial increased, two reporters testified, which was not considered unusual or intrusive. Jacob Dickinson was the *New York Herald*'s man in Albany in 1908. He had interviewed Barnes that year, he testified, and "primarily Mr. Barnes said he had no illusions in politics; that party supremacy was paramount in his mind to all other political considerations." Barnes had told him about a conversation he'd had with Governor Hughes about the racetrack bill, in which Hughes said he had supported it as a matter of conscience. "Mr. Barnes's reply, as he related it to me, was 'Well, if it is conscience and not votes you are thinking of, there is no common ground on which we stand.'

"He told me that Governor Hughes would not get his legislation through."

Walter Arndt had been with the *Evening Post*

in 1911 when he interviewed Barnes at Republican state headquarters in New York. Ivins objected to his testimony, and was overruled—and then listened with astonishment as Arndt recalled Barnes talking about Charles Murphy. "The substance was that (Mr. Murphy) wanted Mr. Barnes to help him defeat the direct primary legislation—and Mr. Barnes' remark was that he replied that that was Mr. Murphy's own business and that he did not intend to take any part, that the Democrats were in the majority in both houses of the Legislature and that they could solve their own difficulties…and that Mr. Barnes was not going to pull Mr. Murphy's chestnuts out of the fire for him… He wasn't going to assist him in any way."

The Colonel sat stone-faced while Barnes chuckled and Ivins outright laughed. Barnes even told Arndt later that it was the best testimony to come out in the trial. Bowers had slipped. By asking a question of a witness without being sure of the answer, he had committed a rudimentary error. And now this witness had weakened the foundations of his entire case. Ivins told the court he had no questions for this witness.

Among the oddest witnesses that day was Frederick Bresler, who was unhappy to be there. When asked by Bowers the simple question, "What is your occupation?", he turned and asked the judge, "Am I obliged to answer that?"

"Of course you are not obliged to answer that if you say it would tend to incriminate you. That is the only reason."

Bresler, who actually had been the clerk of the common council and city clerk of Albany, declared he had no occupation at present. He also appeared to have a very poor memory, failing to remember printing jobs he had ordered as part of his duties, responding with surprise that documents had been printed without his ordering them—three consecutive years—even when shown his testimony in earlier hearings investigating corruption in the printing industry. But when cornered, he admitted that when submitting a printing order he sent it to the Journal Company because "I was a friend of theirs and they were friends of mine."

Often, over days and sometimes weeks, a jury of twelve people can quickly assess what is important and why. Even though they have been instructed not to discuss the case, their shared experience often allows them to think as one on certain matters. When confronted with a hostile witness like Bresler, what he would not say and what he could not recall can become far more important than his direct answers. Why would a witness who had nothing to hide have such a selectively poor memory? Why would a city official want to deny facts when confronted with proof? In the hands of a man like Bowers, who was recovering from his tactical error, the effort to avoid answering questions can be much more dramatic testimony than the straightforward responses.

Charles Winchester, the vice president and general manager of the J. B. Lyon printing company, was called and acknowledged that James Lyon, head of the company, was too ill to appear or give his deposition. Winchester was a member of the board of directors and held several hundred shares of stock in the business. Bowers established that Barnes did not have any business connection with the Lyon company—and yet for some reason apparently had been given 750 shares in that company.

The facts were muddled, but it seemed that something untoward had taken place concerning Barnes's connection to the printing business. While owning the Journal Company, he had been given 750 shares in the competing Lyon company; Winchester had seen him in the Lyon office only one time and never spoke with him about the business. "He had nothing whatever to do with the management of the company," Winchester said. Barnes eventually had sold his shares to the witness for a substantial profit and they were returned to the company.

Ironically, only a day after elevator operator Ed Hoffmeier had described the difficulty in keeping the principals apart, it happened. During the lunch break, the two teams had retired to their offices in the Onondaga Hotel. After the break Roosevelt's team had stepped into the elevator on the eighth floor and was already in conversation when the elevator stopped on the sixth floor—and Barnes stepped inside with his people. All chatter immediately ceased and not a word was spoken nor a glance exchanged as the elevator descended to the lobby. When the doors opened the parties scurried out, taking opposite sides of the street as they walked quickly to the courthouse.

ONONDAGA HISTORICAL ASSOCIATION

Both Roosevelt and Barnes rented "war rooms" in the luxurious Onondaga Hotel. Although it had opened only five years earlier, in 1915 it expanded to five hundred rooms, in addition to an elegant ballroom, bars and restaurants, and a roof garden that offered "breathtaking views of the entire city" for evening dancing.

Bowers spent much of the afternoon trying to get someone from the Journal Company to produce the corporate books that he had subpoenaed, but the only person with authority to do that, it turned out, was the plaintiff. Bowers was getting fed up. Looking directly at Barnes, who was standing in front of the judge's bench with his hands clasped behind his back, Bowers demanded he produce the missing ledgers, stock book and journals, threatening to call him as a witness if he did not do so. Judge Andrews said that would not be necessary as he was certain Barnes would produce those books. Without a word, Barnes sat down.

While the trial was proceeding in full view of

the jury and spectators, few of them were even aware that highly technical legal wrangling was taking place, as well. At issue was when Barnes would be called, and Ivins appeared to be practically gleeful at the prospect of his client being called as a witness for the defense. This would allow Ivins to elicit favorable testimony much earlier than he anticipated.

But whatever satisfaction the Barnes team gained from that threat was short-lived; Judge Andrews had a surprise for both sides.

First though, Bowers called several more witnesses. Isadore Wachsman was questioned about double billing for the same printing work, but like the other witnesses managed to avoid being pinned down. It might have happened, he admitted, but if it did it was due more to a lack of oversight than any intentional effort to squeeze payments out of the city. William Coats, a clerk in Albany's comptroller's office, testified he was responsible for giving printing contracts to the Journal Company then admitted he had never tried to find a competitor who might charge less for the work.

It was then that the judge, without warning, reversed a critical earlier ruling bearing on Roosevelt's state of mind when he wrote the allegedly libelous article. Without explanation, he decided to allow the defense to present additional evidence that helped Colonel Roosevelt form his opinion. "The defendant, simply as bearing on the question of malice, simply as bearing on the question of mitigation of damages, may give evidence which tends to show absence of malice in the mind of the defendant… If by my ruling I have misled you in any way, you may recall any of the witnesses and ask any of the questions which you failed to ask because of that ruling." Whatever the specific legal justification, this entirely unexpected shift now opened the gates for a flood of additional testimony by Roosevelt and the defense about *why* he made the statements at issue.

The appearance of the day's final witness, Frederick Foster, the chief clerk of the State Printing Board, now seemed completely anticlimactic. What mattered was that the Colonel was going to have another go at it, this time with the restraints removed. He would be able to make his full case against William Barnes's reputation. But as the session ended, the defense produced minutes of a meeting about a substantial contract. There had been five bidders for it, and the Lyon company had won it with a bid of $159,550.61.

"When the contract was awarded to the J. B. Lyon Company for the legislative printing," asked Stewart Hancock, a local lawyer working for the defense, "there were three bids which were lower in amount, is that right?"

"Yes, sir."

"And the J. B. Lyon Company was next to the highest bidder, is that right?"

Foster did not respond.

Court was adjourned for the evening with that question looming in the air.

But that evening it was what was happening at

sea that was likely on most American minds. It had just been reported that the American tanker *Gulflight* had been torpedoed by a German submarine while being escorted to a British port by two British patrol ships. The German submarine captain claimed it had been an error, that he had not seen the American flag until he had launched the torpedo. Three Americans died, the first Americans killed by a German submarine. Colonel Roosevelt knew that many Americans of German heritage would sympathize with the Germans, so when he was called to comment by the newsmen he could have resisted, knowing three men of German descent sat on the jury. He did not. "This was an act of piracy," he said, "pure and simple." He went no further with that, refusing to use this as an excuse to push even harder for America to enter the European War, while President Wilson continued to try to defuse tensions and maintain American neutrality.

The trial had gone on long enough for people to be openly taking sides in the dispute. On the morning of May 4, for example, the *New York American* published a letter from its publisher William Randolph Hearst, who came out full throttle for the Colonel, writing, "It is not of immediate consequence that Roosevelt in time past consorted with the bosses he now denounces. It is of no relative importance that he has found virtue in the corporations that favored him and villainy in the corporations which opposed him. Humanity is fallible and you cannot look for perfection in politicians.

Roosevelt is a natural progressive modified perhaps by self-interest and personal ambition; Barnes is a natural reactionary, aggravated by constant corporations's service and association."

That same day the *Post-Standard* printed another letter, this one from a woman named Edith Russell. "The Syracuse women applaud Roosevelt when he appears in the courtroom. Good for you, our Syracuse sisters, our pastor last evening compared his trial with Christ' trial before Pontius Pilate. The women from this state will always applaud a just man and hiss an unjust man."

There was a slight stir that same morning, when Colonel Roosevelt unexpectedly entered the courtroom with his fifth cousin, the thirty-three-year-old New York Democrat and now assistant secretary of the navy, Franklin D. Roosevelt. The two men liked each other; in fact almost a decade earlier T.R. had given away the bride, his niece Eleanor Roosevelt when she married Franklin on St. Patrick's Day, 1905 in a New York City apartment. Young Roosevelt was following his illustrious relative's path. After being homeschooled he also attended Harvard. Spurred on by his admiration for his cousin, he entered politics and won a seat in the New York State Senate. Although he was a Democrat, as his father had been, he too fought the party structure, and often found himself in agreement with Progressive Republican positions. And just like T.R., he accepted the position of assistant secretary of the navy.

FDR was young, smart and charming, and had made friends with the men of the press corps. So he was greeted happily by many of the reporters, who knew him from both Albany and more recently, Washington, DC. He was much admired among those scribes for his frankness, courtesy and availability.

When the session opened, Bowers immediately dampened any excitement that the Colonel might resume his testimony that morning, instead asking Winchester the cost of printing a two volume set of books entitled *Insects Affecting Park and Woodland Trees* in 1907. Winchester could not produce it and was asked to return to court when he had it.

Frederick Foster then returned to the stand, and for the next hour or more Hancock used this witness to demonstrate that there seemed to be no obvious rationale for how printing contracts were awarded; sometimes they went to the lowest bidder and at times that bidder, which appeared to be little more than a shell company, handed the contract over to Lyon or the Journal for a pittance; sometimes the contract was awarded to a bidder in the middle and other times it went to the highest bidder.

The monotony of the technical explanations that had droned on through the morning was finally broken by the acceptance of the Platt letters to, and from, Barnes into evidence. Earlier in the trial, Roosevelt had been under the hot light as a result of personal letters he had written to Senator Platt, but now it was Barnes's turn to sweat. Van Benschoten read Barnes's letters to Platt loudly and slowly, making certain the jurors fully grasped the implications. "Dear Senator," read the first one,

"Mr. McCarthy who is the bidder of record, backed by Mr. Quigg, is an inveterate enemy of the Republican Party… The acceptance of his bid means a fierce local fight for me…

"For six years men assumed to be friendly to you have systematically prevented me from getting anything in the printing line in Albany…"

In a subsequent letter, Barnes was even more forthcoming. "What I didn't want is the establishment of another printing plant in Albany. Already the business has been practically ruined by overcompetition and I can see in the proposal to set up another establishment the beginning of a warfare which I do not court, but which I am ready to meet… Whenever these printing controversies come up I am inclined to be testy, for the reason that since the Republican Party carried the state in 1893 I have never been able to secure a single contract from the Republican State officers…"

According to Van Benschoten, these letters, and several similar pieces of correspondence he introduced, showed the efforts made by Barnes to use his growing political influence to convince state officers to give him these contracts; a quest, the defense intended to demonstrate, that eventually proved wildly successful. Barnes, the defense contended, was in politics for personal profit and not for the benefit of the public, just as the Colonel had written.

Bowers's recital was interrupted by a parade of fifteen hundred Syracuse University men celebrating moving-up day, led by the trumpets and thumping drums of the school's marching band. They paused outside the courthouse and began shouting, "Hurrah for T.R." Judge Andrews was furious at this interruption and ordered the sheriff, "I want that noise stopped!" Just as Van Benschoten resumed reading, the crowd began chanting, "Hail! Hail! The gang's all here," and the band launched into a furious version of the popular ditty "He's a Rag Picker"! The judge told the officers to arrest as many students as necessary if that was required to stop them.

The crowd finally moved on just as the morning session came to a close.

Winchester was back on the stand in the afternoon to explain that several of the ledgers could not be located. He wanted to comply, he said, but the books just didn't exist. So while he was unable to determine the cost of printing *Insects Affecting Park and Woodland Trees*, he could do so for assembly document No. 25, *Plums of New York*, as well as the 1910 job *Birds of New York*.

That apparently made Judge Andrews happy as he chimed in, "We all know *Birds of New York*. I do, because I have them!"

Bowers, who was growing impatient with these excuses, said firmly, "I don't."

His interrogation became testy; the witness zigged and zagged, but when finally pinned down offered to "explain to you the *Birds* if you want me to."

"When we want you to," Bowers responded, "we will ask you."

"But when your reputation is attacked you like to answer."

"No man's reputation has been attacked, certainly not yours."

Winchester took offense at that. "The reputation of my company."

"On the contrary," Bowers said, "we desire to show it as successfully as possible."

After Winchester was sent away to try to put cost information into some sort of fathomable presentation, the next witness was called: Franklin Roosevelt. He stepped smartly to the stand, clearly savoring this opportunity to support his distant relative. The finely tailored dark suit and rimless glasses that he wore added to his somber appearance. Teddy Roosevelt had been an early and consistent booster of his fifth cousin, supporting his decision to go into politics and predicting a fine future for him. The younger Roosevelt had already been elected to two terms in the New York State Senate, perhaps trading a bit on his distant cousin's presidential popularity, and hence knew well how the state senate was run and who benefited most. Franklin Roosevelt was already known to the public and respected; his name brought with it a modicum of charisma, his own hard work reinforcing the general good opinion about the family.

Roosevelt introduced himself as the Colonel's "fifth cousin by blood and a nephew-in-law," and smiled broadly as he said he had known the defendant his entire life. As it turns out, he also had lived on the same street as Barnes at one point. Getting to the issue at hand, Roosevelt had been in the state senate during the bitter 1911 fight between Democrat William Sheehan and the incumbent Republican Chauncey Depew to fill the US Senate seat. The Democratic Party was divided bitterly between Tammany and Independents so even though it held the majority, the Tammany regulars could not muster enough votes to elect Sheehan. The Republicans, in the minority, lacked the votes to elect Depew. As a result the two candidates had been deadlocked for several weeks when Franklin Roosevelt happened to meet Barnes at a social club in Albany. Secretary Roosevelt told Barnes about a conversation he'd had with Democratic Senator Grady "who saw no way out of it because it had been understood and agreed between Mr. Barnes and Mr. Murphy that the Republicans would remain steadfast and continue to vote for Depew so as to give the Democrats every possible way to elect Mr. Sheehan… Grady told me that it was his judgment that the deadlock would continue for a long time as Mr. Barnes had told him that he had an agreement with Mr. Murphy that the Republicans should hold out…so as to give the Democrats every opportunity to elect Depew."

Bowers followed up. "Did you tell this to Mr. Barnes?"

"I did." FDR responded, "I then stated to Mr. Barnes that I thought for the good of the state… a Senator ought to be elected. I told him that the Democrats had a majority in both the Senate and Assembly, that it must be a Democrat and that I hoped he would consider the possibility of…joining with the anti-Murphy Democrats who were opposed to Mr. Sheehan.

"He said no. He said, 'We can't do it now.'"

Weeks later, FDR continued, a letter written by Barnes suggested the Republican minority should join with the Independent Democrats to elect an independent Democrat to the senate. One day later the compromise candidate, James A. O'Gorman, was elected by a vote of 112 to 80 for Chauncey Depew. What led to Barnes's change of heart was left unanswered.

Ivins had only a few questions for the witness, establishing that even though he was an independent Democrat he had voted for O'Gorman, the Tammany candidate. Nevertheless, his appearance had packed an emotional appeal; the loyal young Democrat taking the stand to support his Republican relation and suggesting his own party's leader may have been working in cahoots with the Republican Barnes to elect candidates who did not threaten the fundamental party system. When he stepped down, he pointedly shook hands firmly with the Colonel.

There was some court business to be done, Bowers and Ivins cleaning up paperwork concerning primarily the total of Barnes's interest in the Lyon printing company and the Albany Journal Company. When that was done, Bowers recalled Colonel Roosevelt to the stand.

Roosevelt once again settled comfortably into the witness chair, smiling at the judge, adjusting his glasses and clearing his throat. He was ready to go to work. His task was simply to clear up any difficulties or inconsistences in the transcript so far. This too was part of many trials. On page 269 of the document, for example, "In line 2 of my answer it should be 'initiative,'" or "On page 273, in the third line the word should be 'legislative' instead of 'legislation.'" The editing continued for most of an hour. "I don't think it ought to be 'I will try not to be emphatic' but 'I will try not to be *too* emphatic…'" "On page 572 I don't like that slang phrase. Substitute for the words 'It went through, It accomplished the result.'" And so they worked through the transcript until the round clock hanging above the entrance reached five o'clock and with Judge Andrews's usual instructions not to read about or discuss the trial, the day ended.

The trial had settled into a routine; it had opened almost three weeks earlier and conducted its daily business like any other ongoing concern. Reporters, somewhat dulled by the minutiae of the trial, looked for any subject that might interest their readers. The famed Chicago journalist Richard Henry Little had gotten to know the city and felt comfortable reporting about it. "Syracuse is the most beautiful town in America," he wrote, "and Chicago would not exist if it was not for Syracuse, for otherwise it would have no salt to preserve its meat crop. I am also hesitant to add that Syracuse keeps its face cleaner than Chicago but it has regular water in its lake. Syracuse seems to have more people than Chicago but that might be only because of the trial. I do not approve of the New York Central

Railroad running its trains down on Washington Street in Syracuse, if the Illinois Central drove its trains down State Street in Chicago we would have one thousand fatalities a day but here it is different. In Syracuse I observe that when a citizen strolling languidly across the railroad track is threatened by fast mail that he leaps for his life but he turns around and walks up to the mail train and gives it a kick in the cow catcher…

"All the correspondents have been instructed to remain in Syracuse until the trial is finished and someday when our distinguished conferees are sitting in the old Onondaga Hotel, stroking our long white beards we will have much to say about the great interest, forty years before when in all our youth and beauty we came to Syracuse at the outbreak of the Barnes-Roosevelt libel trial."

The following morning, Judge Andrews announced that based on the "strain of the trial" on the participants, he would be concluding the courtroom activity by 4:00 p.m. each day. With the exception of the jurors, everyone involved from the lawyers to the judge to the journalists were working well past the time that court ended. There were documents to review, legal matters to address, witnesses to prepare and for the journalists, articles to write.

Bowers began the day with more printing evidence, tying Barnes as tightly as possible to the Journal Company. He made an often-complicated effort to demonstrate that profits from state printing business ended up in Barnes's personal bank account. It was long and dry and at times felt like the legal equivalent of a train stopped at the watering station; it was necessary, but it took a long time and very little seemed to be happening. "Here is Mr. William Barnes," Bowers explained, "and the moneys disbursed for his private purposes by the Company and charged to him, against which are credited his salary, and then run the salary over to the profit and loss, and then profit and loss over to the job printing, it must be assumed he exercised this supervision."

It sounded important, but Judge Andrews cautioned the jury not to accept arguments on questions of law as proof of a fact. It apparently was wearing on the judge as he practically begged Bowers to move on, suggesting, "That every individual expenditure that he (Barnes) ever made was charged in that account."

And Ivins added, "The attempt made here is to assume or presume a party is guilty of fraud. You cannot make any presumption of fraud by the introduction of the books of a corporation. You cannot make any presumption of fraud because every man is held to be innocent until proven guilty."

It was eventually established that the Lyon company paid a commission to any person or entity that brought it jobs; apparently most state, city and county printing business was filtered through the Journal to other companies, for which it received a commission—with at least part of the proceeds ending up in Barnes's bank account. That all led up to Bowers asking Winchester, who had been recalled to the stand, "The Journal did not have any plant in which they could do job printing, did they?"

"No, sir." A printing company without a printing plant? Interesting. The point he was making was that they were merely the middlemen. He did not find it necessary to speculate how they won their contracts.

Day by day the defense was exposing the reality of politics to the public; the difficulty Bowers and his team faced was connecting all the disparate pieces and bringing it back to Roosevelt's article. During cross-examination, Winchester testified that, to his knowledge, Barnes never used his political influence to obtain state printing contracts for the Lyon company.

But what was revealed were the many different ways taxpayer dollars were cleverly funneled into political pockets. There were laws, for example, that provided for massive overprinting of various state reports and documents. The former superintendent of insurance William Hotchkiss testified that he had made three different attempts to have those laws amended in an effort to save money by reducing waste, but the legislation he proposed was defeated or ignored and thousands of unneeded sets of books were printed and stored in the Capitol attic. When Hotchkiss wrote directly to Winchester that he desired only 2500 additional copies of a report, Winchester responded, "We are required (by law) to print 5000 copies; it could hardly be expected that we would consent to a reduction…the printing will go forward without further delay."

After hours of tedious technical testimony about printing contracts was finally done, Colonel Roosevelt was recalled to the stand. It was as if someone had shaken awake the somnolescent courtroom. Teddy was back, and now with the judge's revised ruling that allowed him to prove his state of mind when he published the article, he was free to tell the whole story of his relationship with Barnes. Bowers began where he had been cut off by Judge Andrews, repeating that testimony. "I am trying to show what the situation is as it existed..."

To which the judge had responded, "I don't think that is important."

"Now," Bowers asked, renewed, "I respectfully ask...that the witness be allowed to state the conversation that he had with Mr. Barnes on the propriety and nature of the boss and the domination of the machine as tending to support the defendant in reaching the conclusion that he did in publishing the article in question."

It was still a difficult issue for the judge, who wondered if the Colonel's testimony should be heard for justification, meaning the reason he wrote and published the article, or just mitigation, to lessen any potential damages. He finally decided that they "may be competent in mitigation (but) I do not see how they are competent in justification. I think I will take them, because I think they are competent on one ground, at any rate."

Roosevelt began recalling conversations he had with Barnes while serving as governor. The Colonel had met with Barnes in several different places, from the governor's chamber at the Capitol to a train racing from Albany to New York. And during these conversations, the Colonel said that Barnes had "instanced Albany County as an example of one in which it was impossible that the riff-raff could go on in politics without damage to the community if there was not a responsible organization and leader… That the riff-raff could not be trusted to handle political affairs with propriety; that in substance they would misconduct themselves so at the expense of propriety that the government could not go on…"

This was the Teddy Roosevelt the spectators had come to see. He was an explosion of energy, invigorating the courtroom. His voice grew stronger and louder as he seemed to be stiffened by his anger at this dismissive attitude toward voters. "The Colonel had worked himself into a fervor," the *Times* wrote. "He stuck out his chin as he dwelt on Barnes' name, he leaned toward the justice and he pounded his fists on the arm of his chair, using all the accomplishments that Mr. Ivins objected to so strenuously several days ago."

He continued, a single long, loud rant, "…It was not necessary for the boss to issue orders to legislators…that they found out that if they did not support the organization they didn't get their bills through, they were not renominated or they did not have funds given them to carry on a campaign if nominated and that in most cases they very speedily found out for themselves that it was to their

AUTHOR COLLECTION

Political cartoonist Victor R. Lambdin had become nationally known for his work in publications like The Literary Digest *and* Harper's, *traveling extensively throughout the country to bring his own view to current events. This sketch of the Colonel on the stand, for the* Albany Knickerbocker Press, *accentuated his oft-visible teeth jutting forward as he emphasized his point.*

interest to discover what the organization wishes and to do it… If he declined to learn, then he got dropped."

Roosevelt continued with what was essentially a civics class in the corruption of politics: he described Barnes's explanation of the way power and money were employed to compel loyalty. After his election as president, he said his conversations with Barnes continued. In particular he remembered Barnes's statements during the effort to change the primary process. "Mr. Barnes said that the organization had complete control of the legislature; that the effort to pass primary bills represented merely a general effort to break down party government… and that on an issue such as that the Democratic organization would make common cause with the Republican organization and that it had been agreed that they should make such common cause against the primary legislation (which) would not and could not be allowed to pass for it would mean the destruction of party government.

"That was one of several occasions upon which Mr. Barnes said that the people could not govern themselves!" That phrase startled the courtroom.

Bowers read two articles to the jury; the first, from the *New York World* asserted that "a perfect understanding and harmony" existed between the Barnes and Murphy political machines; "As for the Governor's (Hughes) favorable view of the legislature's undertakings," it read in part, "leaders of both machines smiled smugly and let it go at that. Agents of 'invisible government' caressing the favors tossed to them by 'the boys' had little regret over the break between Murphy and the Governor as they sipped cold pints… There was slight chance for anything opposed by the two machines to slip out of Rules."

The second article, also from the *World*, contended that the two parties came together when necessary to block legislation. While Governor Hughes was "brewing war medicine…the allied Barnes and Murphy forces in the legislature directed a steady fire of canister and shrapnel at the Executive redoubts with a grim and sullen humor… The bipartisan combination of the two machines, having accomplished the defeat of the Direct Nominations bill favored by the Governor moved relentlessly on to the slaughter of every recommendation made by the Chief Executive…"

The Colonel asserted that he had relied in part on those articles and two similar pieces "after making inquiries about them."

What had been a long slow day had been transformed in the final half hour into an exciting conclusion. But like any good Saturday morning cliffhanger, no one objected when the plaintiff asked to begin cross-examination in the morning. In a great understatement Judge Andrews suggested, "I suppose there will be no objection to that."

The prelude was done: Ivins was now going to have another chance at Colonel Roosevelt.

CHAPTER ELEVEN

Some libels are easily refuted. In his 1912 lawsuit against the *Ishpeming Iron Ore*, which had claimed he was often drunk, Roosevelt took the stand and testified, "I have never been drunk or in the slightest degree under the influence of liquor… I do not drink either whisky or brandy, I do not drink beer, I sometimes drink light wine…"

The newspaper publisher, George A. Newett was unable to produce a single witness to support his claims and apologized, admitting, "I am forced to conclude that I am mistaken." He agreed to pay Roosevelt a symbolic six cents. That trial was brief and simple, as opposed to this one, which was already long and complex and threatened to last several more weeks. After all, here the entire American political system was effectively on trial.

When court resumed on May 6, Judge Andrews asked all the jurors, as he often did, if they had read any press coverage of the case overnight. When each responded that he had not, as they were instructed not to do, the proceedings began. But the judge then quickly dismissed them again to deal with a serious legal issue. Bowers renewed his argument that the defense must be permitted to tie known political corruption in Albany to Barnes, as a way of showing Roosevelt was not acting with malice.

Each state relied on its own definition of malice, but across the country the laws were often more protective of a person's reputation than of an individual's right to criticize publicly. In New York a published statement not only had to be true—it also had to have been published "with good motives and for justifiable means."

Bowers made a long and reasoned discussion of the libel laws: "The court laid down as a proposition one that everyone concedes, that any publication which tends to charge a person with a crime or makes him ridiculous before the public is prima facie libel and malice is presumed." Citing the decision of a recent Wisconsin case, *Arnold v. Ingram*, he quoted, "Every citizen has a right to comment on those acts of public men which concern him as a citizen of the State, if he does not make his commentary a cloak for malice and slander. Those who fill a public position must not be too thin-skinned in reference to comments made upon them. It would often happen that the observations would be made upon public men which they knew from the bottom of their hearts were undeserved and unjust; yet they must bear with them and submit to be misunderstood for a time, because all knew that the criticism of the press was the best security for the proper discharge of public duties."

Bowers took a circuitous path, drawing on several additional decisions, before reaching the essential point. "I submit to your honor that underneath it all lies the proposition that where a man is saying to his fellow citizens, a man who is a voter and citizen of the State, certain matters in order to put in motion a political campaign and drive out of office two great political parties…(there is sufficient reason to justify) at the very least the reception of any evidence of any character which tended to indicate to the Court or jury that the defendant in uttering the article had reason to believe that substantially his statements were true…

"Mr. Roosevelt should be permitted to give in evidence certain matters which have thus far been excluded concerning information that was brought to his attention…this case, as far as I can glean from the legal situation, the question of whether or not Mr. Barnes had been guilty of corruption is in issue; and it would matter little whether that corruption were in a State act or a County act."

"I agree with you," said Judge Andrews, "that the defendant has the right to give any evidence of any kind which made him believe that the charge when he made it, was true. He can tell what anybody said to him which he relied on. He can tell anything that he read… Now, we agree to that…"

"I do not agree," Ivins piped up.

But in the complex language of legalese, what

sounded very much like a victory for the defendant turned out to be anything but that, as the judge continued his explanation. "This article charges Mr. Barnes with corruption and improper conduct as relates to State affairs…and therefore, I think that any information which the defendant may have received, although he believed it, confined to governmental affairs of the City and County of Albany, is immaterial in mitigation. That is the reason I ruled that this evidence as to local and county affairs of the city and county is immaterial."

Bowers, frustrated, stated once again, "If the act is corrupt, it does not make any difference whether it is state government, city government or county government. This is the ground of the position I take." Nevertheless, the ruling stood.

The jury was brought back in, and Colonel Roosevelt was recalled. It was Ivins's turn to begin his cross-examination. The spectators readied for another delicious confrontation. Instead, Ivins addressed the bench with a smirk. "I do not care to have anything further to do with Colonel Roosevelt." When asked about this decision later in the day, the attorney told reporters, "Mr. Roosevelt came prepared to make some more speeches to the jury. He had both sleeves filled up to the shoulders, but I decided not to give him a chance. I guess I rather disappointed him."

Bowers smiled as he acknowledged, "I guess Colonel Roosevelt will accept the situation."

The Colonel appeared to be taken aback by this unexpected strategy; a veritable groan rippled through the disappointed gallery. He tentatively left the witness chair, his disappointment on display. Theodore Roosevelt took pride in being a man of action. During his presidency, he had a fighting ring installed in the White House basement where he would box and wrestle. His sparring partner, William McKinley Mooney recalled, "'Hit me, hit me hard, just as hard as you can!' he used to say and when I would send one of my heaviest to his jaw he'd come up shouting, 'Fine, that's the way to do it. Now watch me.' And then he would land his heaviest blow on me. He had a good punch too… As an athlete, if he had any fault, he may have let his enthusiasm go beyond his strength."

The inability to maintain control, to sit still and quiet while other men resolved his fate, rather than strike back at what he believed was an obvious wrong, clearly was difficult for T.R. He had chosen the life of a participant rather than a spectator, and now he was being pushed to the sideline.

Bowers moved back to the critical, albeit not particularly scintillating, printing evidence. Through a series of witnesses, he brought out the fact that the printing business was extremely lucrative for Barnes. He presented numerous check stubs representing payments from the Journal Company made to the plaintiff: Barnes received a dividend of $2000 each quarter. In addition, special dividends were paid. On January 11, 1909, "the melon was cut" and Barnes got $8,080. On July 10 he got an extra share of $4,040. On December 21, $16,160. January 11, 1911, $12,120. Check after check, thousands and more thousands of dollars, all paid to William Barnes. His regular dividend payment for the five-year period was $40,400, but he also received extra payments totaling $46,460. All the other stockholders in the company, it was pointed out, received a sum total of $38,765. There was no claim, statement or indication that anything illegal took place, but the relentless presentation gave the impression, fairly or not, that somebody must have done something wrong.

In the midst of this, the court attempted to move things along, asking Ivins if he would concede that the plaintiff knew that on certain dates the Journal company made payments to other printing companies. "We will agree to nothing that these gentlemen ask," the lawyer said angrily. "They are delving into our books and taking out whatever they want and taking unfair advantage of us."

Bowers got to his feet and said with equal fervor, "No advantage is being taken of anyone…" and suggested that Ivins contest it if he believed what he was saying.

When this presentation was done, Judge Andrews tried to bring some legal bearing to it. "Let me see just what you have," he said. "You've got the fact that Mr. Barnes countersigned all the dividend checks…" He went through it step-by-step, finally asking with skepticism, "Have you anything farther which will justify the admission of evidence…"

The argument twisted and turned, but without gaining traction. A good portion of the day was spent debating legal points that were difficult to connect to the original alleged libel. One witness was on the stand for an extended period, and when he was finished, Ivins moved to strike out his complete testimony and the judge agreed. "I think it may go out. I don't think there is anything in that evidence that affects this case one way or the other."

The defense made a prolonged effort to show that the legislature rejected several attempts to pass printing legislation, then attempted to introduce examples of bidding. Ivins objected, saying that material was no more relevant in this case "than the first chapter of Genesis."

The testimony, "shrouded in technicalities," according to the newsmen, "proved dry entertainment for the usual courtroom crowd." Colonel Roosevelt seemed mostly distracted. He flipped through a magazine, occasionally conferring with his lawyers. Barnes appeared no more interested, sitting with his back to the jury box and witness chair, very quietly dictating notes and instructions to his secretary, Cassie Doran. Jurors were yawning overtly, and at one point it appeared that Ivins even briefly dozed off.

It was not a great stretch to compare the pace of this trial to one of the Colonel's famed hunting expeditions: both required great preparation and anticipation, both relied on experience and expertise, and both were dominated by long periods of patient waiting interrupted by bursts of excitement. In an early book, *Hunting Trips of a Ranchman*, Colonel Roosevelt had written, "But many other qualities go to make up the first-class hunter. He must be persevering, watchful, hardy, and with good judgement; and a little dash and energy at the proper time often help him immensely." The lessons learned on those plains undoubtedly came in useful, as sitting at the table listening to this confusing, repetitious testimony for hours required each of those traits. Somewhere hidden in all these debates there were opportunities, and either side had to be ready to recognize them when they came and be ready to pounce.

Late in the afternoon, one of those moments came for the defense. Buried in the voluminous records of the printing company, run by Barnes, the defense produced evidence that the *New York Times* described as having "all the effect of a sudden bomb explosion in the Barnes camp." As it turned out, during the two years ending in 1901, the J. B. Lyon Company got no printing contracts—instead legislative printing contracts went personally to James B. Lyon, and for those two years Barnes was obtaining the contracts directly for Lyon. But what seemed to stun even Barnes's own attorneys, was the fact that Barnes had received a whopping $20,000 in compensation for no identifiable reason. And at the end of those two years, Barnes continued to obtain printing contracts for the company but rather than receiving direct compensation, was handed 750 shares in the company.

While this revelation sent ripples through the courtroom, by the end of the third week Judge Andrews still was not convinced that this printing testimony and evidence added up to very much of consequence in connection to the specifics of this case.

On the morning of Friday the seventh, Winchester was once again recalled to the stand and brought with him more books and check stubs, among them the so-called "unofficial edition" of *Insects in Park and Woodland Trees*, that seemed to have been printed in multiple and entirely unnecessary volumes.

Bowers presented a small mountain of evidence showing how politicians used printing contracts for their profits, claiming as much as ten times the amount of printing was done and billed than was actually needed, and that the same type-composition was reprinted year after year and charged as newly set, but struggled to connect it directly to the plaintiff. When Ivins objected to this, Judge Andrews replied that he had decided to allow the defendant to make his case, and once that was all done he would rule on its admissibility. The difficulty with that, Ivins pointed out in memorable words, was the confounding problem that has plagued jurists forever. "You forget that you may rule this evidence in for the present and rule it out thereafter, but you cannot wipe out yesterday any more than you can create tomorrow.

"You are allowing to get before this jury a series of assumptions where no connection whatever has been made, and where it is beyond your mental or moral power to remove it from the mind of the jury."

It was a question of human nature, Judge Andrews appeared to respond, claiming that the jury was sufficiently responsive to his orders that if he decided to rule out the printing testimony from consideration the jury would follow his instructions.

While an expert witness was testifying that the forty-one lines of type on a page that had been common in 1901 had been reduced to thirty-five lines by 1908, requiring additional pages, Ivins walked over to the defense table and with a smile on his face leaned over the Colonel's shoulder and presented him with a slim green-covered book. "I came across this yesterday, Colonel," he said, "and it struck me that it was a first class translation and if you cared to amuse yourself of anything of this sort while this uninteresting technical testimony is going on, you might enjoy it."

The volume was a translation of *Acharnians and other plays of Aristophanes*. It was an unexpected gesture and one the Colonel clearly appreciated, responding, "Thank you. Thank you, I am dee-lighted!"

This obviously was a cleverly planned move; the inference being that even a collection of Ancient Greek plays was more interesting than the lengthy testimony about printing specifications. The fact that Ivins spoke loudly enough to be overheard by the newsmen, who then reported it, was itself a wry comment on the pace of the trial.

Judge Andrews finally laid down his criteria for accepting this evidence: "First, there was corruption or waste; second, that the plaintiff knew it or shared in it; third, that the corruption or waste was brought about by the exercise of the plaintiff's political influence." Later, he elaborated, "It don't make no difference how much corruption or extravagance you prove unless you prove Mr. Barnes' knowledge of it. Any incident showing corruption or extravagance is immaterial unless you also prove Mr. Barnes had knowledge of that incident." And finally he challenged the defense. "What evidence do you claim that there is which would justify the jury in finding that the wasteful or extravagant nature of these contracts…was brought about by the influence of the plaintiff?"

"If I had that…direct evidence," Bowers admitted, "we needn't be troubling ourselves as to asking the jury to infer that from the facts we brought out."

As Bowers continued his efforts to paste together bits and pieces to make his case, Roosevelt was distracted, thoroughly enjoying himself as he paged through Ivins's gift, at times chuckling at a witticism from this Father of Comedy. His enjoyment was interrupted late in the afternoon as a messenger delivered a telegram to him. He read it in silence and said nothing, holding to himself this awful news.

The luxury British passenger ship *Lusitania* traveling from New York to Liverpool with 1,960 people, including many Americans, had been torpedoed by a German submarine. While it was unclear at that time the magnitude of the damage, Roosevelt had already made clear that he thought the United States should be fighting alongside its European allies. But at least for now, he would sit patiently through more arguments over how much his legal team would be able to attack the questionable business practices of the man suing him for libel.

Bowers was struggling to make the connection. Barnes, he said, through his dividends or the increasing value of his stock or the company was receiving "a compensation and return which naturally would have induced him to do everything in his power to assist the company in which he had such interest, to make a profitable result to all the contracts they had with anyone, including the State…

"He had an interest in everything."

The judge refused to accept a logical chain as evidence. "Mr. Barnes as a stockholder shared in these profits…but that alone does not prove that he knew the bill for these…records was a swollen or unjust bill; it does not prove that he knew the prices received for these…records showed waste on the part of the State."

Bowers once again cited Barnes's letter to Platt complaining that he was not getting printing contracts he deserved, and once again cited Barnes's letter to then governor Roosevelt arguing against the creation of a state printing business. But to little avail as Judge Andrews ruled, "I will hold that the mere fact that Mr. Barnes is a stock holder in the Lyon company is not sufficient to affect him with the knowledge of (corruption or wrongdoing)…

"I will hold that this evidence, and similar evidence…are incompetent unless further evidence is offered connecting Mr. Barnes either with the extravagance of the printer or with the fraud in the rendering of the bill…

"…if they offer a piece of evidence and say they

are going to show affirmatively that Mr. Barnes had knowledge of that himself, I will admit it."

The defense made a valiant effort to forge that connection, offering a list of payments made by the Lyon company to the Journal Company. Things got so confusing that one of the jurors asked despairingly, "May the jury have a little more explanation of the meaning of those things?" The attempt to explain led to more questions from the jury. But finally Bowers had to admit that he had nothing else, and that he would be closing his case on Monday.

What in almost any other situation would have been a devastating ruling that threatened to completely undermine the defense case was cast aside as the courtroom emptied for the weekend; and as the participants and spectators walked out into the street they were confronted by newsboys hawking the extra edition of the *Syracuse Herald* headlined "The Lusitania Sinks."

The true extent of the attack was not yet known. According to the paper, "It is believed that her passengers are safe. No details of how they may have been rescued, however, are at hand."

As more reports began filtering in, however, it became apparent that the passengers were not safe, that most of them had not been rescued. It happened as they had been enjoying a formal luncheon about ten miles off Ireland's Old Head of Kinsdale, in County Cork, when a U-20 German submarine fired seven torpedoes at close range. Two of them struck the ship on its starboard side, one forward and the other in the engine or boiler room, causing huge explosions. The ship was ripped open and began sinking immediately; lifeboats went into the water, and those people who could find life jackets donned them. An SOS went out and rescue operations began, but even before they were fully underway it was too late. Aboard the *Lusitania* life and death decisions were being made in an instant. According to survivors, Alfred Vanderbilt, a friend of the Colonel's, had promised a young mother holding tight to her infant child that he would find a life vest for her; when he failed to do so he took off his own vest and tied it around her, then helped her into a lifeboat. Vanderbilt could not swim, so this gesture was done with the full awareness of the mortal cost.

The *Lusitania* remained afloat for eighteen minutes before going down by her bow. Two ships nearby raced at full steam to rescue passengers. The initial details were vague, but it was reported that only ten lifeboats were put into the water and carried at most five hundred people. German U-20 Captain Walther Schwieger wrote, "Great confusion is rife on board; the boats are made ready and some of them lowered into the water…some boats, full to capacity are rushed from above, touch the water with either stem or stern first and founder immediately."

The true extent of the disaster slowly became apparent; 1,197 passengers and crew—among them 128 Americans—had died in the attack. In addition to Vanderbilt, the Colonel knew several other people who perished.

Roosevelt returned to Horace Wilkinson's home,

knowing he must make a statement. While the magnitude of the loss at sea was almost beyond comprehension, and without comparison, whatever remarks he made now certainly could impact the trial, and the outcome of the trial would help determine his own future. The question was what could he say without alienating the three members of the jury of German descent. His earlier comments criticizing Germany had riled the German-American population. Several of them had even returned autographed photographs to him with angry comments. Finally he told his host, "It doesn't make any difference. It is more important I be right than to win this suit. I've got to be right in this matter." He then retired to his room to prepare his remarks.

The phone rang at midnight. A reporter for the Associated Press asked to speak to the Colonel. "I'll speak with him," Roosevelt said, "I always talk with the boys." The reporter brought him the most recent reports. Bodies of men, women and children, many of them babies, were being brought ashore in Ireland. "That's murder," Roosevelt told the journalist. "Will I make a statement? Yes, yes, I'll make it now. Just take this."

He had made a decision. There would be no caution in his response, no equivocation. "The sinking of the *Lusitania* was not only an act of simple piracy, but that it represented piracy accompanied by murder on a vaster scale than any old time pirate have ever practiced before being hung for his misdeeds… It is warfare against innocent men, women and children traveling on the ocean…

During the trial Roosevelt stayed at the home of shipbuilder and steel magnate Horace Wilkinson, who had joined him in founding the Progressive party in 1912. He built this "chateauesque" mansion at 703 Walnut Street, whose sprawling gardens are pictured here, in 1905.

"It seems inconceivable that we can refrain from taking action in this matter, for we owe it not only to humanity at large, but to our own national self-respect."

The Colonel understood the potential cost of that statement. On Saturday morning he met with Bowers and his son, the young attorney Spotswood D. Bowers, and told them, "Gentlemen, I am afraid I have made the winning of this case impossible. But I cannot help it if we lose the case. There is a principle here at stake which is more vital to the American people than my personal welfare is to me."

Bowers knew his man and knew there was no hope of talking him into a softer stance. Earlier in the trial he had pleaded with him not to "bust out" his feelings about Germany, to no avail. Later that day Roosevelt issued a longer statement repeating his initial remarks. The next day he gave permission to H. J. Wigham, publisher of the *Metropolitan Magazine*, to distribute an editorial he had written for that publication entitled "Murder on the High Seas." It was a call to America to take action, a plea. "We earn as a nation measureless scorn and contempt if we follow the lead of those who exalt peace above righteousness," he wrote, "if we heed the voice of those feeble folk who bleat to High Heaven for peace when there is no peace..."

To Roosevelt's dismay, President Wilson was unmoved, continuing to pursue neutrality. "There is such a thing as a man being too proud to fight," he told a large, cheering crowd at a citizen naturalization ceremony in Philadelphia, Pennsylvania.

The Extra! editions of the *Herald* had kept the trial on the front page, but moved it from column right, the most important space on that page, to the farthest left, and the headline "Great Waste of Printing Says Witness in Libel Trial" seemed almost to disappear among the *Lusitania* stories.

The *New York Times* coverage, however, highlighted the peril Roosevelt's legal team now faced with the judge's latest ruling on the printing evidence: "With this stricken out of the record, the lawyers for the defense must rest their case entirely on mitigation in which event the Justice may direct a jury to bring in a verdict, leaving it to determine only the amount of money to be assessed against Colonel Roosevelt." The paper even went as far as to speculate the next day that this ruling could mean that Barnes might not even have to testify.

Roosevelt was so concerned about the impact of the ruling that he gave up horseback riding that weekend to confer with his lawyers for the day.

The trial resumed Monday morning with even more testimony about the printing business, with Bowers and Ivins arguing whether moneys paid from the Lyon company to the Journal Company could accurately be called "commissions," or was it more accurate to describe them as "trade discounts" or "discounts." The defense appeared to be pushing a rock uphill, as Judge Andrews repeatedly pointed out, "This does not prove it as against Mr. Barnes…

"It is one thing to prove the face, which you have already done and it is another thing entirely to prove an admission of a fact made by a third party does not bind the plaintiff…"

In many ways the judge had erected legal roadblocks. "The city makes a contract with the Argus company to print this book at a certain rate at 35 lines to the page, the Argus company prints it itself, but only prints 28 lines to the page. It collects from the city as if it had performed it properly and turns over to the Journal a certain percentage of what it got from the city. Now we will assume for purposes of this argument there was fraud… Does that connect the Journal, to say nothing of the plaintiff, with knowledge of the alleged fraud which the Argus company had committed?"

The defense continued to argue that Barnes was the Journal Company and the Journal Company was Barnes, and that no business happened without his knowledge and approval. Bowers insisted, "The Journal Company was a corporation which Barnes controlled in almost every detail." Unfortunately for the defense, that was not a winning legal argument. Bowers and then Van Benschoten tried to introduce every possible link until finally, in the early afternoon, Van Benschoten said simply, "We rest."

The judge excused the jury, knowing the motions that were coming might change the course of the trial. Barnes's team took the floor and reviewed the entire defense case, asking the judge to strike all of it out as being irrelevant and immaterial. "It is our contention," began Barnes's attorney Henry Wolff, "upon this motion that in no case where evidence has been offered in justification of this libel has that connection been made (between the plaintiff and claims of malfeasance or fraud)." Wolff then dissected the defense case, issue by issue, witness by witness, claim by claim, from Agnew at the beginning to Franklin Roosevelt near the conclusion. He did his job, putting the plaintiff's slant on every issue. The job of politicians was to conduct politics; sometimes it was messy, but "a difference of opinion…is not evidence of corruption." If arrangements existed between the parties or the players, "there is nothing whatsoever to show that it was corrupt or wrong…

"The record utterly fails to disclose any corruption or even impropriety. It does not appear that such an arrangement (between Barnes and Murphy) if it existed, was contrary to the public interest, that it came about through improper motives or that it was induced by improper influences."

When Wolff asked that all testimony relating to an agreement made between Barnes and Murphy to select a US senator, especially that of Franklin Roosevelt, be stricken out, the judge had an unpleasant surprise for the plaintiff. "I think I will deny the motion," he said. "I think on the face of it such an arrangement between the heads of the two parties is improper."

Wolff clearly was puzzled by that, and asked, "Your honor rules that that is evidence of a corrupt combination?"

"Improper," Judge Andrews corrected, "not corrupt in the sense…"

"That is the charge in this article," Wolff protested.

"No, not necessarily… I think the meaning of the libel is an improper alliance between the leaders of the two parties."

This was a significant reinterpretation of the charge, and one that neither side had anticipated. Wolff was on his feet, pointing out, "Of course the word 'improper' doesn't occur anywhere in the article." He continued with disbelief, "Your construction of 'corrupt' is 'improper'?"

"Yes," Judge Andrews agreed. "I don't confine the word 'corrupt' in other words, to pecuniary corruption."

Colonel Roosevelt beamed and exchanged pleased glances with his team. Then he leaned over and whispered a few words to Bowers. This appeared to be a significant victory. Barnes frowned and was caught looking directly at Roosevelt, an angry expression on his face.

Minutes later Ivins entered the discussion, asking the judge in the most polite way, "Whether it was your intention to construe 'corrupt' as synonymous with 'improper' or whether we shall submit authorities as to the legal construction, use, and meaning of the word 'corruption' from the textbooks, from the cases, from the dictionaries. Because we are not confronted with the charge of impropriety; we are confronted with the charge of corruption of a character which has resulted…

"I simply want to inquire whether or not your honor means to confine the use of the word 'corrupt' to the narrow equivalent which you have stated?"

It had gotten down to this: the precise meaning of the word *corrupt*. Judge Andrews would not be pinned to the mat on it. "I don't think I will define anything that I don't have to in this case… I will rule on this question, this motion to strike out which is now made, and deny it, but I don't believe I will be bound down by any definition of anything at present."

Ivins demurred. "At present possibly not, but I think the time will come when your honor will be bound by some definition."

"I may have to," Judge Andrews agreed.

Wolff went through each issue raised by the defense, asking in turn that it be dismissed: Judge

Andrews refused to strike out the testimony concerning the Hart-Agnew racetrack betting bill; he refused to strike the testimony alleging the Republican and Democratic machines conspired to elect William Sheehan to the Senate, and the testimony concerning the defeat of the direct primary legislation.

As the session came to an end, Ivins agreed that he would continue arguing his motions when court resumed in the morning. The impact of the ruling loosely defining corruption had hit him hard; he had not met regularly, on the record, with reporters, but this afternoon he had a statement for them. Judge Andrews's ruling was "decidedly unexpected," he admitted, and he intended to fight hard to get a precise definition of the words *corruption* and *improper*. His tone made it clear he believed this ruling itself was improper.

CHAPTER TWELVE

As these legal squabbles took place in Syracuse, the attention of the country had turned to the coast of Ireland, where searchers continued recovering the bodies of those killed in the submarine attack. Stories of heroism filled the front pages, but none greater than Roosevelt's friend Vanderbilt. The bishop of London told reporters, "There is one incident the world will remember in connection with the sinking of the *Lusitania*. When Alfred G. Vanderbilt was face-to-face with death he said to his valet, 'Come and let us save the kiddies.'"

While the world was still staggering from the shock, Colonel Roosevelt was lured into the politics of it. Having made his position clear and much to the consternation of his legal team, he continued his outspoken criticism of the German government as well as President Wilson's tepid response. Fully aware of the potential risk to the outcome of the trial, Roosevelt remained steadfast and called for the end of all commerce with Germany: "Let us, as a nation, understand that peace is worthy only when it is the handmaiden of international righteousness and national self-respect."

The president essentially ignored him, instead attempting to secure a firm, public apology and reparations from the Germans. Wilson's approach to the crisis utterly frustrated the action-oriented Roosevelt, who rarely hesitated to brandish his "Big Stick" philosophy when he believed it necessary. While both men were progressives, Wilson's academic background contrasted sharply with the Colonel's derring-do. During the campaign of 1912, the former president of Princeton University summed up the essential difference between them, admitting that Roosevelt "appeals to (voters') imagination; I do not. He is a real, vivid person, whom they have seen and shouted themselves hoarse over and voted for, millions strong. I am a vague, conjectural personality, more made up of opinions and academic prepossessions than of human traits and red corpuscles."

T.R. was anything but vague in his beliefs. "In life as in a football game," Roosevelt had once said, "the principle to follow is: Hit the line hard, don't foul and don't shirk, but hit the line hard."

It was that part of his character that made it impossible for him to remain quiet after the brutal attack, even accepting the potential cost to himself. German organizations in America lobbied hard against joining the war, and seemed to have the support of a majority of Americans. And even members of Roosevelt's Progressive Party in Brooklyn, New York, turned on him. It was reported, "Most of the members of this district are German-Americans, they took exception to these remarks made by Roosevelt on the sinking of the *Lusitania*."

After more than three weeks of testimony and arguments, observers were confidently declaring the outcome of the trial. The *Toledo Blade* had decided: "What action the jury at Syracuse may take is no matter of consequence, the verdict of the people is already in. Theodore Roosevelt emerges from the clash with the enemy, his good name untarnished and his splendid public service unbesmirched. After two long years of vilification and abuse, he stands before the country today as he stood as he rose to power, the greatest citizen of his generation."

While Massachusetts's *Fitchburg Sentinel* had reached quite a different conclusion: "There ought to be no dangers from now on that Roosevelt will be a possible candidate for the presidency."

But this was a court of law, and Judge Andrews could not be swayed by public opinion. He had to remain focused only on the equal application of the law, and as the trial resumed he was preparing to announce a decision that would stun many observers and participants.

When the morning session began, the plaintiff once again challenged the judge's interpretation of the article. Among the sources on which Barnes's attorneys cleverly based their argument was Judge Andrews's father, the former chief justice of the state and recent visitor to the courtroom, who had written in an earlier decision, "Defamatory words, in common parlance, are such as impute some moral delinquency or some disreputable conduct to the person of whom they are spoken."

The plaintiff's counsel had been placed in a difficult situation. Ivins had to convince Judge Andrews that his prior ruling allowing the defense wide latitude to present evidence of Barnes's "improper" conduct was completely wrong, but without alienating him. It required a great deal of polite dexterity to make that argument without being unduly critical of the judge. Dressed to the nines as usual, with his skullcap in place, Ivins demonstrated why for so long he had been among the most respected practitioners of his trade. "Now, your honor has held this article to be libelous per se and has therefore, necessarily held, that it tends to bring the plaintiff into hatred, contempt and ridicule by charging vicious or degrading conduct, not merely an impropriety but something which goes far beyond," he began. By asserting what the judge "necessarily" held, Ivins was putting words in the judge's mouth. Critical words if he was going to succeed in striking from the record evidence about the supposed alliance between Barnes and the Democratic leader Murphy. Ivins sought to portray the judge's initial ruling, that the statements were libelous, as starkly as possible so that only evidence that supported that level of treachery would be admitted to justify the statements.

Then he took that reasoning a step further and basically accused the judge of contradicting himself: "The ruling that proof of a mere impropriety establishes the truth of the libelous portion of the article appears to be inconsistent with the ruling that the article was libelous per se...

"We submit that this libel has a far graver significance. It was an attack upon the character of the plaintiff, its purpose being to render him despicable in the minds of its readers...

"The question," he continued, reaching for an applicable definition of libel, "is not what this article means to a trained mind like your honor's, but what does it mean to the ordinary man who reads it? What it means to a neighbor, what it means to a man and his friends, what it means to the community in which he lives. We submit to your honor that it is beyond all dispute that to the general public this article charges the plaintiff with the prostitution of political influence to his personal gain and advantage. It means he is charged with vicious, fraudulent and unlawful conduct...that he is filling the part of a Judas (or) Benedict Arnold..."

If Judge Andrews's broad definition of *corrupt* was to be allowed to stand, Ivins argued, there would be no basis for the entire libel suit. A libel, he contended, wasn't any sort of common criticism; in fact it was a heinous charge, it was a claim that unless corrected would expose an individual to shame and ridicule in his daily life. It was a statement that would damage a man's reputation forever, not simply an aspersion that might easily be tossed aside and forgotten as the judge's ruling might lead someone to conclude. This wasn't a place for someone as eminent and learned as the judge to impose his belief, but rather it was simply what the people a man encountered in his daily tasks thought about it. Did it make his neighbors feel differently about him? Did it make his friends lose trust in him? Ivins made the argument with respect and passion.

And then he came around to the heart of the matter, defining the word *corrupt*.

"I desire to call your honor's attention to the common and ordinary meaning of the words 'corrupt' and 'corruption.' In *Black's Law Dictionary* it is defined as: 'Illegality…the act of an official or fiduciary person who unlawfully and wrongfully uses his official character to procure some benefit for himself or for another person, contrary to the duty and rights of others.'" Ivins cited definitions from dictionaries and from court decisions. In *State v. Johnson* (Ohio) it was "a wrongful design to acquire or cause to be acquired some pecuniary or other advantage to the person guilty of the act." In the *Oxford English Dictionary*, "probably the greatest linguistic document that has ever been produced," it was defined as "debased in character, infected with evil, depraved, perverted, evil, wicked…influenced by bribery or the like; venal."

Ivins went on, trying to convince the judge that his definition of *corrupt* didn't square with the common understanding of its meaning, and that relying on this much broader standard lowered the legal bar for the defense. "We maintain that no part of this libel is justified by anything which may be termed an impropriety or mistake of judgement. We maintain that the language of this libel has brought disgrace and dishonor upon this plaintiff for all time, that it was done purposely, done maliciously…"

Finally, after weeks of strained good manners, it was time, Ivins had decided, for the gloves to come off. That phrase had only recently come into common use; it is believed it referred to boxers removing their padded gloves, so the more brutal bare-knuckle fighting could begin.

This wasn't just any man making these accusations, Ivins said, this came from Theodore Roosevelt. "A man who has tremendous influence."

"We maintain that the language used in this libel pictured (Barnes) as a debased, degraded and vicious character, and places him outside the pale of decent society, which was the purpose, the malevolent purpose of the defendant…and if the acts which have been proved fell short of justifying an assault which is utterly destructive of the plaintiff's character then it cannot be said to be justification for the libel."

As Ivins finished his long, impassioned plea, his voice high and thin and at certain times cracking, he told the court that he would sit down and his colleague Henry Wolff would continue reviewing the defense case "because of the condition of my voice." It was not an especially unusual remark but as it turned out, this weakness was far more telling than anyone might have predicted.

But before Wolff began, Judge Andrews interjected a response that did not show a willingness to pull back, repeating his belief that the article was libelous per se because it charged a corrupt alliance between Murphy and Barnes. "By corrupt alliance," he continued, "I do not necessarily mean that Mr. Barnes and Mr. Murphy were venal about it. It does not necessarily mean that they obtained money by reason of that alliance. I use the word (to mean) 'to act unfaithfully in regard to their duties.'

"...I have also admitted evidence bearing upon the condition of printing affairs on the theory that they might by that evidence possibly show a corrupt alliance between business and politics..."

With the courtroom calmed, Wolff resumed the broader challenge to the defense case, asking the judge to throw out most of the testimony with a witness by witness rebuttal. Not surprisingly, considering the length of the trial, even the judge was a bit confused about his earlier rulings and the attorneys had to go through the transcript to remind him of what he had allowed and prohibited. In the end, the judge remained mostly consistent with his initial decision to allow a wide range of testimony and rejected almost every plaintiff request. After fierce arguments on both sides, the judge did, however, agree to exclude the testimony of Senator George Agnew who had described how Barnes coerced another senator into voting against a bill that would have effectively banned racetrack betting.

Judge Andrews deftly maintained his balancing act, reminding the defense, for example, "You have shown more or less a combination between the Republicans and the Democrats...you have not shown there was anything corrupt or improper about that."

Then they reached the much debated printing evidence and the plaintiff requested that all testimony about it be struck from the record. Judge Andrews had imposed severe restrictions on that testimony but had still permitted certain testimony to be heard by the jury pending a final decision on whether the defense adequately linked it back to corruption by Barnes. But before they could make their whole argument, Van Benschoten, for the defense, was able to interject a sweeping argument about the foundation of the entire legal system: the right of a jury to hear all the evidence and reach its own decision. In a stirring presentation, he claimed that this was precisely the type of issue "that the law commits to the decision of a jury. Twelve men of the average of the community, comprising men of education and men of little education, men of learning and men whose learning consists only in what they have themselves seen and heard—the merchant, the mechanic, the farmer, the laborer—these sit together, consult, apply their separate experience to the affairs of life, to the facts proven, and draw a unanimous conclusion. This average judgment, thus given, it is the greatest effort of the law to obtain…

"…the very fundamental principle upon which the whole jury system is based, that men will look at things from different viewpoints and will, perhaps, draw inferences which could not be drawn by the court."

That remained the key word for the defense: *inference*. Where did that belong in this courtroom? Where precisely was that line? In Arthur Conan Doyle's *A Study in Scarlet*, the detective Sherlock

Holmes had said, "From a drop of water a logician could infer the possibility of an Atlantic or a Niagara without having seen or heard of one or the other." Conversely, the scientist Antoine Lavoisier wrote in *The Elements of Chemistry*, "We must trust to nothing but facts: These are presented to us by Nature and cannot deceive." And the scientific method demanded reproducible results before a theory could be accepted as a fact.

So where between the whimsy of Holmes and the certitude of Lavoisier did the legal system belong? What line had to be crossed for speculation to become admissible evidence? It was a knotty problem on which the case might turn. Both sides argued it forcefully throughout the day. "The argument proceeds upon this theory," explained Ivins, whose voice had recovered sufficiently for him to state his case. "That because a man is a lawyer and some people dislike lawyers and believe them to be implicated in practices they do not like, that any inference which may be drawn by anybody can be drawn from the mere fact that a man is a lawyer. There is a feeling in the community with regard to stockbrokers. Some people have an idea a stockbroker must naturally be doing crooked business; that proof, therefore, that a man is a stockbroker is proof that he is crooked and is proof that he is a gambler and proof that he had betrayed his trust. There is a similar prevailing opinion in regard to printers: All public printers are thieves; the plaintiff in this case is a printer, therefore he is a thief. But the conclusion is a false one.

"...We are perfectly willing to admit that Mr.

Barnes was a public printer... This question of public printing came up a long time ago...in the autobiography of Benjamin Franklin. 'My first promotion was my being chosen, in 1766, clerk of the General Assembly... Besides the pay the place gave me a better opportunity of keeping up an interest among the members, which secured to me the business of printing the votes, laws, paper money and other occasional jobs for the public that, on the whole, was very profitable.' I am perfectly willing to admit that Mr. Barnes belongs to the Benjamin Franklin class...rather than that he belongs to the class of the defendant...

"...There is not one word of evidence to the effect that Mr. Barnes knew of or shared in any corruption or knew of or shared in any waste... That Mr. Barnes' influence was used knowingly, with design, with purpose, with motive to produce and bring about a corrupt condition of affairs...is utterly unproven and to prove it by inference is just as impossible as it is for a man to put his arms around a hole in the ground. The thing can't be done; it can't be done according to law.

"The connection has not been made. (The defense) has failed in their promise, and we should not be put to proof of the impossible because of the possibility of certain minds to reason in ways that do not conform either to the rules of law or logic."

With that he took his seat. Judge Andrews banged his gavel twice, three times and court adjourned for lunch.

When court resumed, Bowers tried to put the

case into a larger perspective, telling Judge Andrews, "The motion that I am making is perhaps the most important motion I have ever presented to a court of justice… It is doubtful if your honor will often have to pass upon so serious a matter. Striking out this evidence completely destroys one of the main defenses of that part of the article that your honor has held libelous."

In response to Ivins's argument, he continued, "If Benjamin Franklin one hundred and fifty years ago used his position to obtain printing matter at wasteful rates, the law probably was the same as it is today, and the truth of that fact would have been a defense to the charge of the kind that is included in the article. The granting of this motion will be treated by every political wrongdoer in the nation as calling upon him to incorporate…"

Bowers reviewed all the printing evidence one more time, bringing special attention to the mysterious $20,000 Barnes was paid by the Lyon company for unexplained services. "What could those services have been? Can not the jury have anything to say about that?…

"There is room for the minds of jurors to say upon that, that the plaintiff used his political position to obtain these orders…we have established a case sufficiently plain for your honor to say that there is enough in it, even if you have grave doubt about it, to leave it to the jury."

The quality of the lawyering on both sides had surpassed even what these venerable advocates had displayed in previous arguments to this court. And the timing was right since Judge Andrews's decision whether to allow the jury to consider all or some of the printing evidence might well determine the outcome of the trial. There was no obvious answer. While the law gave the judge a blueprint by which to conduct a trial, this decision would rely on his wisdom tempered by experience. It was Socrates who had laid down what was expected of a judge: "Four things belong to a judge: to hear courteously, to answer wisely, to consider soberly, and to decide impartially."

But in practice the function of most judges was similar to that of the referee in a boxing match: to make sure the combatants fought fairly and by the rules, and as much as possible not be noticed.

When Judge Andrews was selected by the legislature to fill an open seat on the state supreme court in 1899, the year before he would be officially elected to that position, he promised only to endeavor to earn the respect of members of the bar. In that he had succeeded admirably. He was admired as an indefatigable worker who immersed himself in whatever case he was adjudicating, whether it be a capital murder or a contested divorce. But none of those thousands of cases were as closely scrutinized as this complicated libel action, and whatever ruling he finally made about the printing testimony certainly was going to be met with deep resentment from the losing side.

Summing up the importance of this aspect of his case, Bowers said flatly, "The denial of this motion practically denies us the benefit of this entire defense… It goes beyond all reason…that we must be left to stand without this evidence, that all goes to the winds—is too much to believe."

To which Ivins responded, "The argument as finally presented really amounts to this: that a coroner's jury would be justified in finding that a man died by eating too much plum pudding because he had complained of hunger. That is what it amounts to; does it amount to anything?

"Lewis Carroll was probably one of the greatest mathematicians and probably one of the greatest logicians of his time. He wrote *Alice in Wonderland* and *Alice in the Looking Glass* to prove what a logician could do when dealing with a mind that carried nothing but logic. Since I assume your honor's mind does carry out logic I am not going to present that authority of *Alice in Wonderland* and *Alice in the Looking Glass*."

Judge Andrews finally announced his decision, "I think I will grant the motion." He would not allow the defense to use Barnes's alleged involvement in printing industry corruption to justify the claims made in the article. He continued, admitting his difficulty in this ruling, "I am not sure about all this evidence. What I say is this: I shall not submit to the jury as justification of the alleged libel any evidence with regards to this printing situation in Albany. Now just what particular sentences in the evidence you ask me to strike out I don't know."

Lacking any evidence of a direct connection between Barnes and the alleged corruption in the printing industry, Judge Andrews had decided, the defense claims could not go to the jury to justify the statements in Roosevelt's article. The defense simply had not demonstrated, according to the *New York Times*, "that Mr. Barnes was in a corrupt alliance between corrupt business and corrupt politics."

The defense team sat quietly, absorbing the magnitude of that decision. Bowers and Van Benschoten had spent much of the last few weeks carefully constructing a circumstantial case to show that there was corruption throughout the printing industry and that Barnes was in a position to influence contracts and profit from them. But the defense had been unable to produce a witness, a note, a contract, anything at all that proved Barnes was aware of the corruption. To the layman, perhaps even to jurors in their normal lives, it was easy to make the short, logical jump that ensnared Barnes, but in a court of law it had to be proved. Judge Andrews was clear: the fact that Barnes profited from his work in the printing industry was not evidence that he had any knowledge of wrongdoing.

Both sides asked for and were granted an exception, a legal term signifying that they did not agree with the ruling, which would permit them to show that disagreement to a higher court on appeal. When Ivins asked for a further explanation, Judge Andrews said wisely, "I have ruled on it distinctly enough to give both of you an exception." His meaning was clear; on appeal, judges could disagree with his ruling and he was providing to both the plaintiff and the defense a platform to make certain they got that hearing.

The reaction of the principals was just as might be expected. The defense team sat glumly at its table,

ONONDAGA HISTORICAL ASSOCIATION

This Herald *sketch portrays all of the principals in the trial, among them (3) Barnum, (4) Ivins, (9) secretary Cassie Doran, (10) Judge Andrews, (12) Barnes, (14) attorney Stewart Hancock, (15) Roosevelt, (19) Bowers, and (20) Van Benschoten.*

absorbing the blow. Bowers's shoulders slumped, and it seemed like all energy had drained from his body. A seasoned lawyer does not make a show of either excitement or disappointment, but this was difficult to absorb. Colonel Roosevelt moved close to him and began whispering urgently into his ear, as if to inject him with newfound determination. A few feet away a broad smile appeared on Barnes's face as the ruling was announced; Ivins couldn't help grinning and looking around the courtroom to share his delight.

The ruling seemed devastating to the defense. The *Times* called it "the hardest blow the Colonel has received in this trial." But looking at it most closely, it might have actually been, to quote the eighteenth century British Reverend James Hervey, a blessing in disguise. "The evidence is still in the record," Ivins complained, "and not stricken out."

"I think you will not be bothered about that," Judge Andrews replied, then added almost as an aside, "Of course I will not allow you to give any evidence as to the Albany situation on your side of the case."

And that condition of the ruling had the potential to become a serious problem for the plaintiff. The testimony painting Barnes as a corrupt politician who used his influence for personal profit already had been heard by the jury. Now Judge Andrews had prevented Ivins from offering any rebuttal or explanation for it. The plaintiff could not present witnesses who might further explain how business was regularly conducted within the industry or show that Barnes's actions were commonplace or benign. Rather, it locked into place the image of corruption, and there was nothing Ivins could do about it. He had gotten his motion, and now he would have to live with that result.

With that decision the defense case ended and the plaintiff began its rebuttal. Ivins intended to refute those defense claims that had survived his appeals. His first witness was Francis Stetson, the former president of the American Bar Association, an organization that had been formed in 1878 to "promote the advancement of the science of jurisprudence, the promotion of the administration of justice and a uniformity of legislation throughout the country..." Essentially, to turn lawyering from a trade into a profession with recognized standards. Stetson, a respected political player and a longtime friend and correspondent of T.R.'s, had been the go-between sent to Barnes's home by Democratic insurgents who had met with Franklin Roosevelt to see if Barnes might join them in finding an alternative candidate for the US Senate to Sheehan. "I went there...to find out what was Mr. Barnes' attitude toward the insurgents." His attitude, Stetson said, was not to support them. "I was to take back his rejection, not his acceptance, but his rejection."

Bowers on cross-examination asked, "Did you know at the time that he was not a member of the senate?" Stetson did and the meaning was clear. The Democrats had sent him from New York City to Albany to speak with Barnes, who held no elective position, but was recognized by the Democrats as the person who controlled Republican votes.

That accusation hung in the air as Ivins tried to rehabilitate his witness, showing that Stetson had made the trip at the behest of Senator Brackett, then the official Republican leader in the state senate, for several reasons.

As Stetson left the stand he paused by the defense table, as if drawn by a magnet; Colonel Roosevelt rose to greet him and the two men warmly grasped hands and whispered to each other. Even when sitting quietly the Colonel remained the center of this universe.

As they embraced, state senator William F. Sheehan, the unsuccessful candidate for the open United States Senate seat in 1911, was called to testify. For the spectators this trial was like watching the front pages of the last decade come to life. The political leaders they had been reading about appeared one by one in the flesh. There had even been strong rumors that if he felt his case was failing, Ivins intended to request former president William Howard Taft and Elihu Root, who had served as the Colonel's secretary of state, come to Syracuse to testify. Both men once had been close to Roosevelt and subsequently had broken with him, and both of them would have fascinating stories to tell. Few men knew the Colonel as intimately as these two, and their testimony could shed bright light on his political dealings. Ivins hinted to reporters that he would ask Taft directly whether Roosevelt had asked for political favors in return for his support in the 1908 presidential election. But thus far Barnes was reluctant to ask these political titans, and friends, to join in the courtroom mudslinging.

Sheehan acknowledged that before seeking the senate seat, he had been the Democratic leader in Buffalo and later lieutenant governor of the state. When Ivins asked him if he believed Murphy was the leader of the Democratic machine, Bowers objected, stating it called upon the witness to draw conclusions. "They can ask him facts."

Ivins turned and said, heatedly, "I am doing as you did. I can go about it in a roundabout way."

Bowers nodded. "You will follow a very excellent way if you do it my way."

"Personally," said Sheehan, "I never recognized him as a leader of the Democratic party in the state." In response to several questions, he denied that Murphy had suggested he run for the Senate post and that he had never, either orally or in writing, discussed his candidacy with Barnes. Although minutes later, perhaps to hedge his bets, he added, "I will say I believe Mr. Murphy had great influence in the councils of the Democratic party during that time, but I didn't consider it was enough to justify me in considering that he was dominant."

Ivins's last question went right to the core of Colonel Roosevelt's defense. "Did you ever hear or know of any arrangement made by anybody, directly or indirectly, in writing or orally, with regard to any agreement or arrangement, or anything tending to show any agreement or arrangement between Mr. Barnes and Mr. Murphy to further your candidacy?"

"No, sir."

The respected financier August Belmont Jr. was next to the stand. Belmont, a Democrat, was one of the wealthiest men in New York. He had founded, built and served as president and chairman of the Interborough Rapid Transit Company, the city's first underground subway line while also owning and operating several other railroad lines. His passion though, was Thoroughbred racing, and a decade earlier he had built the grand Belmont Park in Queens, which he had named after his father. In other situations he might have been a star, but here he was simply a dapper supporting player.

As the owner of the racetrack, he had opposed the Hart-Agnew bill, which prohibited betting at the track and fought the effort to toughen penalties for racetrack gambling that had failed by that single vote in the state senate. He admitted having contacted President Roosevelt to ask for his assistance. "He knew my views," Belmont said. "I took the view that racing was an institution that ought to have the support of the State rather than its condemnation; that racing represented an important element in improving the breed of horses because it was an elimination test which was a guide for the breeder, and that in view of the automobile coming in use the light horse, which was necessary for military purposes, would gradually be driven out by the horse of utility, the farm horse, which did not answer the purpose at all…"

Ivins sought to depict the Colonel as an active political broker in New York state politics even while in the White House. Belmont was asked to read a letter he had written to President Roosevelt suggesting progressive policies that Charles Hughes should embrace in his campaign for governor, pointing out, "The Republican platform refers to nothing that directly touches the labor interests locally. With reference to the eight-hour (workday) law…the tenement law, the child labor and 'sweatshop' laws of the state, it seems to me, are questions which Mr. Hughes could make an excellent point at the outset of his campaign.

"You well know how important these are to the welfare of the laborer and they appeal to his wife and children… It would be essentially good policy for Mr. Hughes to make some sane and convincing statement on these questions…"

According to Belmont, Roosevelt responded that no more important suggestion had been made and he had handed the letter to Hughes, who was delighted to receive it.

Belmont also testified that Roosevelt had asked if he would meet Barnes to discuss the racetrack gambling matter, reinforcing the impression that the Colonel and Barnes had once worked together to further common interests.

As Belmont concluded his answer, the Colonel could be heard not quite whispering to his counsel, "That's right, that's exactly what I told him!"

And finally, Belmont testified that as far as he was aware, and clearly contrary to previous testimony, the opposition to the racetrack legislation had been completely proper, without deceit, and that if it were anything less he would not have been personally involved with it.

When his testimony concluded, he walked directly to the defense table, just as others had done, and chatted amiably with the Colonel. That too was subtle but important evidence; each man on the jury could see for himself the respect powerful men like Belmont had for the defendant, even when the testimony might not benefit him. As the two men chatted, Judge Andrews gaveled the day to a close.

Horace Wilkinson had scheduled a dinner party that evening, and even this distressing day in the courtroom did not prevent Roosevelt from attending. Among the invited guests was Wilkinson's neighbor, Syracuse University chancellor James Day. The chancellor had been a longtime and highly vocal critic of the Colonel, complaining that he had tried to turn the presidency into a monarchy. But the two men had come together over the crisis with Germany. As they greeted each other,

Roosevelt told him, “I am dee-lighted to renew our former acquaintance.”

Chancellor Day later told reporters, “I am far away as ever from him on big business, the recall and the referendum, which I thought were socialistic views, but personally I regard him as an exceptionally interesting man because of his limitless fund of knowledge derived from books, travel and experiences with men. Colonel Roosevelt is probably the most remarkable citizen of the republic at the present time.”

A large reception was held following the dinner, attended by business and educational leaders of the city. Among them was Reverend Dr. Jerimiah Zimmerman, a recognized expert on ancient coins, who spent a considerable amount of time discussing that subject in depth with Roosevelt and came away marveling about “Colonel Roosevelt’s breadth of knowledge.”

The next morning the *Syracuse Journal* reported dutifully upon the Colonel’s legal setback and Wilkinson’s grand dinner, but perhaps as a reminder of simpler pleasures also told readers that “next Saturday is straw hat day, when Syracusans can put their soft fleece hats and derbys on the attic hook and…observe the passing of the chill bleakness of Spring breezes and the debut of summer zephyrs.”

CHAPTER THIRTEEN

While the trial had exposed the sordid reality of state politics, revealing how a few bosses had controlled the process, New York's current political system still seemed a great improvement over the recent past. Rather than gentlemen in fine clothes making deals behind closed doors, only half a century earlier politics had been a business of brute force. Stories were still being told about the notorious political boss Bill "the Butcher" Poole and his gang and their two-fisted work for the Know-Nothing Party.

The Know-Nothings, or Nativist Party, had been founded in the 1840s as the anti-immigrant, anti-Catholic alternative to the Democrats. It had succeeded in attracting a significant following. Nativist James Harper, a partner in the Harper Brothers publishing concern, had been elected mayor of New York, while Know-Nothing governors, members of Congress and state legislators had won in other states. In the New York City mayoral election of 1857, Poole and his boys had threatened to break down the doors of election headquarters and seize the ballot boxes if their candidate did not win. In response, Tammany Hall hired noted "everything goes" brawler John Morrissey, in addition to Yankee Sullivan, Paugene McLaughlin and their men to protect its interests. When Poole and his gang reached the headquarters at noon, they were stunned to find themselves outnumbered by fifty Tammany thugs and wisely retreated to allow the ballots to be counted.

While the days of the knuckle-dusters had passed into history, the revelations of this trial threatened what little confidence the public had in the fairness of the political process. Barnes didn't deny that he believed the boss system remained necessary. Now it was his turn to prove that his way had answered the needs of the public. The Colonel had alleged that in 1911 Barnes and Murphy formed a corrupt alliance to determine who should get the open United States Senate seat. Buoyed by the ruling excluding the printing testimony, Ivins launched his legal counterattack on that claim.

The powerful state senate president and majority leader Elon R. Brown was called. He had only recently fought for, and won, the right to make all the important committee assignments—and determine which legislation moved forward. When he was first elected to the Senate, he said, the leader of the Republican Party in the state was Senator

Platt, and he was followed by former governor Benjamin Odell. And he was succeeded in 1906 by…

"Colonel Roosevelt…"

Who continued in that position, said Senator Brown, "until shortly after the close of his presidential term, when he left the country, came back, and there was a contest again immediately over the matter in the 1910 convention in which he won out, and assumed the leadership of the party, naming the candidate for governor…"

The two sides then battled back and forth about who was dominant in the party in what years until finally Judge Andrews once again paused the proceedings to explain the difference between justification and mitigation for the jury. Certain evidence was being presented to prove the truth of Roosevelt's contentions to "justify" it. Failing that, to minimize or mitigate the damages. The jury had to somehow divine from all of this Roosevelt's state of mind—what he believed based on these facts—when he published the article. Andrews's instruction took the form of a simple legal lesson: "The defendant in justification of his charge has attempted to prove one specific instance which occurred in 1911… That bit of evidence requires the jury to find that at the time of this occurrence in 1911 Mr. Barnes was dominant in the party (and) being so dominant made an improper and corrupt alliance with Mr. Murphy with regard to this Senatorial contest. As meeting that charge (the plaintiff) may prove that at that time Mr. Barnes was not dominant in the party.

"So far as mitigation is concerned it does not make much difference whether Mr. Barnes was dominant or not, if the defendant believed that he was. In mitigation you are concerned not with the fact but with the belief of the defendant's mind… The bare fact that Mr. Barnes was not dominant was wholly immaterial as having any bearing on mitigation."

To make certain the jury understood, Ivins repeated, "In mitigation, we have to take the issue as one of belief and one of good faith in the expression of the belief… If we make it appear that as a matter of fact, being of sound and competent mind, and a reader of newspapers and acquainted with public affairs…was in a position to have known what the actual facts were…"

Judge Andrews returned to the attorneys' arguments, pointing out the irony of the plaintiff's position. "You are asking me to rule in your favor now in regard to inference not based on proved facts; a ruling which you were very strongly objecting to yesterday…"

Brown eventually testified that he had spoken with Barnes about the 1911 election. He met with Barnes, he said, to see if he might consider forming a coalition between Republicans and Independent Democrats to elect a suitable candidate. In response, Barnes had said "he would take it under consideration and he was unable to say whether such action would be feasible because he was not then advised what the opinion of the members of the legislature were, but that he would find out."

After several subsequent meetings and negotiations, Barnes agreed such an alliance to break the deadlock might be possible—but said the party would not support the proposed candidate "because they believed, if he was elected that he would, after election, train with the dominant element of the Democratic party, Tammany Hall."

Brown conceded that Barnes wielded substantial power in delivering Republican votes, but his testimony that Barnes turned down a man who might align himself with Murphy's Tammany Hall undermined Roosevelt's claims that the two bosses were somehow in league with each other.

Banker, lawyer, businessman and longtime state senator Edward Brackett stepped up next. Brackett was typical of the line of men who had been summoned to speak for Barnes, men who had been ruling the state for the previous two decades. They were men of standing, who regularly appeared during election years but whose wealth and power put them above the public fray. Until this trial none of these men had been compelled to answer in public those sometimes pesky questions about the way they conducted their business in private. Brackett, like Brown, like all of these witnesses, was well-known and respected, but never before had he appeared this vulnerable.

Senator Brackett recalled a meeting of the Republican caucus at Barnes's home, held there because a fire had rendered the Senate chamber unusable, to determine if Republicans could be persuaded to vote for a Democrat to end this deadlock.

The consensus, he said, "was that they would vote for such a one as they choose, and didn't think that was a caucus matter...

"I had been feeling out the Independent Democrats so-called to see if anything could be agreed upon with Frank Roosevelt and my impression was that they, even themselves, could not unite on any one; I had gone so far as to have Mr. Frank Roosevelt write out three or four names of men he thought they would vote for for Senator and have him initial it, so that I would feel that I had something on which to start. But after I took it up I found that other members of his independent brigade would not stand for those that he had put on, and that I feared they were all Generals without any men."

Ivins's co-counsel Barnum eventually got to the heart of it, asking, "Was there any agreement between Mr. Barnes and Mr. Murphy in reference to the vote on this question of a United States Senator you knew of?"

"I never knew of it."

Bowers, when his turn came, brought out the fact that in the end "the final result was that Mr. O'Gorman was elected Senator." Judge James Aloysius O'Gorman was the Grand Sachem, or leader, of Tammany Hall. He was Murphy's candidate and could not have been elected without the votes of some Republicans.

William J. Wollman came next. Wollman was a managing partner of the securities firm J.S. Bache. His own story was well-known: Decades earlier, while Cuba was in revolt against Spain, he had bought Cuban bonds at $20, and his fortune was secured after that war ended and those bonds were redeemed for $130. He had used some of his gain for the public good, and was celebrated for providing many thousands of dinners to New York's homeless each Thanksgiving. Adams, for the plaintiff, intended to use this witness to dispute the testimony of William Loeb, who had related a damning conversation with Barnes during lunch at the Bache company offices in 1911. Loeb had recalled Barnes describing an "arrangement" with Democratic boss Murphy that prevented Barnes from trying to impact the 1911 election. Wollman testified that was not possible; "Mr. Loeb was not in our offices until November or December of 1912."

Under cross-examination he clarified that, claiming he actually had first met Loeb at that time and it wasn't until "the Spring of 1913, or the Fall" that he had come to the brokerage office. There was little drama in his telling of it, but the impact of it was enormous. If Wollman was correct, it threw serious doubt on the veracity of Loeb's testimony. He was calling one of the most respected men in America, President Roosevelt's close ally, a liar.

He was followed by an attorney, John Hutchinson, who told of a chance meeting with Roosevelt in the lobby of the Harvard Club in 1914 during which he tried to heal the rift between Roosevelt and Barnes. "I told Colonel Roosevelt that the issues that had divided the Republican party were no longer being considered by the people…that the situation was such that we ought to get together.

He said that was certainly so. That he, Colonel Roosevelt could get after President Wilson on his foreign treaties, and tear it to pieces, and that the Republican party had no one who could do it, and that the Republicans had to have him."

This testimony appeared to jolt Roosevelt; a glum look appeared on his face as he shook his head as if to make clear those comments weren't true. Then he began whispering excitedly with his counsel.

Hutchinson continued, "But he said after what happened at Chicago (when he was denied the 1912 nomination) he would not stand for Barnes, that the party was not big enough to hold both of them." This trial might well be described as the legal version of George Seurat's recently popular pointillism technique, in which numerous dots of paint together formed an image. Testimony like Hutchinson's added a point of information, which combined with the rest would reveal the true picture. If Hutchinson's testimony was to be believed, it could help the plaintiff show that Roosevelt was acting with malice when he made the statements at issue.

When questioned by Bowers, Hutchinson elaborated, "I meant that the Republican party which divided in 1912 ought to get together again. The Progressive party was through and might as well die."

Bowers had his way with this witness. There was a snarl in his voice as he asked him to confirm the very words he had just said. When pressed, Hutchinson admitted he didn't say that exactly or mean that. "What I said to Col. Roosevelt was that as far as the organization was, he was the whole Progressive party."

Again, Bowers repeated Hutchinson's own words. "But he would not come into the party because it was not big enough for him and Barnes?"

Hutchinson, defused, admitted, "He did not say that."

Question by question Bowers tore down this witness until finally reaching the end, asking, "Is it not a fact that in commencing this conversation what you did say to him was this: 'We need your help in the Republican party.'?"

Thoroughly chastened, Hutchinson admitted, "I have no recollection of commencing it that way. I probably said that sometime in the course of the conversation."

The roster of witnesses included those men who had led the party in the past as well as the rising political stars such as Franklin Roosevelt and the next witness, forty-two-year-old Democrat Alfred E. Smith, the majority leader of the state assembly during the 1911 fight and a celebrated crusader for better conditions for the workingman and -woman. What might have been fascinating testimony fizzled quickly. Barnum asked the central question: "Do you know, Mr. Smith, of any combination between Mr. Barnes and Mr. Murphy that affected the election?"

But before he could answer, Bowers objected and Judge Andrews sustained it, explaining, "The Republican Senators might be supposed to know something about such a combination, if there was such a combination. You do not prove anything, however, by proving a Democratic Senator knew nothing about it."

"Assemblyman," Barnum corrected, then pleaded there could not have been any such combination or arrangement without Smith knowing about it. Judge Andrews was not persuaded and Smith was dismissed.

Fred Hammond, the clerk of the assembly, then testified he had not been instructed by Barnes how to cast his vote in the stalemate. Thaddeus Sweet, the current Speaker of the assembly, followed him and said essentially the same thing; he had no knowledge of any arrangement between Barnes and Murphy to select a senator and had received no such instructions from Barnes.

Benjamin B. Odell, who had succeeded Colonel Roosevelt as governor, drew a hearty laugh from the gallery and even from Judge Andrews, when he responded to Ivins asking, "Were you the dominant leader of the party in the state?" by shrugging and claiming self-effacingly, "Well, I don't know. I might have thought so, but it is rather questionable in my mind as I view the past now!"

Odell was a significant figure in state politics, having been among the first to support Colonel Roosevelt for governor and going on to manage his campaign. Eventually he stood up against Platt and made his own run for the office, breaking the Republican machine's hold on state politics.

Ivins wanted to use Odell's knowledge of state politics to disprove claims in the article, among them that Barnes was dominant in party politics in 1899 and 1900 and that Barnes had urged the Colonel to oppose the Franchise Tax Bill because important financial interests had contributed to the Republican campaign fund. Odell said that to his knowledge no such requests were made by the financial men, and no promises were made by legislators. The impact of that acknowledgment, coming from a Roosevelt supporter, was quickly and masterfully negated by Bowers, who asked at the beginning of his cross-examination, "There were contributions that were made of which you have no recollection?"

"Possibly, yes," replied the witness.

"Were there not some prominent Democratic officials…who made contributions of corporate funds?"

"Yes, there were."

The former governor's appearance on the stand was brief but, as he told reporters, it was quite worthwhile. As with all of the participants, the trial had entirely disrupted his life. He didn't seem to mind at all though, for it had put him back in the public arena. He told reporters that he had motored up to Syracuse with his family ten days earlier and while waiting to be called "toured here in the machine. We went to Niagara Falls!" Declining to place Colonel Roosevelt or Barnes in the "political morgue," he reminded the journalists how much each man's future depended on the result. As for his own participation? "All I can say is that I enjoyed my vacation immensely!"

Having laid down the gauntlet, suggesting that Loeb had not been truthful about when his lunch with Barnes had taken place, Barnum began producing witnesses to support that claim. With all the complex and sometimes confusing testimony, this was something the jury easily could understand: Was Loeb telling the truth or lying to support Roosevelt? Alfred Towsley, a railroad man, was questioned next. Towsley testified that he had shared lunch in the J.S. Bache dining room with Barnes and Loeb "some time in the latter part of 1913 or the early part of 1914." Whenever it was, it was considerably later than Loeb had testified. If that was accurate, Loeb's contention that he had been told by Barnes that he'd made an agreement with Murphy not to interfere with the Democrats' senatorial pick was even more unlikely.

Next up was railroad executive Newman Erb, who also had been at lunch with Barnes and Loeb and was certain it took place long after Loeb had claimed.

Changing course, Barnum then put witness after witness on the stand to testify that contrary to Roosevelt's claim, Barnes had not instructed any Republican legislators how to vote in the senatorial contest. These legal points began to form a shape. State senator J. Henry Walters had no memory of "any conversation I had with him in relation to the United States senatorial contest."

Assemblyman Harold Hinman (not to be confused with Harvey Hinman who Roosevelt supported for Governor) recalled Barnes telling him the

Democratic Party held power in the state and "was responsible for the election of the United States Senator" and had failed to do so and that it was most important that New York had its full representation in the Senate—but at no time did Barnes direct him how to vote. He did tell Hinman, however, "that he preferred Mr. Thomas Mott Osborne for the reason that he would be the worst man for Tammany to stomach."

Assemblyman William Nolan averred that he "at no time" spoke with Barnes in reference to the election.

Senator George F. Argetsigner had no talk with Mr. Barnes at any time "in regard to the contest."

Assemblyman James T. Cross did not talk to Mr. Barnes, nor did he get any word from him directly or indirectly with reference to the vote.

George Cobb, who served as a state senator from 1903 to 1912, testified he never had a conversation with Barnes "about the election of a United States Senator."

Assemblyman Simon L. Adler was in Albany throughout all the votes taken for the Senate and never had a conversation with Barnes about it.

Assemblyman Frank Thorn "had no conversation with Mr. Barnes…in regard to that matter at any time."

It was just before noon when Ivins said sharply, "Mr. Barnes, please take the stand." At last, it came time for the plaintiff himself. Barnes stood, solemnly raised his right hand and promised "to tell the truth, the whole true and nothing but the truth,

ONONDAGA HISTORICAL ASSOCIATION

On the witness stand, wrote the Outlook, *Barnes was "cool, self-controlled, wary, taking care to see that there were no rocks ahead...before he answered. When he smiled it was the smile of the cat about to eat the canary... His voice sank almost into a whisper and the Court admonished him to speak louder... He appeared to be the defendant in the suit and not the plaintiff at all."*

so help me God," precisely the same oath that has commonly been heard in courtrooms since thirteenth-century England—when fear of God's wrath for lying was far greater than any secular penalty the state might render.

William Barnes was a large man, bigger than the Colonel, and his deep voice reached the farthest corners of the courtroom. Barnes was reputed to be a hard, even gloomy man; a *Post-Standard* reporter had described his attitude when the Colonel was testifying as "resembling a thunder cloud a good deal of the time," but the person who took the stand displayed none of that. The spectators had anticipated "a sullen and angry witness," wrote the same scribe, but instead "there appeared a joyous Barnes, with a fetching smile, actually with a dimpling smile, with an air of engaging candor and an eager zest for the truth...when Ivins questioned him he turned toward the jury with good faith and innocence fairly pouring out of his face and answered them, not the lawyer." There was no hesitation in his answers, making it clear he had been waiting anxiously for this day, and within minutes he had begun his attack on Teddy Roosevelt's honesty. He began by taking responsibility for the editorials published in his newspaper, the *Albany Evening Journal*, saying, "The man who is supposed to be in control does not permit those who are employed by him to suffer or bear the burden, but that he takes it on himself, whether it be proceeding for criminal libel or a proceeding of any other character of that kind."

It was an odd statement coming from the man who brought suit against the author of this article—but not against any of the numerous newspapers that had printed it. Under the traditional gatekeeper theory of libel, anyone who transmits the libelous material is equally guilty and subject to penalties. But Barnes had chosen to take action only against Roosevelt.

Bowers made an effort to confine Barnes's testimony to politics, but Judge Andrews would have none of that. "He may give his general history," he ruled, reminding Bowers, "There was considerable testimony given as to the Spanish War and matters of that kind which did not have any direct bearing on the case."

Barnes's political career had begun in 1889 when he was elected a delegate to the state convention and thereafter was appointed to a series of Republican Party posts. He was thirty-two years old when he met and supported the recently returned war hero Roosevelt during the gubernatorial campaign of '98.

The Colonel leaned forward to the edge of his chair as if to catch Barnes's words before they might go any farther. Occasionally he would turn and say something to one of his defense team, but even as he did he would not take his eyes off the witness.

Ivins reminded his witness that Roosevelt had testified that he, Barnes, had asked the governor not to remove Payn from his post as superintendent of insurance because he was supported by contributors to the Republican Party, then asked if that conversation had ever taken place?

"No," he said, calling Roosevelt a liar. The courtroom was still. His own relationship with Payn, he continued, "was quite unfriendly." The two men were "not on speaking terms." By comparison, his relationship with then president Roosevelt remained quite amiable, he said, as the Colonel reappointed him to a four-year term as surveyor of customs.

Ivins methodically took him through the Colonel's testimony, and Barnes's memories of their conversations differed greatly; he contradicted or denied almost every claim Roosevelt had made on the stand about their interactions. For example, Ivins quoted Roosevelt, recalling, "'I discussed with him (Barnes) most of the important matters that grew to be at issue between me and Senator Platt.' What are the facts in regard to that?"

"I never knew there was any issue between Senator Roosevelt and Senator Platt. They discussed things together and came to a conclusion." He added that "to his knowledge" he had never had any such discussions.

Ivins read response after response, and Barnes denied they happened or that they took on the color that Roosevelt gave them. "Did you ever have any talk with the defendant about 'Where Mr. Platt and the organization were antagonistic to what I proposed to do?'"

"No, not in that way at all."

After several such exchanges Barnes began to hedge, admitting, "Well, I can't testify that he didn't talk to me."

"He didn't talk to you?"

"I can't testify that he did not."

Even Ivins was confused by that use of the language. "You can't testify that he didn't talk to you?"

"No."

"Can you testify that you didn't talk to him?"

"I cannot testify that I was absolutely silent… I mean, I was in the position of a listener. I listened to what he told me…"

At times Barnes's answers seemed intentionally vague. Asked if he had ever discussed the Franchise Tax Bill with Roosevelt he replied, "It is not impossible. I mean as a matter of history... I never discussed it with him prior to its passage. It is possible that in future years it may have been referred to as history."

But at other times he was direct. When Ivins asked, "Did you ever say to Mr. Roosevelt directly or indirectly in terms or by implication that Mr. Brady had been a contributor to the Republican organization in the country?" he responded flatly, "I certainly did not because he hadn't been to my knowledge."

His testimony was a complete repudiation of Roosevelt's claims. "Did you ever make any remark to the effect that Mr. Payn should be reappointed because of his connection with financial institutions?"

"Not the slightest."

The Colonel's most memorable claim, that Barnes had told him that the people were not fit to govern themselves, called for a longer explanation. Left to stand, that was the kind of comment that might resonate with the men on the jury and stick in their craw so it had to be addressed and discredited. The result was Barnes's description of the necessities of bosses to the political structure, the political theory on which he had based his entire career. "I unquestionably said to Mr. Roosevelt, as I have said to a great many men, that if we were to maintain in this country a system of party government that it was necessary for those parties to be organized, and that no movement of any character whatsoever could ever come to achievement unless it were organized.

The idea that people moved en masse, without order, without rule, without any discipline is absurd upon its face. They do not so move, in political parties, in any organization known to human operation. They must move in order or they do not move at all.

"Unquestionably I said, as I believed, that no political organization can possibly conduct its operations unless it is financed or is conducted by men who give up their entire time to it, which might in times of wonderful stress occur, but in the ordinary process of human operations no political organization ever has existed from the beginning of time, does not exist today, let it be Republican, Democratic, Progressive, Prohibition, Socialist, Labor or Independent League, that is not so organized. I never said to Mr. Roosevelt or to any other man that political organizations should give protection. Those who believe in the party of their choice have the absolute right to give to it as they will and the answer is that those whom they select to office should maintain the principles upon which they were candidates before the voters…"

As he testified, Barnes spoke directly to the jury. Although Roosevelt was sitting only a few feet away, a sullen expression on his face, their eyes never met. It was clear that Barnes was thoroughly enjoying the opportunity to take the case directly to his nemesis. He seemed entirely at ease in the witness chair, smiling modestly on occasion and, unlike the Colonel, rarely emphasized his words with any sort of gesture or tone. Several times he raised his hand to his brow and passed it slowly across his forehead, giving the distinct impression of a man in deep thought. He sat calmly, never raising a defiant fist or grandly sweeping his arm through the air, never hurling out loudly a single word or phrase to reinforce its importance. While a contrast to the Colonel's effusiveness and natural charisma, his congenial manner seemed remarkably effective.

Roosevelt had testified that Barnes had referred to "the riff-raff (who) were incompetent to govern themselves." Ivins asked his witness if he had ever uttered those demeaning words, and Barnes responded, "I cannot recall that I ever used such a word in that connection. I do not know exactly what riff-raff is, but I am very confident that if you look it up in the dictionary..."

Bowers finally objected, "This is way beyond all reason."

And Ivins agreed. "Never mind."

The two attorneys resumed their battle minutes later when Bowers objected to an overly detailed response, pointing out that he had not found it necessary to do so. To that, Ivins suggested to the court, "I was not quite as contentious as my friend."

Bowers was taken aback, responding wryly, "If you are not more contentious than I am I should be surprised."

At intervals throughout the day, Judge Andrews interrupted Barnes's testimony to allow the plaintiff to put even more legislators on the stand for a few questions to underline the plaintiff's claim that he had not interfered in the selection of the

Senate candidate. Assemblyman Alexander McDonald did not "have any talk, at any time, with Mr. Barnes with relation to the United States Senate contest." Assemblyman Fred Ahearn never spoke with Barnes about it. Assemblyman Edward Ebbets, from Brooklyn, also voted for Depew on every ballot and never spoke with Barnes. Neither Assemblyman Harry Haynes nor Assemblyman Thomas Smith had any such talk with Barnes, either.

That brief interlude done, Barnes resumed his testimony. Rather than protecting his contributors as Roosevelt had alleged, Barnes testified that it was actually the Colonel who engaged in that sort of political payback. He recalled being invited by telegram to the White House to visit the president, who asked him to do a political favor. "He told me Mr. August Belmont had been to see him, and he wanted me to go to New York and see Mr. Belmont. That legislation (prohibiting racetrack betting) should be defeated. That Mr. Belmont should be considered and that I should go. I demurred… I finally consented." While this placed Roosevelt behind the scenes engaged in political deal making himself, perhaps more importantly it reminded jurors that no matter what the Colonel wrote, he held the real power in the party.

While Barnes was saying this, the Colonel leaned over and pointed out to his counsel that this directly contradicted a letter that he had written to the plaintiff, already placed into evidence, in which he wrote that he would not take a side in the racetrack dispute.

It was clear Ivins was concerned that the racetrack matter left his client vulnerable as he kept returning to it to close up any loose ends. Earlier in the trial, defense witness Jacob Dickinson, a *New York Herald* reporter had testified that during an interview Barnes had told him that "party success was paramount in his mind to all other political considerations and that he had no illusions about politics." In response, Barnes told the jury about the quoted conversation he'd had with then governor Hughes: "During the evening I said to him 'I think you are making a mistake on the proposed racetrack legislation…' that it would 'cost the Republican party twenty-five thousand votes at the coming presidential election.'

"He said, 'We will gain two for every one we lose.'" Then, after further discussion, he added, "'My conscience would never be clear if my term in office should expire and that iniquitous law should remain upon the statute books.'

"I said, 'I thought we were discussing votes. If it is your conscience, it is no affair of mine.'"

Ivins read from Dickinson's testimony where he claimed Barnes had actually told the governor, "'Well, if it is conscience and not votes you are thinking of, there is no common ground on which we stand.'" Then he asked, "Did you ever say such a thing to Mr. Dickinson?"

Barnes responded resolutely, "Absolutely not! I said no such thing!"

The court day ended as Barnes told one final story. He had met with Roosevelt and several other men at the Colonel's home in Oyster Bay to discuss the renomination of Governor Hughes. "I entered my objections to the nomination… Mr. Roosevelt made the statement that he did not intend to make his friends cut their throats again…" by publicly taking an unpopular political position.

It was clear Barnes had done a good job defending his actions. In response, Bowers announced he would be recalling both Colonel Roosevelt and Secretary Loeb to the stand to testify once again about that lunch.

After weeks of this trial, it had come down to the confrontation everyone had envisioned: Theodore Roosevelt against William Barnes. Only one of them could be telling the truth.

CHAPTER FOURTEEN

Outside the courtroom the world continued to roil. After failing to receive a meaningful apology or reparations for the victims of the *Lusitania*, President Wilson sent a warning to Germany that the United States was prepared to do "its sacred duty" should there be another attack, but still attempted to remain neutral. In the Dardanelles, a submarine sunk the British dreadnought *Goliath* with a loss of five hundred men. In New York, Harry K. Thaw's second trial for the murder of Stanford White had begun. A Chicago police officer was reprimanded for wearing a wristwatch, a relatively recent innovation, while on duty, although he protested that aviators, explorers, hunters and mountain climbers were known to wear them without embarrassment. In Syracuse, the *Post-Standard* offered a public service piece entitled "The Importance of the Dentist," noting, "One mistake that modern science is trying hard to correct is thinking that teeth are about as important as fingernails and that except to relieve pain the dentist is hardly more necessary than a manicure."

In the evenings Roosevelt continued meeting with his defense team, while taking time to mount his campaign to prepare America for a coming war. Dealing with the inevitable conflict, he told reporters, was "not only our duty to humanity at large, but our duty to preserve our own national self-respect, demand instant action on our part and forbade all delay." A day later he added, "We earn as a nation measureless scorn and contempt if we follow the lead of those who exalt peace over righteousness, if we heed the voice of those feeble folk who bleat to high heaven for peace when there is no peace."

In a typically cautious response, the White House issued a statement that Wilson "feels the distress and the gravity of the situation to the utmost and is considering very earnestly, but very calmly the right course of action to pursue. He knows that the people of the country expect him to act with deliberation as well as with firmness."

But at precisely nine o'clock the morning of Friday, May 14, all of that was put aside as the trial headed for its climax. William Barnes was recalled by Ivins and immediately resumed ripping apart Roosevelt's sworn testimony, painting him as a habitual liar. It quickly became clear that the previous afternoon had been but a preparation for the attack on the Colonel's supposedly infallible memory and his credibility. To save his own career, it had become necessary for Barnes to destroy Theodore Roosevelt's reputation. Many of the spectators were aghast at this attack on the former president of the United States, while others saw their suspicions being confirmed.

Ivins opened with a discussion of the Blauvert bill, the direct primary legislation that, as Barnes patiently explained, took the nominating process away from those people who actually knew the strengths and weaknesses of the candidates and gave it to those who might easily be swayed by promises and slogans. It was a bill he strongly opposed.

After some parrying between the sides, the judge allowed the testimony to remain, "not as showing any improper conduct on the part of the plaintiff, but as bearing upon the question of his dominance in the party." It had become clear that this question, exactly how powerful Barnes was in the party, had become central, putting the plaintiff in the odd position of attempting to prove that he had been little more than a functionary rather than a leader. Tensions in the courtroom had been rising as the trial neared its finish, and now they erupted into plain view.

The legal triangle of Ivins, Bowers and Judge Andrews had been sparring for weeks, with the two attorneys always looking for any edge. There had been some minor sniping, but when Ivins once more exceeded his bounds and addressed the jury directly, the pot had finally boiled over. "I think I shall make my own statement to the jury," Judge Andrews scolded Ivins. "The jury will take any statements of law from me and not from the attorneys in this case… I think you better simply ask me to make statements and not make them yourselves. I think you better simply ask the witness the questions in an ordinary way."

Ivins held his ground. "I thought I was doing it in the ordinary way."

"Oh, hardly," Judge Andrews chided him.

"In view of what your honor has just said…"

"Hardly," the judge repeated.

"…in the hearing of the witness and in the hearing of the jury."

Judge Andrews would have none of that. "I said myself what I chose to say to the jury. I do not think that attorneys on either side need repeat, for the purpose of paraphrasing or even stating in the same language, what I said to the jury."

In a legal form of apology, Ivins said, "I will withdraw the question."

Barnes then began telling how and why he had broken with Roosevelt. At the meeting of the state committee in the summer of 1910, shortly after the Colonel had returned from his celebrated African expedition, Roosevelt had attempted to reassert his party leadership. "He told me that I took the direct nomination matter entirely too seriously. I replied that he had been out of the country for fifteen months, that we had gone on with the program along this particular line…and the question would be settled (at the coming convention) where the Republican party stood on this question.

"He then stated that he did not understand my

action in voting for Mr. Sherman as temporary chairman…he stated that he thought I should have supported him (Roosevelt)…

"I said that I did not support him because I was not entirely clear as to what his ideas were and that, as the temporary chairman of the state convention is known to be the man whose expressions are taken as the expressions of the convention…that I did not believe in his doctrine called the 'New Nationalism' and that I could not as a Republican have voted for him as temporary chairman."

But even without Barnes's support, Roosevelt was elected the temporary chairman of that convention. Using the leverage of that position he secured the Republican gubernatorial nomination for his candidate, Henry L. Stimson—but also caused the rift with Barnes that would never be healed.

Ivins took a roundabout route but eventually came back to the 1911 senatorial election, asking the plaintiff, "Did you ever have any conversation with Mr. Murphy at any time with regard to the election of a United States Senator?"

"No."

"Do you know Mr. Murphy?"

"I met him once at a dinner called the Amen dinner." That dinner was an annual gathering of Republicans and newsmen.

Bowers objected, protesting, "We are entitled to a yes or no."

While the answer clearly was yes, the truth of it, as claimed by Barnes, was quite different. In contrast to Roosevelt's article, which claimed an alliance between the two men, the plaintiff was testifying that he barely knew the man. Barnes continued that he had been introduced to him at that dinner. "Did you have any talk with him?" Ivins asked.

"No."

"Have you seen or talked with him since?"

"No."

"Have you ever since that time seen or talked with him on any subject whatever; directly or indirectly, by or through his or your agent, in writing, orally or by telephone."

"No."

Ivins then brought up a dinner attended by both the plaintiff and defendant where Barnes described showing Roosevelt a letter written by Abraham Lincoln to Barnes's grandfather Thurlow Weed, one of the first and most influential Republicans leading up to, and during, Lincoln's presidency. According to Barnes, the Colonel "took it out of my hand" and put it in his pocket, proposing to discuss it with a Dr. Abbott. The courtroom broke into laughter at the thought of Teddy Roosevelt swiping a letter and just stuffing it in his pocket. Judge Andrews quickly gaveled the courtroom back to order. But instead of handing it to Dr. Abbott, Barnes continued, the Colonel turned it over to the newspapers and said incorrectly "that he had been asked by Mr. Barnes to incorporate it into his speech."

Bowers objected and when the court sustained it, Ivins protested, telling the judge, "This goes directly to the credibility of Mr. Roosevelt."

Judge Andrews then offered a hypothetical situation, supposing Colonel Roosevelt had stolen the letter, forged some sentences then gave it to the newspaper; "Would it have any effect…on Mr. Roosevelt's credibility in this case?"

Ivins responded, "If we proved that it would certainly show that Mr. Roosevelt's credibility was not worthy of attention."

Justice Andrews disagreed and sustained the objection.

Barnes finally had the opportunity to tell the jury how he proceeded in the 1911 senatorial contest. As the Democrats had won the majority in the state legislature in the 1910 elections, Republican Senator Depew could not attract sufficient support to retain his seat. "Two months had passed and no Senator had been elected to take the place of Senator Depew." Barnes said he had to take action and spoke with various members of the Senate and assembly. Whatever the resolution, the objective was to elect a candidate who was not beholden to Tammany. Eventually he was given a list of candidates acceptable to the Independent Democrats, which meant by joining forces they could elect a senator. But he was unable to rally sufficient Republican support behind any one candidate to put that plan into action. The leader of the Independents, Franklin Roosevelt, finally informed him that Democrats had coalesced around Senator James A. O'Gorman and "that closed the situation."

Ivins then jumped ahead to the Republican Convention of 1912. When Bowers once again requested answers be confined to yes or no, Ivins wondered sarcastically, "You don't desire my friend the plaintiff to be as loquacious as your defendant was?"

Bowers had a ready answer. "I am quite willing he should be and I make no objection to it. The more he talks the better I like it, but I don't want to be trying issues that have nothing to do with the case."

Ivins took umbrage at that. "You tried a good many which had nothing to do with the case, and I didn't object."

Bowers appealed to the judge. "Am I to be forced into this discussion?"

"Simply ask your questions, Mr. Ivins," Judge Andrews instructed.

Again Ivins started, again Bowers interrupted, wondering how this line of questions was going to be connected to the Colonel.

Ivins told him, "I am going to show the relation with the malice of the defendant, and the cause of the defendant's malice."

Barnes proceeded. He was a delegate at large and favored President William H. Taft for the nomination. There also was considerable support for Colonel Roosevelt at the convention, which resulted in a bitter dispute over which delegates should be seated. Barnes sided with the Taft people, and Taft eventually won the nomination. Barnes did not speak with Roosevelt ever again.

The next issue concerned Loeb's testimony in which he claimed to have met Barnes during lunch at the Bache brokerage house in 1911. Did that happen, Ivins asked. "No, he is mistaken… I never met him there in 1911. I was not there at luncheon in 1911." However, he did remember meeting him there—after the election of 1912.

"Do you remember Mr. Loeb's testimony as to having had a conversation with you with regard to an arrangement between yourself and Mr. Murphy in respect to the election of a United States Senator?"

Flatly, with complete confidence he answered, "I had no such conversation."

Ivins looked to the bench and said, "That is all," turning his witness over to Bowers for what promised to be a tough cross-examination.

But before that began, Judge Andrews told the jury he wanted to explain the rulings he'd issued while they were out of the courtroom the previous day. "I have held," he reminded them, "that the article is libelous per se…because it charges a corrupt alliance between Mr. Barnes as head of the Republican party and Mr. Murphy as head of the Democratic party in relation to state government. I use the word corrupt…not as meaning necessarily something connected with pecuniary gain.

"I have also held (it) is libelous per se because it charges that Mr. Barnes worked through an alliance between corrupt business and corrupt politics." He had permitted the defense to offer evidence regarding printing contracts to justify that claim, but then he explained, "I have held while you were absent that…the defendant has not been able to produce sufficient evidence to justify you in finding that there was corruption in the printing situation… Therefore I have taken from your consideration that question.

"So too in regard to various other pieces of evidence in the case," he continued. "With regard to all those matters I have held that you can't find any corruption or crime on the part of Mr. Barnes with regard to his position.

"I have left in the case evidence of alleged admissions made by Mr. Barnes as to contributions received under an implied pledge, and evidence as to Mr. Barnes' position and action in the Senatorial contest. But ruling that way I express no opinion as to the truth of the evidence… I am going to leave it for you to say…"

And then he asked the impossible. "I am going to ask you gentlemen to disregard, put from your minds entirely this evidence which I have stricken from the case."

With that instruction made, Bowers began his highly anticipated cross-examination of William Barnes. The manner in which an attorney asks his questions to a witness is often as important as the actual questions; a tone can convey respect or disbelief, even incredulity. The jury gets the message. This jury had spent weeks watching Bowers and Ivins, and their teams, approach witnesses with various styles. Rather than being brusque or aggressive, Bowers treated Barnes with respect. There was little challenge in his tone; it was rather conversational. *Let's you and I work this thing out together as professional men*, he seemed to suggest.

He asked about details, such as when Barnes was in Albany and when he was in New York City. Barnes answered warily, unsure where this line would lead. The confidence he had displayed throughout the morning was gone; he seemed nervous, continually clasping and unclasping his hands as he waited for the attack sure to be coming.

Bowers eased into it, establishing that Barnes had acquired the *Albany Evening Journal* in 1899, that he controlled the paper's editorial policy, that he wrote, supervised or approved the editorials published in that newspaper. "My principle activities were in writing and supervising the policy of the paper," Barnes agreed. Whether he gave more attention to the content of the paper than to the business side he could not determine, he said. "I certainly did what I did."

The newspaper, Bowers continued, had become an important voice in Republican politics. Barnes agreed to that flattery too, saying, "The object of the editorial article is, of course, to influence the mind."

Bowers's purpose was revealed when he offered into evidence an editorial concerning the selection of a senator, his point being that Barnes did not have to speak directly with Republican legislators. They would ascertain the party position by reading the *Journal*. "The duty of Republican members of the legislature," the paper editorialized, "is to vote for the Republican candidate for Senator, the caucus nominee… If they should begin to gyrate and make an exhibit of personal antagonism and personal ambition similar to that which the Democrats are showing, they should justly become, as well as the Democrats, the laughing stock of the state."

Bowers read several such editorials, still maintaining his congenial attitude. Then he asked, "You believe that when a man accepts a nomination for any office he takes upon himself the obligation to stand by the principles of the party and to do as the majority determines?"

Barnes had no recourse. "As a general principle, of course… It was intended to refer to any movement or any man in a legislative body who do not cooperate with the party by whom they are elected."

The editorials provided substantial material for Bowers to attack Barnes's testimony. For example, although the plaintiff had testified he supported Independent Democrat Thomas Mott Osborne as an acceptable compromise choice for the Senate, *Evening Journal* editorials read in the courtroom by Bowers criticized Osborne and praised the Tammany candidate, William Sheehan.

As the cross-examination continued, it became obvious that Roosevelt was growing restless at his attorney's conversational approach. He was in motion at the defense table, whispering to other members of his team. At the plaintiff's table Ivins was sitting back contentedly, his entwined hands resting on his chest, a confident pose that suggested his man was doing well.

Bowers was maneuvering carefully through the strict confines left by Judge Andrews. His questions did not dwell on the specific elements of each article as they did on the much broader charge: politics is corrupt, the people are not being represented and power brokers such as Barnes, and Murphy, are the root cause of the problem. What Barnes appeared to be admitting was that elected officials had a greater duty to their party than to the populace. It was the type of emotional issue that might well be embraced by jurors, some of whom undoubtedly already were suspicious of politicians. If Bowers could get jurors riled up over political insiders determining their destinies, it could be much easier for them to find for his client.

Ivins finally recognized this and objected to the cross-examination "of this witness as to his views. His views are not an issue here. The other witnesses have not been examined in regard to their views. I cannot recall him and have him go through an extended line of examination in regard to his views."

Judge Andrews was skeptical, raising his eyebrows in surprise at that claim. "Did you not examine the defendant somewhat lengthily about his views?"

"In so far as he testified to them," Ivins said. "I gave him all the line he wanted and after he had testified, I cross-examined."

Bowers couldn't resist: "And he was glad to take it." The entire courtroom once again burst into laughter, requiring the judge to bang his gavel again on the wooden sound block several times.

Moving on, Bowers made an effort to substantiate Barnes's importance in the machine. He established that during the senatorial deadlock, Barnes was receiving messages every day asking him to use his influence to resolve it. Bowers then expanded his question, asking, "Was it a usual thing that you should receive communications, requests, bearing upon the question of legislation, to do things for people, to assist them?"

"Very constantly, yes. When I was in Albany and since."

And then Bowers moved to the relationship with Colonel Roosevelt. Barnes said he saw him infrequently when he was governor, but later saw him more often and they became "fairly well acquainted." During those meetings, he said, they never discussed any differences between Roosevelt and Senator Platt. Bowers asked the witness if he had testified previously "that Mr. Roosevelt talked and you listened. Now, was there anything of that kind said? Because you know, I may have dreamed it."

Barnes admitted he had said that.

In contrast to Ivins's sarcasm, Bowers's tone dripped with exaggerated confusion. Perhaps the plaintiff might help him sort it all out. Colonel Roosevelt had testified that he and Barnes had discussed the issues he had with Platt as a party boss, but Barnes had testified he had no knowledge of the issues separating those men.

Barnes offered slight help, suggesting, "Issues and relations are not the same thing."

"That is what I want to know," Bowers continued. "When you testified that you knew of no issues, you had in mind, did you, that the word used was a mistaken word?"

"The word 'issue' involves a division."

"A division." Bowers considered that. "Now, then we will drop the word 'issues' as Mr. Ivins did, and put to you the question he did, 'I ask you if you ever talked with him, that is Mr. Roosevelt, about any such thing?' And you answered, 'Well, I cannot testify that he did not talk to me.' Will you be good enough to tell me what you meant by that?"

"I cannot recollect exactly what I said," Barnes began. To the ordinary man that might well appear to be an attempt at evasion, whether it was or not. Those members of the jury who recalled that testimony might think it odd that the witness did not recall. Barnes continued, "Of course Mr. Roosevelt did talk to me in relation to Senator Platt… to get from me what information I had in regard to affairs in Albany."

With condescension underlining his words, Bowers offered, "Now you recollect that he did do all that, is that right?"

"Yes, I think that occurred."

Getting the plaintiff to admit he or she is wrong, even on a minor point, is a significant victory for a trial attorney. While the facts might be of minimal importance in the case, the impact of it can be great. Scottish philosopher Thomas Reid wrote in his 1786 *Essays on the Intellectual Powers of Man*, "In every chain of reasoning, the evidence of the last conclusion can be no greater than that of the weakest link of the chain, whatever may be the strength of the rest."

Bowers pressed further. "Did you talk with him about some appointments?"

"I did."

"Did you make one or more requests of that character?"

"I made more than one, of course."

Barnes tried to fight back. Bowers asked the witness: "Stop and think for a moment. You were good enough to talk with him about his relationship with Mr. Platt. Did he at the time tell you he had any differences with Mr. Platt?"

"No."

"Did he tell you that they were of different views upon any question?"

"He may have; I can't remember whether he said he had a different view."

"You say he asked you to give him what knowledge you had acquired in any way in Albany. Did he ask your advice in any way, or your assistance?"

Barnes drew knowing laughter when he responded, "I am more inclined to think he told me." When pushed by Bowers he went further. "I think he asked my opinion and then told me what he was going to do… I think he told me he was going to get along with Senator Platt and at the same time conduct his office as Governor." He told me this, the plaintiff continued, "Because I suppose he assumed that I thought it would be impossible."

Bowers wouldn't let go. Barnes was on the defensive, doing his best to avoid answering questions:

"I can't remember that."

"I could not swear that he said that, no."

"I have forgotten the letter."

"I cannot remember everything that Mr. Ivins does."

"I remember the letter was read. I didn't recollect that letter."

"I mean, I can't distinctly testify to anything Mr. Roosevelt may have said to me eighteen years ago."

The witness had lost some of his previously marked swagger. Bowers smelled blood and continued his pursuit. "Now, do I understand that the talk you had with reference to his relations with Mr. Platt was limited to times you were at the Executive Mansion?"

Again, leaving himself an escape route, Barnes said, "That is my judgment."

He admitted to speaking with Roosevelt about Platt only once. Bowers asked, "Did you have quite a long talk with him on that evening?"

"I cannot say how long it was."

After Bowers guided the witness through his previous testimony, he reached perhaps his most vulnerable territory. While Judge Andrews had thrown out using the printing testimony to justify the libelous statements, some of it still could be addressed to potentially mitigate damages, or more simply to establish the relationship between Barnes and Roosevelt. "You wrote a letter to the Governor in the Autumn of 1899 in which you said, in substance, that if a State printing house was established it might be your financial ruin. Do you remember that letter?" He did, indeed, although when questioned further he could not recall if he had discussed it with Roosevelt. Bowers seemed puzzled by the proposition that a State printing house would hurt the newspaper business, especially when "the Journal Company had no job printing plant of any size."

The company was doing some job printing at that time, Barnes explained, and would have been hurt because wages would increase. It also would have been hurt, he continued, "If you establish a state printing house…"

Bowers finished the thought for him. "There will be no state printing to bid on."

Bowers was performing a neat trick, continuing to raise questions about Barnes's conduct in the printing business without violating Judge Andrews's decision barring the jury from considering Barnes's conduct in the printing business. Ivins objected to it, but Judge Andrews allowed it to continue. Bowers very patiently was catching the witness in contradictions and equivocations. None of them were especially damaging in and of themselves, but altogether they had an impact. For example, when he asked, "Had you any special interest at that time in any other corporation other than the *Journal* engaged in the printing business?"

"No," Barnes responded. "I had no interest in any other corporation."

"None whatever?"

"No."

"You had some interest in Lyon at that time?"

"Yes."

"Were you engaged in business with Lyon?"

"Yes, Mr. Lyon and I were the owners of the state printing contract for the year 1899… I had purchased it from Mr. McCarthy."

"You purchased it?" Bowers repeated.

"I did," Barnes said confidently.

And with the real meaning of that admission hanging in the air, the trial ended for the week.

Colonel Roosevelt returned to New York City for the weekend, for the first time since the beginning of the trial. Just before the trial began his wife, Edith, had been hospitalized with what was termed "a mysterious illness," but in actuality was a hysterectomy. Granting her privacy, the newspapers wrote very little about it. After a successful operation at Roosevelt Hospital, she had just returned home to Oyster Bay and her husband joined her there for the weekend.

As Colonel Roosevelt had feared, his response to the sinking of the *Lusitania* had led to serious rebukes from the German-American community. The *New Yorker Staats-Zeitung*, the largest German-language newspaper in America, reported that Roosevelt had been dropped as an honorary member of the League of Old German Students and the General German Language League.

While journalists continued to fill column space with speculation, there remained no consensus

Harry J. Westerman was among the nation's leading political cartoonists. His illustration "The Whole Show" from the Knickerbocker Press *satirized Roosevelt's attempts to take complete control of the courtroom.*

about the outcome; both sides had made their case so well that more and more it began to look as if there might be no clear verdict. An unidentified intimate of Roosevelt's told the *Times* reporter, "It will be absolutely impossible for the jury to reach an agreement, even political considerations aside. A verdict of anything over 6-cents for Mr. Barnes will mean politically that in the heat of a campaign a speaker on the stump has no right to criticize a political boss. Such a proposition strikes too deeply at the fundamental right of free speech.

"It is practically certain that Mr. Roosevelt will ask for a re-trial if damages over six cents are awarded to Mr. Barnes. Mr. Barnes, on the other hand, cannot possibly be satisfied with either a 6-cent verdict or a disagreement. Either will be a verdict for Mr. Roosevelt. Both men are appealing to a greater jury, the American people, and nothing but a clean-cut decision will satisfy either."

If the jury was to reach the required unanimous decision, the *Times* predicted, the trial would be turned by the summations of the two sides. "Lawyers who have followed the case closely agree that the summing up may have a decided effect upon the verdict." Both teams were already at work on their summations. Barnes's libel expert, former congressman John J. Adams, had been at work reviewing every other similar trial of importance, including the full stenographic transcript of the scandalous Tilton-Beecher "alienation of affections" trial from 1875. The opening statements and closing arguments in that trial had lasted nearly two months and were considered some of the best presentations ever. Not only had Ivins clerked for the judge on that case, but he considered that case so significant that he hired a former reporter named Hugh Hastings who had covered Tilton-Beecher for a New York paper, to help out here.

But before any final arguments would be made, there were still witnesses to be called and Ivins claimed to reporters that he now had "a surprise witness," a man he refused to identify. Anticipation remained high as the trial resumed Monday morning. In addition to the mysterious witness, Barnes would complete his cross-examination and then Teddy Roosevelt would retake the stand one last time.

The Colonel had enjoyed a pleasant weekend with

his recuperating wife. He arrived early to the courtroom, wearing a new Scotch tweed summer suit. And rather than proceeding straight to the courtroom, as had been his practice, he paused and posed for several photographers before taking his usual seat.

Before Barnes was recalled, Ivins announced that it had been agreed "to interrupt the examination of Mr. Barnes to take testimony from fifteen to twenty members of the legislature."

And Bowers got the week going with a hearty laugh when he said, "I have no interruption to the interruption."

As promised, a parade of current or former legislators marched to the witness chair and testified to the political purity of William Barnes. Former assemblyman William Keys testified that he had been told by Barnes, "It would be a good idea for the Republican members to form a fusion with the insurgents or Independent Democrats for the election of an independent Democrat for the United States Senate." This was in contrast to the testimony of Franklin Roosevelt and others who said that Barnes wanted to protect his relationship with the Democratic Party boss Murphy and would not agree to that sort of independent meeting of the minds. Assemblyman, and publisher of the *Middletown Daily Times*, John Stivers swore he had never had any conversation with Barnes on this subject. Assemblyman William Coffey did not have a conversation with Barnes about the election of a senator. One after another these distinguished men, lawyers and merchants, farmers and financial men said the same thing: they had not discussed the subject with Barnes nor were they following any party instructions when they cast their votes. "Mr. Barnes was very anxious to elect an Independent Democrat," remembered Eugene Travis. Aiden Hart had never even spoken to Barnes. Caleb Baumes, Ellsworth Cheney, Henry Constantine, Frederick Filley, Fred Cray, one after another raised their right hands and swore that they had not spoken with Barnes about the senatorial matter and had not been influenced by him. August Pepper never spoke with Barnes about the matter, James Shea never spoke with him, and so on throughout most of the morning as twenty-six more men joined the twenty-two who had testified previously that Barnes had not forced or influenced their vote.

Ivins's point was hammered into the minds of the jury: contrary to the testimony of Roosevelt, Barnes did not use his supposed influence to resolve that 1911 deadlock.

Roosevelt made his opinion of this strategy obvious; he sat quietly at the defense table listlessly paging through several magazines, ignoring the repetitious testimony. He paid special attention to a short story entitled "Broke I; or, The Busted Lady" in the latest issue of *McClure's Magazine*.

There was only one discordant note in Ivins's symphony of legislators: former senator J. Mayhew Wainwright. Wainwright had been summoned to Syracuse by Roosevelt, and when he was not called to testify for the defense, Ivins made a careless mistake; he assumed Bowers had abandoned this witness because his answers would not square with his strategy. So, apparently without interviewing Wainwright, he called him to the stand. It was an entirely avoidable error, certainly not typical or expected from someone of William Ivins's legal caliber. Wainwright testified happily that when a Democrat named John Kernan was suggested as a possible compromise candidate for the Senate, "Mr. Barnes told me that he had an agreement with the Democrats not to interfere, but to let the Democrats fight it out among themselves." Ivins did not give away his obvious distress at this answer, instead managing to save some ground by getting Wainwright to admit that Barnes had not tried to influence his vote; and that, after all, was the charge.

It was almost noon before Barnes finally returned to the witness box. Whatever nerves he had exhibited when this cross-examination had begun were gone; instead he once again appeared completely confident, smiling easily as he answered questions, often looking directly at the jury as he did. It seemed he was now enjoying this sparring match with Bowers.

The editorials in his paper had made it clear, Bowers suggested, that Barnes "was not politically friendly with Governor Hughes." Barnes did not dispute that, agreeing that "I exercise my right of criticism." His attorney, however, objected, reminding the court it is possible to "be friendly in respect to some things and not in respect to others."

The constant objections began to wear on Bowers. When he asked Barnes a simple question about his "interest" in the racetrack betting bill, Ivins objected once again, asking for "some definition of 'interest.'" Bowers responded irritably, "I think the witness understands the English language pretty well."

Ivins apparently took offense at that, responding loudly, "Well, you do not."

Bowers smiled at his foe's indignation, responding sarcastically, "Well, I know that, but that is unfortunate for me. I am trying to learn from you gentlemen."

The racetrack gambling bill had assumed an exaggerated importance in the trial. With alleged corruption in the printing business ruled out, one of the last threads remaining for the defense was to prove that Barnes had formed a corrupt alliance with Charles Murphy to influence legislation. Bowers intended to use the Hart-Agnew racetrack bill as his way in.

Barnes reluctantly agreed he had an "interest" in the bill. Asked if he remembered making a speech at the Republican club, the Unconditional, against the bill, he replied he did not—at least not until Bowers produced an article quoting him that had been published in his own *Journal*. "If the *Journal* says that," he admitted, "I unquestioningly made that statement." Once again, his casual denial seemed far more damning than the answer.

Bowers asked, "The *Albany Evening Journal* opposed the repeal of that law upon the ground that it was not conducive to public morality but would increase rather than lessen the evil it was intended to destroy. Do you remember that?"

No, the plaintiff said, he did not remember making that speech. Placed in the uncomfortable position of questioning the accuracy of a story about him published in his own newspaper, he said, "I cannot certify to the accuracy of that report...but I can say in general that the report is apparently correct, as correct as most newspaper reports. I cannot go any further than that."

Bowers was surprised by that answer, wondering to the benefit of everyone in the courtroom how Barnes remained "unable to tell whether you ever made that speech?"

"I want to visualize it," Barnes said. "Where was it?"

Bowers read more of the story, which included the passage, "William J. Barnes Jr., at the annual dinner of the Unconditional Republican Club last evening made clear his attitude toward the anti-racetrack message of Governor Hughes," then asked if that assisted his memory.

Barnes still appeared to struggle to recall it, asking if it was at "the hotel or the place?" He then claimed that he was not trying to avoid any statement.

"You have already answered the question," Bowers continued, "but I did not understand your answer, because perhaps I am not sufficiently gifted in English, so I will put it in this form. Is your recollection refreshed so that you can state whether or not you made that speech that is published in the *Albany Journal*, and which I think you have examined at some considerable length?"

"Is the date April 27th?"

Frustrated, Bowers snapped, "I don't care what time it was made, at or about that time. It is published in the *Journal* of the 26th. You can answer that yes or no?"

Barnes still refused to admit it. After all, that would directly contradict his prior testimony. "I made a speech at the Unconditional dinner of which that purports to be a correct copy; I cannot certify that it is a correct copy, or the correct words that I used. It is probably very nearly correct."

Barnes's problem was that he had claimed in his testimony that he took no position on the bill, while at the same time his newspaper was strongly editorializing against it. Trying to explain that, he said, was simple. "I am responsible for the articles that appear in the *Albany Evening Journal* as I am the editor of it. It has no relation whatsoever to any political act of mine."

Bowers was not going to let go of that obvious conundrum. "I don't know that I quite understand you," he said. "You have stated that you were the editor and responsible for all the articles in the *Journal*, have you not?"

"No. I have not testified to that."

Bowers raised his eyebrows in surprise. "You haven't?"

"Not exactly that…" Then he repeated, "I am not trying to avoid responsibility for this article." His answers became more convoluted; he accepted responsibility for the editorials published by his newspaper, "but I won't be responsible for every article that has been printed in it to be held up against me individually."

This head-scratching testimony continued, as Bowers appeared to be chasing Barnes in circles. The plaintiff added, "I think I testified that I either wrote the article or directed its publication."

So, Bowers said quite logically, "Then may we assume that the paragraph was what you personally believed?"

"I should not think that would follow."

Bowers continued his pursuit of the answer. "You would not think that would follow?… Did you or did you not write or direct that that paragraph should be inserted in that editorial?"

"I did not… I mean that I either wrote that article, which I very much doubt, or that I telephoned to the editor and asked him to write an article, or that he may have written it of his own accord without consultation with me at all. I happen to know I was not in the office on that day… I think that this article stands for itself."

"Then, as I understand you now, you do not assume responsibility for the statements contained in that article? Would you mind answering that yes or no?"

Instead, Barnes asked, "What does responsibility mean?"

Ivins sat perfectly complacent, uttering not a word, as his client fended off this attack like a lion tamer deftly manipulating a defensive chair. "There is legal responsibility," Barnes continued, "and moral responsibility."

"Well, there is moral responsibility here. Do you assume moral responsibility for that statement?"

"Will you show me any moral proposition involved in it?"

Earlier in the trial William Ivins had made a reference to *Alice in Wonderland*, that strange world in which reality is turned inside out. At times this testimony might well have reminded spectators of that nonsensical dialogue. Bowers said, "I ask you this simple, plain question: Did you read the article?"

But clearly, for Barnes that question was neither simple nor plain. "When?" he responded.

"At any time."

"I can't answer that because I don't know whether I wrote it."

The jury sat in their box absorbing every word. During a trial, lawyers can rarely know with any confidence what testimony might sway jurors toward or away from their client. But it was becoming increasingly obvious that Barnes was taking great pains to avoid answering what seemed to be a simple, plain question. And the failure to do so had its own impact. Bowers tried to move forward. "If you wrote it, you wrote the paragraph that I have read, didn't you?"

"Certainly! I have said so all along."

"Do you mean to say that that imposes no responsibility, financial, legal, moral or otherwise upon you in that article?"

"It opened me to a suit for criminal libel."

"Is that the only thing you are afraid of?"

Barnes smiled at the jury as he responded, "I am not worried about anything."

Bowers asked if the plaintiff even understood the consequences of the bill that was proposed to make anti-gambling laws have some bite. The existing law eliminated all penalties for placing bets at a racetrack other than the loss of whatever money had been wagered. As a result, betting and bookmaking at racetracks flourished. The debate revolved around the effort to repeal that soft-on-gambling law and to effectively end the practice. "Don't you know that the great issue between Governor Hughes and the legislature at that time was whether the act should be repealed which permitted acts to be done at a racetrack without imposing criminal liability which at any other place would impose criminal liability?...

"And to that you expressed yourself as opposed, or at least your *Journal* expressed itself as opposed, from the moment Governor Hughes suggested it?"

The bill failed when eight Republicans joined seventeen Democrats to vote against it. The Democratic leader of the opposition to the bill was Senator Patrick "Long Pat" McCarren, the acknowledged boss of Brooklyn. Bowers's questions established that McCarren had met with the plaintiff at his Albany home four days before the bill was defeated. At that meeting, Barnes testified, McCarren told him "the measure would be defeated" if Republican Senator Grattan would vote against it, "and asked me whether I would not talk with Senator Grattan about the matter."

Suddenly realizing the danger to his client, Ivins stood and objected. When Judge Andrews told him to wait until the question is finished, to the surprise of the courtroom he said, "No," and continued talking.

"Sit down, Mr. Ivins," the judge ordered sternly. "When he has finished his question you may object."

Until this moment the cross-examination of William Barnes by John Bowers had been a respectful exchange that had delighted the courtroom. Bowers had jabbed at him successfully and even connected with a couple of bruising rhetorical blows, but now he had maneuvered him into a corner.

But just as Bowers got ready to press his attack, an unusual-looking package was delivered to the Colonel. Throughout the trial an attendant had brought the Colonel's mail to him hourly without incident, but this was different. Roosevelt examined the wrapped package carefully; curiously, it had no recognizable markings. The Colonel still carried a bullet in him; he had survived many life-threatening situations, so he certainly recognized danger when it was close.

And at that moment he sensed danger.

CHAPTER FIFTEEN

This trial was entering its final stretch, and once again the principals were back on center stage.

There is no prescribed length of time in which a trial has to be conducted. The Tilton-Beecher trial, for example, had gone on for six months. Two decades later, in 1895, when former president Benjamin Harrison represented a plaintiff suing the former executor of a relative's estate, the trial lasted four months and ten days. So the month that this trial had taken thus far was long, but hardly remarkable.

Before the cross-examination of William Barnes could continue, that strange package delivered to the Colonel at 3:40 in the afternoon had to be dealt with. Roosevelt's outspoken criticism of the kaiser combined with his insistence that the nation should be preparing for war against Germany had engendered substantial animosity. It was not impossible that someone who disagreed with his position might take action to stop him. The first "mail bomb" had been sent more than two centuries earlier, and bombs had now become the weapon of choice for radicals and anarchists. By 1908, the *Times* reported, an average of one bomb a month was discovered or detonated in New York. Detectives had even disrupted a plot to blow up St. Patrick's Cathedral. The possibility that this package might be an infernal device could not be discounted.

Judge Andrews briefly halted the proceedings as the Roosevelt and Barnes teams discussed how to proceed. Attorney Stewart Hancock finally carried the package out of the courtroom and handed it to the Colonel's bodyguard, Syracuse Police Department Detective Pasquale Bennett. The brave detective took it outside the courthouse and carefully unwrapped it. He first found a picture of a whisky bottle. And when he was finally able to fully open the package, he discovered it contained a badly scarred potato.

No one would speculate about the intended meaning of the potato, assuming, of course, there was one.

The brief respite offered Barnes an opportunity to gather his thoughts and try to fight a new round. Bowers asked him again about his conversation with Senator McCarren regarding the critical vote on the anti-gambling law. "I told him that I would see Senator Grattan and talk with him about the matter, that I didn't want to become involved in the proposition at all, but that I would talk with the Senator and find out what he would do."

Senator Grattan had already announced his support for the racetrack bill. But at McCarren's request, Barnes met with him. Bowers did not ask him to repeat the conversation, instead eliciting the fact that prior to this meeting Grattan supported the bill, and apparently after this meeting he turned against it and cast the deciding vote ensuring its defeat. He would let the jury make that short and logical leap.

Barnes did his utmost to fend off the questions, at times avoiding answering a question then claiming his nonanswer was his answer. In an attempt to untangle some of this, Bowers asked a complicated question, which caused Ivins to wonder, "Why the counsel asks three or four questions in succession?"

Bowers, who had proven to be a fine match for Ivins, was pleased to respond, "So as to get an answer to one."

According to Barnes, McCarren told him very little of consequence beyond the fact that there were twenty-four votes against the bill, one less than necessary to defeat—and that did not include Grattan's vote. Bowers wondered, "Did you or did you not tell him that you would advise Mr. Grattan to vote against the bill?"

Barnes avoided a direct answer, saying only that McCarren left without knowing whether or not he would speak to Senator Grattan. "There is no doubt about that in your mind?" Bowers asked.

"Not the slightest."

Once again the impression left with the jurors was arguably more important than any specific information. With these questions Bowers had shown that the plaintiff was consulting with Democratic leaders on pending legislation, just as Roosevelt had charged.

Bowers then changed subjects to the printing matters. He read a letter the plaintiff had written in 1894 to Senator Platt in which he complained that a well-placed politician "undoubtedly will stick to his determination not to give the Journal company the stationery business and appurtenances thereto," then asked for an explanation.

It was no surprise that Ivins objected vehemently "to going into this printing business. It has been ruled out, unless it be stated on what ground it is gone into."

Bowers made his argument. "On the ground of credibility and character."

Judge Andrews reminded the attorneys that he had closed that door. "Of course you gentlemen understand that I have ruled out evidence as to the printing business in so far as it is admitted to claim there is justification in this libel..." And then he opened it again. "Of course it is true that you may ask the witness with regard to any moment of his career with the purpose of showing that he had committed some crime, and is, therefore unworthy of belief on the stand."

In other words, Bowers was free to ask away in an effort to impugn Barnes's honesty and credibility.

The meaning, Barnes explained, was that the clerk of the assembly has the power to buy supplies and job out printing work. A new clerk apparently had decided to give that work to a different company, and Barnes had written to Platt asking for that work. In later letters read to the jury, Barnes continued to complain: "I have never been able to secure a single contract from the Republican State officers, but have uniformly been ruled out by some friend."

At the time these letters were written, the plaintiff testified, he had no interest in the Lyon company.

Bowers asked his questions crisply, making certain the witness answered in brief sentences, cutting him off when he tried to go longer. It was clear the lawyer was bringing him to an intended answer, although at first it was not clear what he intended to reveal. In the contract under discussion, the Lyon bid was significantly higher than that of Henry J. McCarthy, the owner of the *Albany Knickerbocker Press*. But somehow McCarthy won the job and almost immediately sold the contract to Barnes, who in turn sold it to Lyon.

The pieces were beginning to fall into place. Americans were still fondly quoting the words written only a few years earlier by the very popular "Hoosier Poet," James Whitcomb Riley: "When I see a bird that walks like a duck, and swims like a duck and quacks like a duck, I call that bird a duck." While never intended to become a legal maxim, in fact it described perfectly Bowers's courtroom strategy. He might not be able to make a direct connection showing Barnes had corruptly used his political influence to profit from his printing connections, but he certainly could show all the moving parts and once again let jurors reach their own conclusion.

"Did you buy it?" he asked.

"I took an option and I sold it to Mr. Lyon."

"And then you had a claim against him for $20,000 for services?"

"That was not for services... I was the owner of the McCarthy contract and I sold it to Mr. Lyon for $20,000 and an interest...in the neighborhood of $11,000."

Barnes assigned his agreement, a claim against J. B. Lyon for a $20,000 salary, to the Journal Company. For salary? Bowers wondered. "What services had you rendered him?"

"I told you he owed me money and I sold him the contract."

The attorney took hold of that fact and squeezed every last bit of inference out of it. "You sold him the contract for $20,000?"

"I certainly did."

"What was the contract for salary for?"

"That was the $20,000 Mr. Lyon owed me."

"Is that not the $20,000 he paid you for the contract?"

"That is what I said."

Bowers emphasized his confusion for the benefit of the jury. "Why would it be in the form of salary?"

"That I do not know. Mr. Lyon did that."

Bowers phrased his next question perfectly, suggesting something to the jury without having to make the accusation. "As a matter of fact, was the claim of $20,000 against Mr. Lyon for services you had rendered to him in obtaining the contract, or was it because you sold it to him at the sum of $20,000 beyond what you had paid for it?" The subtext was obvious: Wasn't this actually a payment for using your political connections to secure the contract?

"Why, it is absolutely the latter."

"And (Mr. Lyon) put the obligation in the shape of salary?"

"That is it exactly."

Almost as an aside, Bowers wondered, "Did you say there was more than $20,000 that was due you on that transaction?"

"Yes, I said that… It was for $20,000 and some interest in the contract. That interest he did not definitely, as I remember, specify."

When Ivins again objected that this whole area had been thrown out, Judge Andrews suggested this line of questioning gave him "the opportunity to explain what was denied to you before."

Ivins responded with one of his grand exaggerations, "You might as well ask him to explain the solar system… It has no relevancy to it, and your honor has so ruled. I don't want to explain the solar system because he drags it in."

The judge cited the complexities of the law to explain his reasoning. "It is competent as bearing on the credibility of the witness. You can ask a witness if on such-and-such a date he committed murder, and if he says yes that bears on his credibility. Or you can ask a witness regarding facts which would lead the jury to infer that on such-and-such a date he committed murder, and if they do infer it, it bears on his credibility. Of course, if he denies it they are bound by his answers."

Bowers disagreed. "What I intended to bring to the attention of the jury was that the correspondence and the McCarthy contract and his visits to state officials all show a situation which justifies the jury in forming a conclusion that it does tend to affect his character and his credibility." He was effectively making the "duck" argument.

Judge Andrews offered him some latitude to proceed, but Bowers explained he was almost done with this subject; then added wryly, "I knew I was bound by his answers and I only intended to ask questions where the answer could only be one way."

Bowers continued, producing a transcript of Barnes's testimony before a legislative committee in 1911. "Question," he read from the document. "Are you aware, Mr. Barnes, of this transfer by McCarthy to the Lyon company? Answer: No, I was not. Do you remember so testifying?"

Ivins objected strongly, complaining, "He can't contradict his own witness."

Bowers objected to the objection. "As cross-examination."

The judge sustained the objection, reminding Bowers that he would permit him to go forward if he intended to prove the plaintiff had committed some crime or been guilty of a moral lapse, which would raise a question about his integrity. Bowers admitted, in a wonderfully honest description of the legal process, "I am not going to claim what I may fail to prove."

Which proved a good place to end the day.

While it had appeared throughout the trial that the Colonel had won the affection of the women of Syracuse, Barnes also had his admirers. One of them penned a little ditty that appeared in the next morning's *Journal*:

Three cheers for Mr. Ivins who the libel suit enlivens, When a witness testiphones or telephies;

The Colonel cannot beat him, Mr Bowers can't defeat him; when he has that saucy twinkle in his eyes;

There's nothing quite so charming, so seraphic or disarming, as the smile that lights the face of William Barnes;

As he gazes on each juror, it occasions quite a furor—and reverses the effect of Teddy's yarns!

When the morning session began on May 16, Bowers leaped back into the fray with his first question, wondering if the $11,000 interest Barnes had mentioned was finally paid.

Ivins objected immediately, and the session was back in full swing.

Bowers admitted he was perplexed, that he did not know if he could show a criminal act or moral turpitude. But he still managed to throw an unexpected roundhouse at the plaintiff. "Assuming I get what I believe to be the truth then I do know what I am going to show, and it will involve one or the other." It was a wonderfully no-lose argument: if he failed to show Barnes's guilt, it must be because Barnes is lying. To make certain that was understood, he added, "I believe that when the full truth is received that there will be matter obtained from the lips of this witness which will justify the jury in considering it upon the question of credibility."

The two principals jabbed back and forth over

what printing testimony was excluded, what would be allowed in and how it might be considered. "I have felt that we ought to, before this case is summed up," Bowers said, "have determined exactly what is out and what was in. But it seems impossible to do it."

He then tried to pin down the witness about when the $11,000 was paid. Barnes admitted nothing; he wouldn't even confirm that it was exactly $11,000 and couldn't remember precisely when it was paid. When shown competing bids for contracts, he testified he hadn't seen pertinent documents.

In his usual calm, conversational and curious tone, Bowers then asked when the witness had met with New York State attorney general John C. Davies. It was during the bidding for the printing contract, he was reminded. "You saw him as you stated in your letter daily?"

Barnes dismissed that thought. "Oh no, I didn't see him daily."

The attorney then quoted a letter the plaintiff had written to Senator Platt, highlighting the portion that read, "'I was in almost daily conference with Mr. Davies, and tried several times to meet Colonel Morgan but failed.'… I thought you said you didn't see him daily?"

Barnes's own confidence wavered as his words were turned around on him. He looked for a safe exit. "I can't testify whether I saw a man daily seventeen years ago."

"But you wrote the letter?"

"'Almost daily.' It may mean whatever it may mean. I can't define."

Bowers cited a somewhat obscure point of law, a small reminder of the extraordinary breadth of experience and expertise the litigators brought to the courtroom. "It is a rule of evidence that where a record is made in the usual course of business, in a letter or in an entry of any kind, and the witness has entirely forgotten it, and he says he has made a truthful entry, it is accepted as evidence."

Bowers had taken control of the spotlight and placed himself in it. By catching the plaintiff over and over in these contradictions, he was painting a powerful picture for jurors. After all, if Barnes was not telling the truth about minor items, how could he be trusted to be honest about meaningful facts?

Bowers moved on to the regular meetings with the attorney general, which Barnes claimed were to try to convince him to award the contract to the Lyon company. Yet why would he need to be lobbying the attorney general on behalf of the Lyon company, when their bid was nearly $100,000 more than McCarthy's, Bowers asked. "I was very much surprised to see those figures," Barnes admitted.

What happened next was once again like trying to pin down mercury. "After (McCarthy won the contract) it was then he came to you and asked if you would buy it?"

"Yes, sir?"

The Colonel was leaning forward now, his eyes locked on the witness, who answered each question without hesitation.

"Didn't he go to Lyon?"

"That I don't know; he might have."

"Didn't he agree upon a price with Lyon?"

"He might have."

"Don't you know that he did?"

"Well, I didn't know it."

After bringing out several more murky details about the contract, Bowers read from a letter written by Barnes to Senator Platt, in which he said, "I have no quarrel with Mr. Dady (the practical owner of the McCarthy bid) and I am willing to take his contract at the price agreed upon between Mr. McCarthy and James B. Lyon." After Barnes acknowledged that he did remember that, he was asked, "Then there was a price agreed upon at the time that letter was written between McCarthy and Lyon?"

The witness said reluctantly, "There must have been from my letter, but I have no knowledge of it."

"Did you buy at the price agreed upon between them?"

His answer, after all this, arguably was the worst of all responses. "I don't remember."

Bowers was making significant progress in his effort to show that the $20,000 was just a payoff from Lyon to Barnes, rather than a negotiated deal between Barnes and McCarthy that Lyon then acquired. Instead, it was looking more like Barnes had helped ensure that McCarthy got a sweetheart deal so that he could then sell it to Lyon at below market rates.

And from there, it proceeded to get worse for Barnes. He claimed there was no price agreed upon. "The letter does not state there was a price agreed upon."

But Bowers read the pertinent portion: "I…

am willing to take his contract at the price agreed upon," and asked, "That is a distinct statement that there has been a price agreed upon between those two men, doesn't it?"

"Yes," the witness agreed, "but it does not mean that there was any agreement between them."

The increasingly incredulous Bowers asked for a clarification. "It means a price had been agreed upon between them?"

"Certainly not, to my mind."

Attempting to highlight the confusion, Bowers asked later, "Now then, did you buy at that (agreed to) price or at a different price?"

Barnes was reduced to this: "I don't know anything."

Bowers remained curious about that additional $11,000 that was referred to as "interest," and asked for additional details. The witness explained, "I had an agreement that a certain portion of the profits of the contract…my recollection is that this was an understanding between Mr. Lyon and myself."

As this cross-examination headed to a conclusion, it came down to the core of the Colonel's claim: the money. "You appreciated that when you signed that paper you had done nothing to justify your claim to a salary from Mr. Lyon?" asked Bowers.

"Certainly."

"Did you perform any services for Mr. Lyon during the years 1899 and 1900 or 1901?"

"Not to my recollection."

The point was made: Barnes had been paid $31,000 for what appeared to be no effort beyond utilizing his political connections to obtain a large contract for James Lyon. There was more; Barnes had written to Platt that McCarthy, "the bidder of record," was an enemy of the Republican Party and had often assailed Senator Platt, and yet, wondered Bowers aloud, he "of his accord" came to Barnes to sell the contract he had bid hard for?

It seemed odd; this was the first bid Barnes had ever purchased. It was done without a written agreement—and eventually, in addition to payment, Barnes "became the owner of 750 shares of the stock of the J.B. Lyon Company."

Ivins was furious that the judge was allowing such leeway to the defense. Whether it would end up in or out of the record, the jurors were present for all of this testimony concerning the printing business and undoubtedly it would figure in their deliberations. Ivins appealed to the judge that Bowers had made one statement about his intention a day earlier and then the exact opposite this morning, then threw his hands in the air and said, "He may state something else tomorrow morning."

Bowers agreed, "Very likely."

Judge Andrews explained his duty. "I have to rule on the statements that are made when the evidence is offered."

Those 750 shares, apparently given to Barnes for no identifiable reason, loomed large. "The purpose of it," Barnes protested, "was that Mr. Lyon and I would carry on this printing business. The stock was valueless. There was no consideration whatsoever for the stock…

"…It was given to me because I wished to be associated with the Lyon company in the business, not to be in any way connected with any possible State printing contract, with which I was not thoroughly known and understood to be connected." The smiles that had been so much in evidence were gone now.

The trial had boomeranged on Barnes: his reputation had been attacked by Roosevelt and he had sued him for it, yet the Colonel could only win this trial by further destroying Barnes's reputation. Bowers might not be chopping it down with one swing, but he was certainly chipping away at it. Barnes had been on the defensive all morning; now it was time for him to stand his ground, time to show that he had done nothing wrong. With rising indignation, he told how those shares of Lyon's company had been earned: "I had bought the McCarthy contract in 1899 because Mr. McCarthy offered it to me and it was a bargain to make the purchase and I bought it. I received my pay for it from Mr. Lyon. In 1901 I was in a position either to go on and bid for the Journal for the work or for me to bid for the work as I had a perfect right to do, as the Journal had a right to do. I talked the situation over with Mr. Lyon and we decided the best thing for me to do was have an interest in the Lyon Company, which I did and for which I had no consideration whatever. I had no further interest in the company."

What had previously been established, but was left unsaid at this time, was that after this Barnes had helped build up the company whose once-valueless shares were sold back to J. B. Lyon for a profit of nearly $60,000. It would not have been difficult for jurors to make the desired connections: William Barnes had acquired for himself at absolutely no cost partial ownership of the J. B. Lyon Company. He had used his political influence to secure state and local printing contracts, for which he was well paid when he sold this stock.

The tension between the two principal attorneys that had been leaking out as wit and sarcasm for several weeks finally exploded into bitter accusations as Bowers attempted to put into evidence information contained in a letter, then suggested if he was not permitted to do that he would elicit that information in another form of questioning. "Is there any denial of my statement," he asked the court, "that the other form has been allowed in this trial?"

"You, decidedly," Ivins snapped. "I should be very much ashamed of myself if I had done what you are doing."

"I am afraid you do not know what shame is," the courtly Bowers responded.

This type of exchange between men of such stature was highly unusual but apparently Ivins did not take these clashes to heart. Often after making a biting remark to his opponent, he would slyly turn and smile toward the gallery, making it clear he remained unperturbed by the rancor. This courtroom charm won him admirers of his own. Several women from the audience even surrounded him during a break and commented on how much they enjoyed his smile. "What's the use of getting sour?" he responded.

Rather than responding to Ivins, Bowers turned to the bench. "Of course I will do whatever your honor says."

"I think he may answer," Judge Andrews decided. Whether or not the men of the jury understood the intricacies of the legal matter, it was clear to them that Bowers's point of view was upheld.

Then Bowers, in a magnanimous gesture, announced, "I will put another question."

In rapid-fire fashion he took his witness through a range of subjects, asking only a few questions, then pursuing a different line. He elicited testimony that Barnes's Journal Company had been designated by both the state and the county to publish so-called "session laws." The company had printed them once but been paid by both the state and county—leading the state to sue and recover more than $12,000. He showed that Barnes had set up an annual "honorarium" for his father with the Mutual Life Insurance Company. He produced materials that demonstrated the plaintiff's skill at soliciting funds for the Republican Party: William Rockefeller donated $10,000. Henry Flagler, $10,000. Oliver Payne, $20,000. Mary Harriman, $10,000. He asked the witness if he had read the article in *Collier's Weekly* that had included similar allegations to the ones made by Roosevelt. After Mr. Barnes acknowledged he had done so asked, of course knowing the answer, "Did you ever bring an action against that paper?"

Ivins interrupted, "He has a right to choose his game!"

Bowers agreed, then moved on to his next subject matter, promising to return to this later. And finally, at precisely noon, after the witness admitted that banker Robert C. Pruyn had contributed substantial sums on a regular basis to the Republican Party, Bowers smiled and said, "That is all."

When Barnes stepped down, his attorneys immediately set out to repair the damage. They began, once again, having those people accused indirectly by Roosevelt of voting as directed by "boss" Barnes, proclaim that never happened. Five more legislators took the stand and testified they never spoke with Barnes "in reference to the election of a United States Senator."

Then the plaintiff was recalled by his lawyers for redirect examination. And this time, as Winston Churchill had written in *My African Journal* only a few years earlier, "the boot (was) on the other leg." Now it was Bowers objecting regularly. Asked why he had supported a plan to unite with Independent Democrats to elect a senator, Barnes explained that he urged Republicans "to join hands with those Democrats who had asserted their independence of Tammany Hall."

He told his story with renewed energy. Bowers had worn him down but once again he had regained his footing.

He was firm that he had never, never once, advised any Republican to stay away from a legislative session to make it possible for Democrats to elect the machine choice.

Ivins attempted to clean up the unexpected testimony of Mayhew Wainwright, who had told jurors that Barnes had talked about an agreement with the Democrats not to interfere in senatorial selection process. Bowers objected, protesting, "They called that witness; they accredited that witness and they cannot contradict him."

"You cannot contradict your own witness," the judge agreed, "but you can contradict a witness by calling for independent evidence."

Barnes said he "did not recall" making that statement, and moreover he did not make any such arrangement with the Democrats, and anything and everything he did during this senatorial contest he "deemed to be in the best interests of the Republican party," while doing nothing at all to assist the Democrats. He went even further, denying that he ever had any conversation with "boss" Murphy or any representative of the Democratic organization about this matter.

When asked about an editorial published in his newspaper criticizing Thomas Mott Osborne, the Democratic reformer he later supported, he responded that at that time he was not a member of the Republican state committee, and "There was a good deal of satire and humor in the article." He only came to support Osborne because he believed it would "cause a breach in the Democratic party."

And so it continued for almost three more hours: The plaintiff defended his statement that a man who runs under the party banner owes allegiance to the expressed will of that party. He claimed he never discussed the racetrack bill with Democratic leaders, nor did he urge Republicans how to vote on it; in fact, he said, he told Senator Grattan—before he changed his vote—"Whatever you may do, of course this action rests entirely upon you. You take whatever course you desire." He explained that he had read the offending article in its entirety when it appeared in print but had not reread it in the complaint. When asked if he ever had "any conversation with anybody in your entire life in which you promised any person contributing to the campaign fund protection in legislative matters?" Barnes responded that he had not.

He finished with a passionate defense of his father, who had been the first superintendent of insurance in New York State and whose lifetime service to that industry had earned him that honor. That done, he stepped down and the defense asked the Colonel's secretary, William Loeb, to return to the stand.

At issue was precisely when Loeb had met the plaintiff; he had claimed that luncheon occurred in 1911, but the plaintiff and two of his witnesses had sworn that was not accurate, that the meeting had taken place considerably later. Van Benschoten asked Loeb if Wollman's testimony that this meeting took place in late 1912 was correct. "It is not," Loeb said flatly. "I met him in February 1911 in the office of J. S. Bache and company."

Loeb testified that he had enjoyed several luncheons there to discuss a position he had been offered as president of the International Banking Corporation. That caused Ivins to object derisively, "We do not think the defense wants to go on lunching forever."

Skirting numerous objections, Van Benschoten set out to prove his point in a different manner. The witness had turned down the job offered at that meeting and instead had joined Guggenheim and Sons in January 1913. Thereafter he had visited Bache to discuss possible investments, including copper in Chile and mining shares in China.

Adams handled the cross-examination. Each attorney has his own preferred way of questioning a witness, and several different times Adams appeared to resort to a slight bit of trickery; for example, while supposedly trying to pin down the date he asked, "Will you fix the date that you met Mr. Barnes and Mr. Towsley together?"

"I do not ever remember having met them together."

Or, "Do you recall that you met (Mr. Gleason) on the corner of 35th street and 5th Avenue and inquired about his trip to Europe?"

"No. I met Mr. Gleason on 5th Avenue last year (1914) and exchanged a few words of greeting."

Adams asked Loeb, seemingly with a yet-to-be-revealed purpose, "Do you positively swear that you did not meet him about the 18th of May, 1911?"

Loeb had no difficulty doing so. "I positively swear I did not see Mr. Gleason for four years before last year."

"You will swear that he didn't send a letter from Paris to you in 1911?"

Adams was asking the impossible. "I won't swear that he didn't send a letter to me, but I never received a letter."

But the lawyer persisted, asking again, "When you met Mr. Gleason, assuming rather you did meet him on 5th Avenue in May 1911, did you make any inquiries about Mr. Barnes?"

Objected to and sustained. Adams came at it again and finally found a way to slip it through. And with his own disdain Loeb told him flatly, "I see no earthly reason why I should inquire of Mr. Gleason about Mr. Barnes."

Adams continued trying to attribute words to Loeb, but the witness deflected those attempts.

Former United States senator Simon Guggenheim, a principal of the firm Guggenheim and Sons, then raised his right hand, took the oath and confirmed everything Loeb had said. "Mr. Loeb became connected with M. Guggenheim and Sons in February 1913… He was in the office during the month of January."

No one had to point out to the jury that it was highly unlikely he was continuing to discuss the bank presidency with Bache at the same time. When that point was finally settled, the defense recalled Theodore Roosevelt. The courtroom suddenly came alive, the *Times* reported, and "The Colonel was in the witness chair in a twinkling."

Teddy Roosevelt was back in the spotlight.

CHAPTER SIXTEEN

This was to be the final confrontation and Teddy Roosevelt seemed primed for it. He took the witness chair with a nod to Judge Andrews and immediately seemed ready to pounce. Thus began what the *Post-Standard* described as "One hour of the most violent testimony in Part 1 of the Supreme Court in Onondaga County ever heard."

It was Van Benschoten's task to correct the record where his client might be vulnerable and prepare him for the onslaught that was sure to come. They started with the testimony of John Hutchinson, who had testified that during a 1914 meeting he asked the Colonel to come back into the Republican Party and Roosevelt had told him that he was the only person who "could get after" President Wilson and tear his foreign policy "to pieces." But he could not rejoin the party, he supposedly had said, as it was not big enough for both him and Barnes. If

Hutchinson's claim was true, that statement seemed to show that malice existed between the two men.

But Roosevelt's version of that meeting was quite different; and once let free to explain it there was no holding him back. Hutchinson, he recalled, "said to me in substance that in my Pittsburgh speech and in what I said about the Panama treaty I had handled the administration as no Republican seemed to be able to handle it, and I said I thought so too." At that, the Colonel could not prevent himself from breaking into an amused chuckle, once more grinning at the jury. Judge Andrews quieted him and he continued.

"Then he asked me why I could not get back and support the Republican party that fall. I told him I was anxious to support the Republican candidate for governor, provided they would put up a governor who we could be sure would war on Republican crookedness just as much as upon Democratic crookedness, but that it was idle to ask me and men like me to come back to the Republican party while it was dominated by and its principles given it by men of the stamp of Mr. Barrrrrnnnnnes."

He drew out his adversary's name to such length that the courtroom was convulsed with laughter. Judge Andrews had to pound down hard with his gavel and warned the gallery that he would clear them out if there was any further commotion.

Again, Roosevelt grinned with delight, those famous gritted teeth very much in evidence as he savored every moment of this. He remained perched on the very edge of his chair, and across the way both Ivins and Barnes also were leaning forward on their table to hear every word. "The face of Mr. Barnes reflected every emotion within him," wrote the *Post-Standard*, "for a moment William L. Barnes dropped a smug smile to which he had listened to all the proceedings."

When quiet was restored, Van Benschoten asked, "Did you in that interview at any time use the phrase that the Republican party was not big enough for you and Barnes?"

"I did not," Roosevelt practically shouted, slamming his fist down hard on the arm of his chair. The Colonel was back in the saddle.

The plaintiff's attorneys tried every tactic to disrupt him. When he was asked about his conversation with Loeb, for example, Ivins complained, "He has stated it already."

Wolff, also representing the plaintiff, chimed in, "It is the same conversation."

Ivins added, "It will be a different version of the same conversation."

The Colonel explained that while he had already testified about the conversation, "It was not until Barnes got on the stand that he himself refreshed my memory…"

Given permission by the court to tell his story, Roosevelt began and…

…was interrupted by Wolff asserting that this was the same story he had told before.

He pressed on. "Mr. Barnes stated that if we alienated big business men we would go down into defeat, and he instanced what happened in Albany County the preceding fall as a case in point…"

ONONDAGA HISTORICAL ASSOCIATION

As local celebrities like Syracuse University chancellor Day squeezed into the courtroom, revealing letters Roosevelt had written years earlier were entered into evidence. Set against the noble trappings of justice, the trial had become a bitter personal fight between political enemies. Whoever wins, the Herald *reported, "Roosevelt is buoyantly confident that he has wrecked Barnes' chance of ever going to the United States Senate and Barnes, likewise is buoyantly confident that TR will never again rise to prominence."*

And Wolff objected again. "That is precisely what he testified to already."

Judge Andrews told the Colonel, "You never stated that particular sentence, but what troubles me is whether he has already given this conversation."

"He has," Ivins said firmly.

Nevertheless, Roosevelt continued, "He stated that the year before, when I was running that Mr. Brady had flooded the county with his money and had beaten us; that he was very sorry but it could not be helped, and he said ordinarily Messer's Brady and Pruyn had been his—he may have said our supporters instead of his supporters—had been the supporters of our side and heavy contributors..."

After an objection, the Colonel cleverly said what he was not supposed to say: "Then you don't wish me to repeat what I have already said about expressing surprise?"

After additional chatter between the sides and the court he was told to continue, and so he did, recounting a damning conversation: "(Barnes) said in substance that the big business men had to contribute to the conservative side that would take care of their interests, and that they contributed to the Democrats or the Republicans indifferently, to the organization, because there had to be this connection between the party organization and big business of mutual helpfulness properly from the standpoint of protecting big business from the demagogue and the scoundrel."

As he spoke, his entire being seemed infused with anger at that thought; he turned to the jury and practically vaulted out of the witness chair, his arms flailing as he spoke of this corrupt relationship between the political parties and business interests—with the interests of the people being ignored.

Ivins was up too, objecting again. This time Judge Andrews was troubled, as well. "He has testified to that," he agreed, then ordered the reference to demagogues and scoundrels stricken from the record.

The Colonel acknowledged sheepishly that he had already made that point, admitting, "So I did."

Ivins did not appreciate his amusement. "I do not want to be put in the position where I have got to ask this very eminent witness precisely what is new in this testimony as distinguished from what is old," but then he did exactly that. After a discussion about new and old, about complete and incomplete and forgetting and remembering, Ivins reached back into his own distinguished past, recalling, "One of the earliest cases which it was my fortune—while my colleague was still a very young man—to take part in was the Beecher trial; and I recollect very well the decision that was made there, and I have a memorandum from the decision in that case, that whatever evidence is offered or omitted in the original case could not be given in reply; that the only evidence that can be given in reply is that which cuts down the case on the part of the defendant."

This was a matter of law and few men knew more about that than Ivins. "It is corroboration of their own witness," he explained, "and it is corroboration of their own witness under such circumstances that it is not receivable in rebuttal at this time…

"They have introduced certain testimony from Mr. Loeb which does not conform at all to the recollection of the matter as given by Mr. Roosevelt. I do not mean to say for a moment that I impugn the integrity of the defendant's recollection, but the testimony is entirely different." Nevertheless, Van Benschoten was eventually given leave to question Roosevelt about his conversations with Barnes, and asked him about the discussion he had with the plaintiff about the racetrack bill.

That was not what Roosevelt wanted to talk

about. "I want to talk first about the evidence as to the dinner when Mr. Platt was there." The whole room erupted in laughter at the witness's audacity, and again Judge Andrews gaveled the gallery into silence, said firmly, "That goes out!" and warned against such outbursts.

But that would prove difficult. The Great Roosevelt was on full display, the adventurous, sometimes reckless, always headstrong and extremely confident man who already had secured his place in both real history and legendary tales. Now he was barging his way through the laws, and no one seemed able to stop him. "He swept the lawyers and spectators off their feet," the *Times* reported, "and even Judge Andrews was powerless at times to stem the tide of his pent-up energy. The jurors smiled with the Colonel as if they welcomed an old friend."

Van Benschoten acceded to the Colonel's request, asking him if he remembered that dinner, then letting him loose. Judge Andrews's memory was short, and he asked Ivins, "You asked him about this dinner?"

"I did... And if the witness has refreshed his recollection and is prepared to swear that on this particular occasion there was another conversation, the only question that remains is should he swear to it at this time, or whether he should be confined to his original testimony?

"If your honor rules that it is proper for them to reopen the case...then of course I acquiesce in the propriety of the latter course."

This conciliatory, albeit somewhat sarcastic response surprised the judge, who wanted to strip away the sarcasm about "reopening" the case and get to the issue at hand: "Acquiesce unwillingly?"

"No," Ivins protested again somewhat facetiously, "I acquiesce willingly, because I am entirely willing that Colonel Roosevelt should say everything that he can say and wants to say that is within the rules of law, curbed by the customs of the courts."

Judge Andrews now seemed truly incredulous. "Do you mean that you don't object to it?"

"I mean just a minute ago when he reached over and said..."

"Do you object to the conversation or don't you object to it?"

"I object to the conversation on the grounds..."

That's what Judge Andrews had been waiting to hear. He banged his gavel and said, "I don't think it is competent! I think the witness should have given that on direct testimony."

Van Benschoten retorted, "You were pretty kind to our friends on the other side in their re-direct of Mr. Barnes, but we will pass it." He moved his witness along, asking him if "you recollect that (Barnes) testified that you said the racetrack legislation should be defeated?"

Roosevelt looked directly at Barnes, his face clenched with anger as he replied, pronouncing each word distinctly, "It. Is. Utterly. False."

There ensued another lengthy discussion over whether the Colonel was permitted to respond to Barnes's claim that Roosevelt had "cast some reflections" on former governor Woodruff—who had died two years earlier—during their discussion of the racetrack bill. Ivins made the legal argument that the witness had given direct testimony "to what we were justified in believing was the entire communication as he understood it. Barnes then testified to what occurred as he understood it. He said that Mr. Roosevelt had made certain remarks about Mr. Woodruff which he regarded as unimportant and therefore did not repeat." It seemed improper to the lawyer that they "bring in a conversation between this man and a dead man."

Why this testimony was so bitterly contested was revealed moments later, when Roosevelt was permitted to offer his version of that meeting. "Mr. Barnes asked me why I did not go to Governor Woodruff...and I said that Governor Woodruff was not the man that had the power...that Mr. Barnes did and I would go to him, and so I went to Mr. Barnes."

Van Benschoten then brought up a conversation between the witness and Barnes that had taken place at his home at Oyster Bay during which the renomination of Governor Hughes was discussed. Barnes had testified that Roosevelt had said to him, "Of course you will continue your opposition to Governor Hughes?"

The Colonel literally shouted his answer, which reverberated through the courtroom. "I did not say it! I said to Mr. Barnes, 'I suppose you will oppose Mr. Hughes to the end, but I have hopes for the others!'"

Then there were questions about another meeting with Barnes, this one at the Manhattan Hotel in 1910 to discuss the Colonel's support of Governor Hughes's direct primary bill, as well as his personal ambitions in the forthcoming presidential election. Roosevelt's obvious intent was to provide evidence of Barnes's control over the Republican machine. In extremely animated fashion, as if relating a grand story to a group of friends, he revealed, "Mr. Barnes said in substance that he and the organization…felt more kindly toward me than toward Mr. Taft…

"Mr. Taft had tried to double-cross them. And he also said that he had warned me before that Mr. Hughes' supporters were my enemies…and that it was against my own interests to take the course that I was taking and allying myself with the followers of Hughes… But that he and the organization were unalterably hostile to the principles I had enumerated…and they would not support me if I continued to stand for those principles and for the primary legislation and would be hostile to me."

This was a juicy morsel of political gossip. After all, Roosevelt had fought long and hard to win the 1912 Republican nomination, and if Barnes and the Republican Party had not opposed him so vigorously, he likely would have become president again. The packed courtroom was at attention. Then as if he were speaking on the hustings, he continued, "I answered…that I was not concerned with the interest either of myself or of Mr. Taft in that matter; that I regarded the points at issue as being of far greater consequence than the welfare of either Mr. Taft or myself; that I was supporting Mr. Hughes' primary legislation as a matter of principle, because I believed in it, and that in (the speeches) I had made in the West that all I had been doing was trying to apply the principles of Abraham Lincoln to the conditions of our own country, and that I could not abandon that fight.

"Mr. Barnes said, 'All right, then the fight would have to go on.'"

With that, Van Benschoten handed over his witness to William Ivins one last time. Here it was then, the final confrontation between these two men. There was not a sound to be heard in the courtroom as Ivins stood, an amused smile on his face. The Colonel turned slightly in his chair to look at him directly.

Ivins picked up the echoes of the Colonel's impassioned defense of Lincoln Republicanism, wondering, "Did Mr. Barnes sit there quietly and listen to a long speech which you made and interpose no objections, and just finally end by saying, 'Very well, then we part?'"

Roosevelt began, "In the…"

Ivins cut him off sharply, his voice a little louder this time. "You have just testified to a long conversation, which I would designate a monologue. I want to know whether it was a dialogue."

The witness could be equally sarcastic; glaring at Ivins, he replied, "Now, do you want me to correct your understanding of it?"

"No," Ivins said dismissively, his point made to the jury, "I understand it."

"You do not!" Roosevelt practically screamed, thrusting out his jaw. These were actions of a man who did not appreciate his word being questioned. "I testified that it was a dialogue. I gave the statements of Mr. Barnes and my answers to them. The way I think it came was in a long statement by Mr. Barnes, and then quite a long statement from me." And then he added, "It may have been occasionally broken up by interruptions."

Ivins did not take his bait. "As a matter of fact that is not the way you gave it."

At the defense table Bowers sat easily, knowing Roosevelt neither desired nor needed any help he might offer with an objection. Instead, he let them go at each other.

"I am giving it to you in substance."

"What you mean now," the lawyer suggested, "is that as a matter of fact in what you just gave you gave the substance of the conversation?"

Substance versus direct quotation? The Colonel recognized the potential trap. "You can test it by reading it."

"Can you tell me now, recalling what you have just testified to, how many times you referred to Mr. Barnes as having broken into your conversation and made a remark?"

The Colonel was taken aback by the question. "How many times I referred…"

Ivins asked directly, "How many times you introduced him into what you call a dialogue?"

Roosevelt considered that, then responded, "My memory is that I gave Mr. Barnes' statement first, and then my own statement. If you have any doubts about my memory being accurate let the stenographer read it."

Ivins looked straight at Roosevelt and said, clearly, sharply, "I have very grave doubts of it."

"Then let it be read," Roosevelt challenged him.

Ivins kept his smile locked in place. "But my doubt is not a matter for consideration or discussion."

"Then why ask me about it?"

And then, in a few words, Ivins summed up the weeks of testimony. "Because I want your doubt."

And that was not within the realm of possibility for the Colonel. In Theodore Roosevelt's entire career, he had never been a man held back by doubt. "I have none," he said, flatly and forever. "I have no doubt."

Ivins had got what he wanted, and asked softly, "You have no doubt?"

"None."

Ivins let those words settle, then told Judge Andrews he had no further questions and turned his back on the witness.

Van Benschoten had only one question for the former president of the United States. "It occurred in precisely the way you have stated?"

"In substance," Teddy Roosevelt agreed. "As I particularly said: In substance the way I have stated."

Every attorney strives to leave the jury with a

final, positive impression. In this instance, Adams for the plaintiff asked the court's permission to call Lafayette Blanchard Gleason, the secretary of the New York State Republican Committee. Gleason was the mystery witness that Ivins had promised earlier to reporters. His purpose was to buttress the plaintiff's case by calling into question Loeb's testimony, about a 1911 meeting with Barnes where he talked of an "arrangement" with the Democrats. The groundwork had been laid on cross examination of Loeb when he was asked about an encounter with Gleason on 5th Avenue. Plaintiff's attorney Adams had indicated it occurred in 1911 but Loeb insisted it was in 1914. "Do you remember meeting Mr. Loeb on 5th Avenue in 1911," Adams asked.

"In 1911," Gleason agreed, "I met him."

The date of this meeting was important because Gleason then testified that Loeb had told him "in substance" that he had not seen Barnes recently. If true, that would tend to belie Loeb's claim of a meeting with Barnes earlier that year. But when asked what day that was he admitted, "I can't recollect the exact day."

Adams persisted, "Did he say to you that he hoped he would make a great chairman, if he would be conciliatory?"

"Not exactly that," Gleason replied.

Judge Andrews stopped this, ruling, "This does not contradict Mr. Loeb in any way. The only thing to contradict him is this first sentence which you have given."

Bowers asked the man a few perfunctory questions, establishing that he had spent his entire career filling appointed offices in the Republican Party, making the point that he owed his career to the Republican machine. As for his qualifications, he was a lawyer, but before getting his political position as a twenty-six-or twenty-seven-year-old, he admitted, "I had been studying law in my father's office and attending Yale College, and occupied by the usual boyish pursuits before that."

Hardly the grand finale that the plaintiff desired. Without any corroboration the jury had no real way to determine when this casual encounter had taken place. It was little more than a he said-he said situation.

Both sides rested and court was adjourned.

Throughout the trial Judge Andrews had done as much as he could to give both sides a fair hearing. At times that had required allowing legally questionable testimony to be heard by the jury. Now the lawyers were going to make their legal case to limit that testimony, making motions to exclude certain evidence from the trial and forcing the judge to finally rule on its admissibility. Before these legal arguments began the jury was asked to retire. Henry Wolff, speaking for the plaintiff, started by challenging how much testimony about the printing industry the defendant's counsel should be able to discuss in its summation, asking in particular that Roosevelt's cross-examination on that topic be struck from the record.

"I think I will deny the motion," said the judge,

adding that he would, however, only allow it for limited purposes.

Next, Wolff asked for a directed verdict, a ruling that allows a trial judge to decide that the evidence presented is so clear that there is only one verdict a reasonable jury could reach. It means the case is so one-sided that under the law there is only one possible conclusion a reasonable trier of the facts could make based on the evidence. In those rare instances, the judge issues a verdict for that side and the case does not even go to the jury.

It is a common tactic that rarely succeeds, but if it had here, the jury would just be deciding what damages should be awarded. Wolff made a long, long argument to support his motion, citing the judge's original ruling that on its face, the comments were libelous, then claiming the defense had not proved directly, circumstantially or inferentially any of its claims contained in that article. "We respectfully refer your honor to the rule of law which provides that the justification must be as broad as the libel," he stated, pointing out, "In this libel there are points which have not even been touched upon…

"We hold that there is no evidence Mr. Barnes committed any act that could properly be called corrupt, even in the meaning of the word given it by your honor…and there was no evidence of an alliance between Barnes and Murphy." The lawyer touched on several different claims for which the defense had introduced no evidence that would support the attack made by the Colonel, then asked if those statements were true would Roosevelt "have associated with him, received him as a friend into his home and asked his advice and counsel?"

Wolff then reminded the court that his client's reputation, his very future, was at stake, that Roosevelt had "characterized Mr. Barnes as a man of the type that whenever the issue is drawn between corruption and popular rights, you will always find him fighting on the side of corruption," and "it is through his aiding and abetting that the present rottenness in the state is due." Harsh words that, he argued, would plague the plaintiff in all his future endeavors and result in irreparable damage.

His presentation was logical, complete and passionate, covering each of the three pillars holding up the defendant's case. First, he challenged Judge Andrews in his definition of *corrupt*, pleading, "We have contended here that the word 'corrupt' has a far deeper and graver and more sinister meaning than that which has evidently been given by your Honor..."

He asked for a broader definition, perhaps making his argument as much to public opinion as to the judge. To the plaintiff's counsel "It means that a person who has engaged in a corrupt enterprise must have secured to himself some personal advantage contrary to the public interest, whether it be in money or in power or otherwise."

The judge found that claim wanting, responding harshly, "In other words you would not say that a man who traitorously betrayed his party or his country simply because he had an evil mind and did not obtain any advantage by it is corrupt?"

Wolff persisted in his claim that the proper definition of *corrupt* in this trial requires that a person must receive some money or personal advantage contrary to the public interest.

He then moved on to another central claim made by Roosevelt, that the relationship between Barnes and Murphy was corrupt. "There is no evidence showing any evil motive or bad purpose, or purposes contrary to the public interest, such as would justify a jury in finding that such an arrangement, if it existed, was corrupt—even in the sense which your honor has used the word."

Finally he brought the court's attention to the charge that Barnes had created a corrupt alliance between crooked business and crooked politics, essentially calling him a crook. Wolff argued that the defense would have had to have proved that campaign contributions were made in return for political favors, that Barnes was aware of this, and that he was a party to the arrangement. Most of the evidence presented on this issue focused on the Franchise Tax Bill, which was enacted long before Barnes had risen to power in the party. "There is absolutely no such proof in this case" that would support that claim.

The Colonel sat with his lawyers at their table, leaning back and occasionally crossing his legs, or whispering to Bowers but expressing no emotion other than a general interest.

Judge Andrews appeared to take a keen interest in Wolff's presentation. Although it would be astonishing for him to intercede at this point to prevent the jury from weighing the case, he gave the argument careful consideration. In fact, based on the totality of the judge's rulings, this was hardly a frivolous motion. Judge Andrews asked incisive questions at several points and when he was uncertain, he pushed for a more specific explanation. There could be no doubt he was giving the plaintiff the opportunity to make his pitch.

Time and again Wolff came back to the proof, or the lack of it. There is no proof that Barnes had any power in state matters. There is no proof that he conspired with Murphy. There is no proof that he profited one cent beyond what he earned from his printing business. No proof that bore any responsibility for any transgressions of the party.

Wolff concluded with a flourish, arguing the Franchise Tax Bill was the only relevant, admissible evidence presented to even potentially justify the comments, and even then "It is not conceivably possible…that conditions existing fifteen years prior to the utterance of the libel constitutes any evidence upon which the jury would be justified in finding that the defendant has established the truth of the charge with respect to conditions in 1914, and there is no other proof in this case."

Despite his best efforts, the motion was denied. In his ruling, Judge Andrews repeated the same general rulings he had followed throughout the entire trial: the article was libelous in its entirety because it charged a corrupt alliance between Barnes and Murphy. The only subordinate charge for the jury to consider was whether the plaintiff worked through an alliance "between crooked business and crooked politics." In regard to that charge, the judge declared that while "the evidence is slight… I think this evidence should be submitted to the jury for what it is worth as bearing on the charge." And then he added, as if to remind the attorneys of the boundaries for the upcoming summations, "I shall restrict the jury's consideration of this article to the two charges which I have mentioned…" Summing up his ruling, Judge Andrews made plain the challenge ahead for the twelve jurors: "If the jury finds that this plaintiff, a public officer has been damaged in his career and his character, it is to consider that the statement was made in the heat of a political campaign; but if it finds that the libel was not justified, it will be instructed to assess punitive damages."

With that, it was time for the sides to present their closing arguments, to knit together all of the arguments and all of the evidence into a convincing yarn. Teddy Roosevelt would not personally take center stage for this, but he would still play the starring role. This was all about him. The case was brought because of his words, and the weight that they carried with the American public remained sufficient to make or break a man's future. Had a lesser man published that same article, it was unlikely it would have sparked more than a stern rebuke, rather than this sensational trial.

But the Colonel had said it, and when given a chance to apologize or at least modify those comments, he had instead doubled down and repeated them. So the crux of both Bowers's and Ivins's closing arguments would be focused squarely on Roosevelt. They would be artists painting his portrait, using the same medium to create two very different likenesses. But while the lawyers were speaking, it would be the Colonel who held the spectators' attention, and it was him they would be watching for some hint of a reaction.

And should his representatives fail to convince these "12 good men and true" that the words published by their client were truthful, it would be the Colonel who would pay a great price, both in dollars and prestige.

Should the jury find for the plaintiff, it would then have to answer a most difficult question: What is the value of a man's reputation? What damage had the plaintiff suffered due to Roosevelt's words? And would a verdict in his behalf be sufficient to restore honor? There was no sense of which way the jury was leaning on these questions.

Both Bowers and his esteemed counterpart, Ivins, had spent long days preparing to make this appeal to the jury. And finally the time had arrived to draw this journey to a close.

CHAPTER SEVENTEEN

Prior to 1166, when Britain's King Henry II introduced the concept of trial by a jury of neighbors, most disputes, but especially those concerning land ownership, were settled by combat. Those "trials" took place at sunrise on staked-out ground sixty-feet square, witnessed by the judges of the court in their scarlet robes. The two parties in the dispute, and their advocates or *champions* as they were known, each swore to their claim, then took an oath against sorcery and enchantment, repeating: "Hear this, ye justices, that I have this day neither eaten nor drunk, nor have upon me any bone, stone or grass, nor any enchantment, sorcery or witchcraft, whereby the law of God may be abased, or the law of the devil exalted, so help me God and his saints."

The two combatants fought until one of them yielded or was killed or until the stars appeared in the night sky. If the battle ended in a draw, the defendant was awarded the disputed property, as he already possessed it.

The battle between Theodore Roosevelt and William Barnes had lasted far longer, and certainly was more civilized, but both sides had struck telling blows. Finally it was time for their champions, Bowers and Ivins, to make their closing arguments, armed with meticulously planned and practiced words along with a dollop of engaging wit.

Coming at the end of a trial, summations are a much-anticipated opportunity for the competing advocates to talk directly to the members of the jury. Not through witnesses, or their own questions, or the judge's rulings, but to look them straight in the eyes and try to persuade them that only one position is just and right. After days or even weeks of testimony and evidence, a case might be won or lost by the quality of this presentation. For the lawyers, it's the chance to bring together everything that has taken place in the courtroom, to emphasize the strength of the totality of their case and the weaknesses of their opponent's, and most of all to lead the jury to rule in their favor.

It's a time for them to talk freely and often at substantial length, mostly unburdened by legal restrictions. Obviously, there are some limits: the lawyers must focus only on evidence admitted, avoid personally vouching for the credibility of witnesses and shy away from irrelevant personal attacks. But generally, they are quite free to appeal to the jurors' intellects or emotions in a sometimes shameless attempt to win their vote.

A closing argument is theater and everything about it matters; from the shine on a lawyer's shoes to the tone of his voice. All part of an effort to make a personal connection with each member of the jury.

Some lawyers have earned their reputation based on their ability to sway a jury. It was written about Abraham Lincoln, for example, that when he stood up to make his argument he was "twenty-feet high" and "no longer was the homely and ungainly man that he was reputed to be; his eyes flashed fire, his appearance underwent a change as though an inspired mind had transformed the body…"

Bowers and Ivins had the benefit of studying what were accepted generally as among the finest closing arguments in American legal history. Like the great Clarence Darrow's closing argument in his 1907 defense of labor leader William "Big Bill" Haywood. Accused of hiring a hitman to assassinate the anti-union former governor of Idaho, the evidence against Haywood appeared overwhelming, and it seemed likely he would hang. That is, until Darrow made the case about a greater cause. "To kill him, gentlemen? I want to speak to you plainly. Mr. Haywood is not my greatest concern. Other men have died before him, other men have been martyrs to a holy cause since the world began. Wherever men have looked upward and onward, forgotten their selfishness, struggled for humanity, worked for the poor and the weak, they have been sacrificed. They have been sacrificed in the prison, on the scaffold, in the flame. They have met their death, and he can meet his if you twelve men say

ONONDAGA HISTORICAL ASSOCIATION

The concept of the aging Rough Rider standing defiantly against powerful politicians in defense of the common man had made this "the trial of the century." Practically every available inch of space in the courtroom was utilized to satisfy the national interest in the trial.

he must. Gentlemen, you short-sighted men of the prosecution, you men of the Mine Owners' Association, you people who would cure hatred with hate, you who think you can crush out the feelings and the hopes and the aspirations of men by tying a noose around his neck, you who are seeking to kill him not because it is Haywood but because he represents a class, don't be so blind, don't be so foolish as to believe you can strangle the Western Federation of Miners when you tie a rope around his neck..." This oft-quoted summation was credited with turning the case in Haywood's favor.

Expectations for these closings were lofty. Two of the finest attorneys in the nation would go head-to-head in one of the highest profile cases of the era. Even Judge Andrews's parents, along with his wife, who had been a regular visitor to the courtroom, were in attendance.

During the six weeks of this trial, neither side had established a clear path to victory. There was a serious legal argument to be made for each side. No one sitting in the rows of journalists was willing to make a firm prediction as to the outcome. The prevailing sentiment as Bowers rose confidently and began was that the jury would be unable to reach a unanimous decision, and both men would go home with enough to satisfy their supporters—but not nearly enough to satisfy either of the litigants.

Bowers acknowledged the court and the jury, then began by setting the stakes. "From time immemorial it has been the custom of the Anglo-Saxon people to settle the differences existing between litigants by the verdict of a jury. For the most part these decisions are rendered in cases affecting none but the individual parties to the suit. At times, however, public questions become involved and the jurors...by their verdict, determine the verdict of the nation. This case is of that character.

"It is undoubtedly the most important case in which I have ever taken a part, one of the most important on which a jury ever passed their judgment on the facts. This suit is not brought with reference to the pecuniary result to Mr. Barnes, but the defendant is selected as the game Mr. Ivins wanted, and the only purpose is to break him down before the people of the United States." While this personal attack on Ivins was of questionable propriety, Bowers was allowed to continue uninterrupted.

"It has been said by Mr. Barnes that I am a Democrat. I am. I did not vote for Mr. Roosevelt for Governor. I did not vote for Mr. Roosevelt for President in 1913. I did not vote for him when he ran for Mayor of New York. Indeed, on every one of those occasions I voted against him. Why am I here? It is because I desire to perform one act in my career at the Bar for the public benefit."

Bowers spoke in a carefully modulated tone, conveying the seriousness of his task. The courtroom was hushed. Colonel Roosevelt sat at the defense table, never taking his eyes from his champion. Barnes, at his table, looked somewhat distracted, his eyes wandering about the room.

"I have uniformly held in the highest respect men of good character who choose to enter the political arena and take part in the government of the country for our benefit… I can live and you can live under a Democratic President or a Republican President—provided the man is worthy of the place."

He then quoted his client's own words from an article entitled "The Man with the Muckrake," written several years earlier, about the worth of a man's reputation. "There are in the body politic, economic and social, many and grave evils, and there is urgent necessity for the sternest war upon them… I hail as a benefactor every writer or speaker, every man who on the platform or in a book, magazine or newspaper, with merciless severity makes such attacks—" he then raised his voice to make certain the point was made "—provided always that he remembers that the attack is only of use if it is absolutely truthful. The liar is no whit better than the thief, and if his mendacity takes the form of slander, he may be worse than most thieves. It puts a premium upon knavery untruthfully to attack an honest man, or even with hysterical exaggeration to assail a bad man with untruths. The effort to make financial or political profit out of the destruction of character can only result in public calamity. Gross and reckless assaults on character, create a morbid and vicious public sentiment, and at the same time act as a profound deterrent to able men of normal sensitiveness and tend to prevent them from entering the public service at any price."

Bowers explained that no man who had written those words would casually or without good reason make such an attack unless he "deemed it his duty."

"Our defense is that they are true… It is a wrongful thing to say something of a man which hurts his character if it is not true. It is a noble thing to do it, if it is true, and if the people of the State ought to know it."

Gradually he moved his argument to the facts of the trial, carefully referring to the printing evidence by reminding jurors he was not permitted to refer to it and did not intend to refer to it, which he had just done. The plaintiff, he said, "had a perfect right to take a stand against Governor Hughes, his racing legislation or any legislation…against the primary bills. But when he wrote urging the Governor not to recommend in his message the establishment of a State Printing House because it might end in his financial ruin he was trespassing upon the verge of propriety of his action."

Bowers reminded jurors that Barnes had received a salary from Lyon for "no consideration," plus the $11,000 interest and the double pay for publishing the session laws, then used all of it to question Barnes's integrity: "Remember that these acts, this payment of $20,000 salary, this transfer of 750 shares of the Lyon company stock took place in 1899, 1900, and 1901 when he was dickering with members of the state printing board and begging the Governor not to recommend a state printing office. Remember this gentlemen, you would be the judge as to whether that man's character is of immaculate purity." The jury might wonder, he continued, looking at each man in turn, "why this gift of (750 shares of stock) was made," and suggested it was done "because Mr. Lyon did not want the opposition of the plaintiff" in bidding for future contracts.

On the subject of character, Bowers then compared that of his client to the plaintiff. He began by quoting from the long letter written to Roosevelt by Quigg on the possibility of his nomination for governor: "You are a rare good fellow, and you have got the American spirit which, with the multitude, I greatly admire. You are dead honest and I like that too; but in the great office for which you are being certainly called you have got to remember that nobody is ever surely right and nobody else ever absolutely wrong. You have got to remember that compromise and adjustment are unfailingly necessary to all human progress… The thing that I fear is that these plausible and poisonous Mugwumps will at some time or other involve you in some of their 'good government' entanglements…"

Reading that letter attesting to his client's character also allowed him to read the response to it from Roosevelt: "In short, I want to make it clear that there is no question of pledges or promises, least of all the question of bargaining for the nomination." And when the Colonel went to Albany, Bowers continued, he willingly worked with Senator Platt and Barnes for the good of the people of the state and the party "and it was only when the organization demanded wrong that he stood his ground…

"Was there anything more wonderful in the history of politics in this nation?"

It did not take Roosevelt long to separate himself from political interests, Bowers reminded the jury, pointing to the Franchise Tax Bill. Platt called the bill "radical legislation bound to strike the conservative business community, which is the strength of the Republican party," warning Roosevelt, "You put the party in a most unfortunate position." He responded, the jury was told, by signing the bill.

"He was a nervy man," Bowers continued, reminding the jury that the former president had spent his career building his reputation and that it would be entirely out of character for him to make such a libelous attack without full confidence in the truth of it. This was the man they were called upon to judge: "He was not afraid to strike. He would stand by his friends, but if his best friend turned against the interest of the State, Roosevelt became his political enemy. Do you recollect when he was shot and when a merciful dispensation of Providence only prevented the bullet taking his life, how he went right on, with the bullet in his body and made his speech.

"The Panama Canal; its construction, its ownership and management by this government for all time to come was the absolute personal work of President Roosevelt.

"This man, this great president. This hero and soldier has been before you on the stand, heckled under cross examination by two lawyers. What have they brought out…?"

As for the article? When it was published, the defendant "was in possession of a vast amount of information which would seem to have justified its publication…" Bowers then began reading from numerous articles and official government reports entered in evidence although not previously read aloud in the courtroom, which tended to support the claims made by his client. For example, until the night before the vote on the racetrack gambling bill "Senator Grattan had told his friends he would support the bill, he could not afford, he said, to place himself under suspicion of being a grafter, any other course would be political suicide…

"The next morning Senator Grattan got word to vote against Hughes and the racetrack bill. He told his friends he had begged Barnes to spare him the humiliation, but that Barnes was deaf to his entreaties."

Bowers told the jurors that the *Evening Mail* wrote that during one political stalemate, "Twice a week Boss Barnes goes to the room of Senator Brown, the Republican 'leader,' and makes known his will."

Through most of this presentation, Bowers held the jury transfixed, but when he began reading long articles or delving into technical explanations, their attention seemed to waver. Bowers appeared to recognize that in real time and adjusted his approach, regaining their full attention. After the first hour, the proceedings were recessed until the afternoon, giving Bowers and the jurors both the chance to renew their energy.

When the afternoon session began, Bowers immediately resumed his aggressive defense. "His Honor will charge you that the article is libelous per se because it charges a corrupt agreement between Mr. Barnes and Mr. Murphy in relation to the state government. The justification which we tender in that regard is that Mr. Barnes was a party to an arrangement with Mr. Murphy directly or indirectly to keep the Republican Senators voting for Mr. Depew in order that the Democrats might settle their own differences…that the act was purported on Mr. Barnes' part from a very early date follows from certain articles which were published in the Journal newspaper which he largely owned and controlled." Bowers then proceeded to read several of those articles praising the Democratic candidate while criticizing his opponent.

Throughout the trial Barnes's team had claimed or suggested that he was mostly a follower rather than a dominant power in the party. Bowers attacked that by pointing out that when a decision was to be made, legislators turned to Barnes for guidance. When an alliance between Republicans and Independent Democrats to pick a senator was being considered, nominal Republican leader Elon Brown turned to Barnes. "Why did he go to Barnes? Well, you gentlemen (of the jury) know just as well as I do why he went to Mr. Barnes…he believed that Mr. Barnes had the power if he chose to exercise it to get that very thing done."

And after Sheehan's candidacy had collapsed, once again Republicans turned to Barnes for an answer. "Why," Bowers mused, "was Mr. Barnes sending for them and asking that they go to his house? Why were they in conference with Barnes? Was he the only man in the State of New York who could change the caucus rules (which pledged them to vote for Depew)? Nobody lifted a hand until Barnes sent for them… (Republicans) didn't do anything. They sat perfectly quiescent until he acted."

After mentioning the numerous legislators who had testified that Barnes had not attempted to control their vote, the lawyer focused on Ivins's biggest mistake, putting former Senator J. Mayhew Wainwright on the stand. He reminded the jury that Wainwright had testified that when he proposed a union of Republicans and Independent Democrats to elect an independent senator, Barnes had replied, "'Well, I have an agreement with the Democrats and we cannot do it.' I don't know if you noticed that evidence," he continued, "but it was of the most powerful character." He reminded them that both Franklin Roosevelt and William Loeb Jr. had testified that such a combination was impossible because there was an agreement that they should stay with Murphy.

Then he put the pieces together: "If you find… that the statements Mr. Barnes made to Mr. Wainwright and Mr. Loeb, and the admission he made to Mr. Franklin D. Roosevelt are true, there is nothing else for you to find but that the preponderance of evidence fairly establishes…that article is justified and the defense is completed in that respect."

Bowers then pointed out that this is not simply circumstantial evidence that "consists of gathering together a certain number of facts from which the inevitable conclusion is reached," but it also includes direct evidence "where a man has seen a thing done, or where there is a direct admission made by him, as there is here by Mr. Barnes and two of the witnesses."

When necessary, Bowers defended his client with basic logic, saying essentially that if he was going to color the truth or outright lie he certainly would have been better at it. In the discussion of campaign contributions to buy influence, he continued, "Why did Mr. Roosevelt select the names of Brady and Pruyn, who had been the contributors, the one a Democrat the other a Republican, if he made it up? If it was a story he made up? He had committed himself to those two names." Barnes denied the details of it, Bowers conceded, but did acknowledge discussing those two men with the defendant. Why would Roosevelt clearly identify two men if he intended to lie? It is not logical.

The attorney then asked jurors to compare the manner in which Roosevelt and Barnes testified. While Roosevelt couldn't wait to take the stand and answered every question directly, "Mr. Barnes did not speak out quickly and accurately to the point: 'What do you mean by that, Mr. Bowers? What do you mean by moral issue? What do you mean by this question? I must have misunderstood what it means. I don't want to make a mistake.' The questions were all perfectly plain. I may not be refined in my English but I know the English language and you all understood them and he understood them. Why was he evasive? Why did he hesitate?

"Well, even on his direct examination it was just the same thing… Now, the witness who testifies in that way is not likely to be accurate as the one who comes out plainly and bluntly as the defendant in this case did… After all is said and done the defendant in this case…did not equivocate, he did not try to tell a story which might be difficult to deny."

Bowers's most powerful weapon was the Colonel's reputation, and he returned to it often. He reminded the jurors that they had been watching Roosevelt on the national scene for nearly two decades, and by this time they had taken the measure of the man. "While you take into consideration the importance of this case to both of these parties you will also take into consideration the character of the two men: No man has ever claimed the defendant sought anything at any time or place, or in any way, for his pecuniary advancement…

"On the other hand, it is as plain as plain can be that the plaintiff's whole attitude in 1899 was the question of his own financial interests and his political position in the Republican party."

Issue by issue, point by point, sometimes witness by witness Bowers took the jury through the trial, finding virtue and honor in the testimony and actions of his client while doing as much as possible to cast doubt, raise suspicion and refute the defendant's case. It was only as he reached his conclusion that there was a tremble in his voice, as his passions became completely engaged.

In a sense, he said, making a personal appeal to the jurors, this trial "is a fight of the machine against the defendant. It is a case of momentous consequence. We are fortunate in having jurors of your experience and your standing in this community. We have been four weeks and more in making one another's acquaintance so far as it can be made under such circumstances. You have seen the ex-President of the United States and the ex-Governor of the state in your presence…

"You have seen the plaintiff on the stand…you have seen the evidence of both parties and have drawn your own conclusions as to their character and the probabilities of their speaking or not speaking the truth… One thing is certain. There is no room for compromise. The issue is clearly drawn… No compromise of the (Michigan) verdict of six cents, no compromises of any kind or character. In Onondaga County the issues are tried. The whole matter passes into your hands as representatives of different professions, different views, different political relations, a jury of twelve men who doubtless represent this community in the highest possible manner."

Bowers then launched into his big, dramatic, patriotic ending. This would be his Darrowesque moment, meant to send the jury rushing into their room and emerge shouting to the whole world that

Theodore Roosevelt was an innocent man. "The people of this nation have lived in the happiest period of the world's existence...we have lived the freest people on the face of the earth. Our ancestors, fleeing from the persecution of foreign governments established in a new and undeveloped country a home for themselves and their descendants, the United States of America...

"These founders of our country were hardy, honest and religious men, law-abiding, self-sacrificing and self-reliant. Then the Declaration of Independence was adopted, it was decreed that all men were created equal; that they were endowed by their Creator with certain inalienable rights, among them were life, liberty and the pursuit of happiness... The only limitation placed upon the absolute freedom of every man is that the same freedom shall be allowed to every other man, and that no act shall be done that impairs the rights of others. This is the perfection of government."

Bowers took the jury through a brief history of America, a country in which "The great majority of men who have attained prominence have been born poor boys." The first of our three great epochs was the Revolutionary period, which was led by George Washington, who gave us our Constitution, thus "securing to the inhabitants of the United States the blessings of liberty! A system of government was established which enforced law and order by the direct act of the people."

The immediate connection of this history lesson to the Roosevelt-Barnes trial was obscured as Bowers continued his lofty entreaty to the jurors' best selves, while subtly reminding them of the place in history occupied by the man they have been called upon to judge.

The second epoch was the Civil War and the Restoration, and "the man at the front was Abraham Lincoln… The nation was saved, saved for the benefit of the North and South." Syracuse, he acknowledged, honored that period with a great city monument.

Which brought Bowers to the sad reality that "Europe is now engaged in the most bloody war the world has ever known… Contrast the blessings of peace under which we live with the awful tragedy abroad.

"The third great epoch in the history of our nation," he concluded, "came about through the Spanish War and this nation becoming a world power… which compelled this nation to accept the responsibility. That responsibility is now before us in a form which requires action of the utmost moment to this nation. That action will be determined by Woodrow Wilson, the president of the United States…"

And just in case the jurors might not realize the responsibility that had been placed in their hands, he explained, "Closely following as a guide to the nation is the gentleman I represent in this action.

"The purpose of this action is not confined to the plaintiff. It is the purported act of the machine to destroy Mr. Roosevelt's usefulness to the people of the nation…the people's true representative. Jurors!" he cried, grabbing hold of their attention.

"It remains with you whether he shall be broken down. Stand for him and thereby stand for good government and for the true interests of the people of the nation. Remember that the next generation is to be dependent upon our action, and perhaps no more momentous action will ever be taken by any of you than the act that you shall do in rendering your verdict in this case..."

His plea to the patriotism—and heartstrings—of this jury as the nation debated war was clear: a verdict removing Teddy Roosevelt from the public arena would strike at the very foundation of the nation, for this was a man who had dedicated his career and actually risked his life on the battlefield for the American people, and was now fighting once more to save the country from a political system that would rob them of their hard-earned rights.

Finally, humbling himself before the majesty of the jury, as sincerely as possible, he lowered his voice and concluded, "My work is done. The responsibility passes from my hands to yours. My voice can be heard no more. I am not gifted as an orator. I have lived a quiet, uneventful life, practicing my profession as I saw it should be practiced. I am here because I felt it my duty to be here. Met on your part with the same clear conscience that have actuated my poor efforts, and Theodore Roosevelt will remain a power for good during the allotted period of his life.

"Now I close with the most beautiful piece of English our country has ever produced, the words of Abraham Lincoln in delivering his speech at

Gettysburg." And to make certain no one in the courtroom would miss his mark, in a wonderful touch he read this from *The Perfect Tribute*, the book written by Mary Raymond Shipman Andrews, the wife of presiding Judge Andrews, who sat in the courtroom listening intently.

Bowers lowered his voice just a bit more and his audience leaned forward to better hear his words. "Fourscore and seven years ago," he began, reading it slowly as if to give the words new meaning, "…highly resolve that these dead shall not have died in vain, that this nation, under God, shall have a new birth of freedom, and that government of the people, by the people and for the people shall not perish from the earth."

Almost in a whisper he beseeched the jury, "Gentlemen, I ask you to find a verdict in this case of no cause of action."

The defense rested.

As Bowers closed his book and returned to the defense table, Colonel Roosevelt stood and grasped his hands. With tears in his eyes, he gratefully thanked Bowers for his effort.

At the plaintiff's table, Barnes was described as looking bored. But not for long.

CHAPTER EIGHTEEN

And now it was Ivins's turn. His task was entirely different. In addition to making the legal argument that his client's reputation had been attacked and severely damaged and for that he deserved to be compensated, he had to counter Bowers's emotional appeal to the jurors' patriotism; that a great man such as Theodore Roosevelt should be rewarded for his service to the nation, rather than castigated for honestly stating his political opinions. As far as closing arguments go, this was the far more challenging presentation; Ivins had to bring down the former president of the United States to the level of the everyman and convince the jury that this was not about exalted patriotic principles, but just a simple tort, a libel, that no American, no matter who they are, no matter their position in life, should be permitted to spread with impunity.

Ivins walked to the podium to open the morning session, May 20, 1915. He began by acknowledging His Honor and the jurymen and then, in a pleasant conversational tone, struck out against his opponent's argument. "Mr. Bowers opened with a reference to himself and his politics and his relations with the defendant," he began. "I shall say nothing about myself or my politics, they are not in evidence and wholly unimportant in this case. We come here as officers of the law…when we were admitted to the bar forty years ago or more we were compelled to take an oath of office. It is not for me to discuss myself, but it is for me to discuss the law.

"The lawyer's place, his work, his duty, his function are confined to seeing that all of the evidence in a case is properly marshalled and brought before the court; to see, so far as lies in his power, that the rulings of the court conform to the law and then, when the evidence is in, to sum up the case on the evidence with the view of coordinating or collating, bringing together all of the evidence which bears on the real issues of the case…"

It seemed a slightly esoteric beginning, until he reached his point; clearly his great fear was that the jurors' awe for the defendant as emphasized by Bowers would color their judgment of the evidence. "…Oratory is destructive of thought as a rule. Oratory is an appeal to passion, it is an appeal to feeling; it is not an appeal to wisdom… I was, therefore, surprised when toward the end of his speech Mr. Bowers in my opinion forgot his function as a lawyer and devoted a long time to political considerations…from the landing of the Pilgrims until the time of the Spanish War.

"It would be as pertinent for me to close my address by quoting the first lines of Cicero's *Gallic War*, that all Gaul is divided into three parts. It may have been, but it is entirely immaterial in this case… You, as jurors each swore that you were entirely competent and qualified to try this case as between man and man, citizen and citizen, without regard to person, without regard to politics, without regard to the offices which had been held by one or by another of the parties to this action. That was your oath, that is your duty and an appeal to you to consider any political qualifications, an appeal to you to consider anything with regard to the future of these parties or their possible activities is something which never, never should be made.

"It was an appeal to feeling, it was not an appeal to reason and it was not an appeal to the evidence in this case. What has the effect on the future usefulness of Mr. Roosevelt have to do with this case? I appeal to you in my function in my position as a lawyer to dismiss all of that from your minds and to consider this as an ordinary action at law. It is not a political controversy… Should any man because of the position which he has held in the past be placed in a position above the law? Should he be beyond the reach of the law?

"Not at all. And when you get in the jury room you must forget your (political stance) and remember simply that you are men; fair-minded manly men, doing your duty, agreeing if you can, disagreeing if you cannot, but under no circumstances let any appeal to passion, any appeal to feeling reach you."

Should the jury find for the plaintiff, the jurors then would have to determine the financial penalty. Ivins addressed that issue well in advance, telling them, "During the last years of his life Thomas Jefferson was in exigencies of a financial kind. Can you imagine Thomas Jefferson going into a court of bankruptcy and saying that the law should be held up because he had been President of the United States and that he should not be declared a bankrupt because of his possible future usefulness? Daniel Webster was a large borrower and frequently in debt. Is it conceivable that because Daniel Webster was one of the greatest orators and the greatest statesmen this country has ever produced, and was a potential candidate for the presidency of the United States that he therefore should not appear before the court like any other man and pay his debts?

"No man is above the law... Here nobody's life is in question, but there is one thing that is in question and that is the life of the law. If you want to see the law live, if you want this jury to take its place in the great historical line of American juries that has built up that system of law which has produced the most marvelous human justice...you should not for one moment forget your duty... If you were in this case to consider it from a political point of view rather than from the point of view of jurors determining the facts, and if your precedent were to be accepted as a universal order, then law would disappear from the land; you would be setting a precedent for the death of the law…"

Suggesting to the jurors that they held the future of the American legal system in their hands, he had raised the stakes. In as many different ways as possible he put forth one idea: "The question is this: Has any man in this land the right to rob another of his honor?"

Reiterating themes he presented in his opening statement, Ivins reminded the jury that once placed in a position of dishonor, a man's life in his community—in his client's case that community being New York state politics—is done. For those who doubted that, he told the story of the butcher's cart, an "old story (that) has been heard time and again, as to the usefulness of racing with a butcher's cart, because if you beat the butcher's cart you have got no glory; if the butcher's cart beats you, you are in a very sad position." The butcher's cart, in this instance, he claimed were the newspapers and magazines. "When what they say is taken up and not only repeated but is fulminated throughout the entire land by a man who is known to be one of the greatest, if not the greatest center of public opinion in certain quarters, then the offense ceases to be negligible; it must be met."

For years, Ivins told the jury, his client had read the "silly stuff" being said about him without being overly concerned, "but when in the summer of 1914, in a struggle for supremacy, the defendant saw fit to spread throughout the length and breadth of this land a libel charging corruption, charging dealing with the enemy, charging Mr. Barnes with being a political Benedict Arnold…then the time had come… we have a situation which justified the strong, the patient, courageous and the determined man finally saying: I must go before a jury of my peers…and have it determined as a matter of law whether it is I who am telling a falsehood or another man who is telling a falsehood. Because if it is I who is telling the falsehood then what the other man says about me is true: I am unfit to live in decent society.

"Now, that is the only issue in this case."

The initial phase of Ivins's closing was intended to convince the jury to treat this case the same as it would if one of the principals had not been among the most important men of the time. When that appeal was done, he began reviewing the case he had presented. "In an action for libel," he said, as if he was explaining the legal aspect to a good friend, "a jury has to inquire into two things: First, it has to decide whether the libelous matter is true. Then it has to decide whether it is so libelous that for the protection of society, and as a warning to others, punitive damages should be given… Consequently, the question is raised as to whether or not the libel was malicious, (and to do that) you have to consider the frame of mind of the defendant…"

Ivins expressed sympathy with the jurors for the complicated two-headed charge that made sitting in judgment of libel so confusing. Evidence may be admitted for one purpose that should not be considered for the other. The example he gave was Franklin Roosevelt's testimony that he had been told by Senator Grady that there was an arrangement between

Barnes and Tammany Hall. If this was entered for justification, for evidence of truth, it would have been deemed inadmissible hearsay. "Evidence of a corrupt fact upon which you would not have kicked a yellow dog..." And then Ivins slipped easily into comfortable sarcasm. "...But the defendant in this case, lacking as he is in experience, credulous as a child, listens to Franklin Roosevelt and sets that up as a reason he should not be punished. But the Judge has to take that evidence, but only as bearing on the state of mind of the defendant and not in any sense as bearing upon the justification of the truthfulness of the matters charged." Determining the difference between justification and mitigation was complicated and inexact, he admitted, but he urged them to be cognizant of it as they deliberated.

Now he turned to the essence of the case, which according to Ivins, was far simpler. It began during the election of 1914 when Roosevelt admitted "with the same vehemence and the same eagerness and the same intensity of the eminent Nimrod, the (Biblical) hunter," that he had written it for the "edification, the illumination, the education of the people of the State." In politics, referring to a man as a boss has come to imply "a tone of dishonor, or a Phariseeical occupation."

Ivins was well-known for peppering his presentations with historical, mythical, biblical and literary references, and this time was no different. It was questionable that many of the jurors understood them, but still they listened intently, as he guided his own tour of the trial as methodically as one would stroll through the halls of Roosevelt's African animals on display at the Smithsonian Museum of Natural History.

One by one he dissected and dismissed all of the familiar topics: "invisible government," "crooked business and crooked politics," "bosses running a machine," "the alliance between Barnes and Murphy." He stood in front of the jury, with just the appropriate level of indignation in his voice, and ridiculed Roosevelt for setting himself up as the nation's moral censor, then characterized the personal attack on Barnes as unjustified "as if he were to charge you with forgery," he said, pointing directly at one juror, then another, "or you with picking a pocket," and another, "or you with perjury," and another, "or you with arson."

Ivins established a rhythm; he introduced a topic, briefly explained the evidence through his filter, then concluded, "There is not one word of evidence as to the existence of a corrupt or machine ruled government...

"There is no evidence that (a) public office and public officer was controlled during the time to which this controversy refers by any one...

"There is no evidence of mal-administration, nor is there any evidence of corruption in public offices..."

Ivins was not so foolish as to deny what the jurors probably believed, that politicians were corrupt. Indeed he surprised them by admitting it, claiming it was to be expected, almost a natural order: "There has never been any government in which there has not been some corruption," he said. "The reason is very simple: It inheres in the nature of mankind. St. Paul said that we were born in corruption…until we attain a higher stage of civilization, until the principles…of Christianity be converted into practice instead of into preaching, there will always be some evil men (who become involved in government) as a source for the protection or advancement of their interests…"

But such corruption was limited. He continued, "The whole government of this country is not deeply tainted… It is the wonder of the world that we live as we do, without autocratic command." And what damage did Roosevelt do to this? "The only two equals of Theodore Roosevelt," he roared with sarcasm, "George Washington and Abraham Lincoln would make a pronouncement to the effect that our whole government system was deeply tainted and discredited, and that the only cure was to attack one or two individuals. And the gentleman who wrote this knew what attack was. He had been at Kettle Hill, if not at San Juan, and he had been in a jungle, and no man on earth knows better what an attack means than he. And he was inviting the readers of newspapers to make this attack upon the personal integrity, upon the personal honor of these two men."

His client, of course, was "a man of courage, a man of profound convictions, a man of dignity, a serious man." A man who has been wronged. "Out of all of the men one arises, dignified, stern, courageous, determined on holding his own and challenges the truth of this statement and asks the eminent defendant to come into court and give you the proof."

In the matter of Barnes's supposed collusion with Murphy in the election of a senator in 1911, Ivins argued that his client could have accomplished that covertly simply by directing a number of Republican legislators to stay away from the process. That would have given the Democrats a sufficient majority to elect their choice; but instead Barnes loudly, actively and publicly joined the fray. "We find ourselves in this position," Ivins suggested, his sarcasm once more amusing the courtroom. "This man is eminently and incontestably crooked because he is so undeniably straight. Undeniable straightness must imply crookedness. That is about the volume of evidence in this case."

The one piece of evidence that Ivins admitted might reasonably prove the alliance between bosses was the contested claim of Loeb that Barnes "confessed to him his dishonor… You have got to determine whether, as you have seen Mr. Barnes on the stand, he is the kind of man to tell a person whom he had met casually at a luncheon that he was guilty of a dishonorable dicker—to volunteer it. We have a phrase in law, *nunc pro tunc*; that is doing a thing now as if it were done then. Here we have the reverse of that phrase turned upside down, it is *tunc pro nunc* doing things then as if it were done now. Mr. Loeb throws his testimony back a year in order to supply the missing link…which Mr. Barnes denies and which we prove was impossible."

At the defense table Roosevelt and his team of lawyers paid respectful attention but displayed no emotion beyond an intellectual curiosity.

Just as Bowers had done, Ivins addressed the complex printing issue by explaining why he would not address it. "I am not going to touch it," he said, "because it has nothing to do with this case. Counsel on the other side thinks it (does) because Mr. Barnes was a public printer." During the trial the jury had been absent when he had quoted Ben Franklin, public printer, so for their benefit he repeated Franklin's words. If Bowers was willing to compare Roosevelt with Washington and Lincoln, it was appropriate for Ivins to point out, "Mr. Barnes, just as much Benjamin Franklin, wanted to do public printing. It is perfectly true and perfectly human that he should have communicated with Mr. Platt the fact that he was being discriminated against in these matters… You are all in business of one kind or another, you all know what would happen to you if we entered into a state of socialism." He continued this reference to Roosevelt's desire to establish a State printing office, which Barnes had lobbied hard against, warning, "If everything was done by the government…many men would be put out of business."

Every trial eventually comes down to the credibility of the witnesses. Who does the jury believe? What exchanges do they remember most? "You saw Mr. Barnes take the stand, you saw his calmness, his deliberation, his precision…you saw him sit there, soberly, dignified and you heard his testimony. He made his impression on you."

Very subtly, without flair or a sense of rancor, Ivins then calmly launched his final attack on Teddy Roosevelt, whom he described as testifying with "not only his mouth but also with his feet, his hands and his head." Then telling jurors what he had perhaps been aching to say for weeks. “You saw him when he was recalled spring at that chair as though it was going to get away from him, such was his haste to tell us his story. (But) one hundred times through his testimony you heard him say, ‘I don’t remember’ or ‘I can’t remember,’ but whenever he wanted to remember he remembered with a rapidity and accuracy, with a certainty, and with an illumination that put electricity out of business.

“But he has a fixed habit. The defendant believes he has the duty of reforming everybody’s character… The whole thing comes out in the psychology of the man. Here is a man dominated by the spirit and desire for power, a man who is dominated by his desire for publicity, a man who, unhesitatingly and unhaltingly attacks whomever he disagrees with. He has got himself in this position for one simple reason: He did not abide by the terms of his own letter declining the Presidency of the United States for a third term. I am not going to read any Gettysburg speech, nor am I going to read the Epistles to the Romans. I am only going to say this, that the whole trouble with the defendant in this case and the reason he has got himself in this position is due to the fact that he did not follow out the advice that was given by Cardinal Woolsey to Cromwell, ‘Cast aside ambition, by this sin fell the Angels.’”

And with that, he took his seat.

An odd silence permeated the courtroom, just as when Bowers had concluded. The gallery had just witnessed a bravura performance from a celebrated lawyer, a man who had faced hundreds of juries, arguing what would undoubtedly become the case of his career.

He had been at it slightly more than two hours and had lived up to all expectations. The natural instinct was to respond with applause or even hurrahs. But this was a courtroom, not a theater, and the spectators restrained themselves. Ivins quietly accepted congratulations from Barnes and his associates, and Judge Andrews recessed the case for the scheduled midday break.

Judge Andrews began the afternoon session with his charge to the jury. In the wrong hands, this can be a tedious process as the judge instructs the jury on the precise, sometimes opaque law that they must use to decide the case. But these are the final words that jurors hear before they deliberate, coming from the objective source, so the judge needs to take great care in choosing those words.

There have been exceptions to this general principle of a judge serving as a fair arbiter of the law. When abolitionist John Brown was tried for treason after his raid on the armory at Harper's Ferry, Virginia, for example, in his charge to the jury Judge Richard Parker supposedly said, "I will not permit myself to give expression to any of those feelings which at once spring up in every breast when reflecting on the enormity of the guilt in which those are involved who invade by force a peaceful, unsuspecting portion of our common country, raise the standard of insurrection amongst us, and shoot down without mercy Virginia citizens defending Virginia soil against their invasion."

But despite his sometimes controversial, and at times seemingly contradictory, rulings, Judge Andrews had earned the respect of the attorneys and jurors alike. This charge, however, was going to be difficult to translate out of legalese. His attempts to separate testimony into justification and mitigation had proved confusing, even to the legal teams. Jurors had been cautioned to consider certain evidence as this, not that. The confusion was not necessarily his fault, however, since libel law was intrinsically complicated and still roughly hewn.

"The time has come when the mass of evidence offered here before you is to be submitted to you for your decision," he began. "Your duty is to follow the law as laid down by the Court. If I am wrong I may be corrected in another court, but here and now you are bound to follow my instructions.

"To publish falsely of another any charge which tends to injure his reputation and so expose him to public shame or derision or disgrace is wrongful, to do such an act is libelous… There is but one defense. That is the truth. If the charges are true there is no libel. The truth of the charges is a complete answer to the complaint. You all know the maxim of the criminal law that a man is presumed to be innocent until he is proved to be guilty. Precisely the same rule applies to civil law: Innocence is presumed…"

But then he had to explain how the burden of proof was turned on its head here once the judge made his initial finding that the statements were libelous per se: "The defendant is bound to satisfy you by a fair preponderance of evidence that what he has said is true." If, he continued, the jury decided that the libel was published with actual malice and "a reckless and wanton disregard of the plaintiff's rights," the jury could go further and award the plaintiff punitive damages, a sum intended to punish the defendant for his actions. The difficulty in making that determination, he explained, was that "malice is a state of mind" and therefore "direct evidence (of that) is impossible." Any evidence offered by the defendant to prove there was no malice is evidence in mitigation; "It simply bears upon the question of how much, if any, punitive damages should be awarded by the jury."

He went issue by issue through the testimony they had heard and the decisions he'd made, the defenses raised by the Roosevelt side and the responses of the plaintiff. Central to the review of the facts was the 1911 Senate election: "If Mr. Barnes, as the leader of the Republicans, and Mr. Murphy as the leader of the Democrats, agreed to keep the Republicans voting for Mr. Depew, not for the purpose of benefitting the state, that is prima facie evidence of corruption…now the question is was such an agreement made? And if so was it a corrupt one?"

And finally, inevitably, he arrived back at the printing testimony. This issue had been the most difficult for the judge, who throughout the trial seemed to show the resolve of a pendulum, moving back and forth slowly and continuously. But now he had to make his final declaration on it. "Until it was all put together, until you could tell just what conclusions were to be drawn from it, it was impossible to rule whether it would finally become competent or not… Now you have heard that evidence. It may be more or less in your minds, but I say to you it has nothing to do with this case; I say to you that if you allow it to influence your verdict in the slightest you will be false to your duty. That evidence is out of this case; that evidence you are to put from your minds."

He then addressed the unusually apt—in this political trial—cliché, the elephant in the room, Theodore Roosevelt. As Ivins had reminded them, the man had dominated the nation's headlines for more than a decade. He was beloved by some and despised by others. But he could not be ignored. It was almost impossible not to have an opinion about the man, and the tricky part here for every juror was eliminating those feelings from his deliberation. Addressing it directly, Judge Andrews warned, "We are not here to be influenced by anything except the evidence in this case. If you allow yourselves to be swayed by passion or by prejudice or by friendship or by sympathy, if you allow your minds to be influenced by anything except the evidence you have heard, you are just as false to your duty, just as unfit to sit on that jury as I would be if I allowed my mind to be swayed by anything except my opinion as to what the law is."

After more review and telling the jury how to consider additional pertinent facts, he concluded, "There is a fair question of fact here, a fair dispute between these parties and when that is so it is your business, not mine, to determine it.

"Now gentlemen, take the case... As I said once to you before, you are here to do equal justice between these parties."

It was a balanced charge, so naturally as soon as he

had finished there was an avalanche of objections to it from both sides. Wolff for the plaintiff objected "to so much of your Honor's charge" and listed his complaints, then requested additional charges be made that the defendant has failed to accomplish this or show that or prove this or refute that, most of which was denied. Other requests asked him to extend or broaden charges already made to the jury. A few of those requests made little sense. At one point, trying to understand the objection, also referred to as an "exception," Judge Andrews asked, "You except to my refusal to charge and you except to the charge as made?"

"Yes," Wolff agreed, then launched into an equally confusing explanation, which in the end was refused.

When Wolff had finished, Van Benschoten for the defense began requesting exceptions or additions to the charge, some broad, such as a request that because the entire offending article was issued during a political campaign—it was therefore "privileged," or exempt from legal consequences; some of it more obvious, for example that the jury might dismiss the entire testimony of a witness who testified incorrectly about any issue. In the end, many of his objections focused on specifics that would likely make little difference in deliberations.

When all that noise was done, Judge Andrews once again faced the jury. It was only a few minutes before the scheduled recess. "Gentlemen," he said, making an understatement so great that the courtroom broke out in relieved laughter, "it is very evident you will not be able to come to any conclusion in the twenty minutes before court adjourns."

ONONDAGA HISTORICAL ASSOCIATION

The fact that a former president would come before this jury of twelve common citizens, pictured here, created a sensation but surprised no one. Years earlier Roosevelt had said, "No man is above the law and no man is below it, nor do we ask any man's permission when we ask him to obey it. Obedience to the law is demanded as a right, not asked as a favor."

* * *

At 3:45 p.m. the jurors finally began their deliberations. In the six week trial, 104 witnesses had taken the stand, 71 for Barnes, 33 for Roosevelt, and of them, 58 were former senators and assemblymen. The fully transcribed testimony, not including Judge Andrews's charge, filled 3,738 pages. A member of Roosevelt's defense team had even calculated that there had been a total of 934,500 words spoken in testimony—exclusive of the 252 exhibits, including letters, newspaper articles and other pieces of evidence admitted into the record.

At 5:00 p.m., the judge summoned the jurymen to the courtroom to see if they had anything to report. After a few moments of silence, juror number 1, Walter J. Zuill, a Progressive like Roosevelt, asked that part of the judge's charge on not allowing political leanings to influence their judgment be reread. Judge Andrews replied that he did not feel it necessary to do so since it should be perfectly clear it was their solemn duty not to be swayed by political considerations. The jurors then returned to their room to continue deliberations.

Throughout the late afternoon and into the evening, lawyers and newsmen moved in and out of the building. At six o'clock dinner was served to the jurors in their room. While the lawyers retired to local restaurants and taverns to wait out the verdict, resourceful scribes engaged in conversation with the bailiffs stationed outside the jury room, hoping for some bit of exclusive information about the proceedings.

There was considerable debate among the observers as they waited. The *New York Times* reported that a "ballot was taken" at the outset of deliberation: "It is not known what the result was, but there is ground for the statement that there was a division along political lines." According to the *Times*, ballots were taken frequently after dinner, and they weren't coming down in Roosevelt's favor: "While no word came from the jury room as to what was taking place, it was persistently rumored that the vote greatly favored Mr. Barnes. One rumor had it that three members were holding out for a verdict for Colonel Roosevelt."

What was not reported at that time was that much to the dismay of Roosevelt, this was entirely consistent with what his legal team had been predicting. Their hope was that the jury would be unable to reach a unanimous decision and warned Roosevelt, quite candidly, that he would be lucky to get as many as four jurors to vote for his position.

The waiting continued into the night. Roosevelt passed the evening quietly in Syracuse while Barnes returned by train to Albany. The Colonel received an amusing gift when he stopped at the hotel. An admirer from Troy, New York, had sent him a small silk-lined jewelry box filled with the tiny blue-and-white buttons marked *T.R.* that had been distributed during the 1912 campaign, accompanied by a note describing them as "An antidote for the crooked politics for Mr. Barnes, one to be taken before each meal."

When asked by reporters to make a statement, Roosevelt maintained the proverbial stiff upper lip, replying, "It would be manifestly improper for me to say anything until a verdict has been rendered. Even then, I intend to let my counsel, Mr. Bowers, do all the talking for me." Among themselves though, the newsmen doubted that, agreeing that no one had ever done all the talking for Teddy Roosevelt.

When it became apparent the jury would not be able to reach a verdict that night, arrangements were made to house them in the dormitory in the jail building on Cedar Street. At 11:30 p.m. they walked together as a group to that facility, ignoring the reporters who shouted questions at them. The papers described them as being "locked up" at the jail for the night.

Some jurors reportedly rose as early as five thirty the next morning, anxious to continue deliberations. Many observers expected a deadlock to continue until the judge would be forced to declare a hung jury. With that possibility in mind, slightly after 10:00 a.m., Ivins, feeling ill, boarded a train to return to New York City.

At about that same time, Judge Andrews called the court to order. Unlike at any point during the testimony, now he looked out on to a mostly empty courtroom. For the first time the newsmen far outnumbered the spectators. But to everyone's surprise Justice Andrews was handed a sealed envelope from the jury foreman, Warren W. Somers, a Syracuse grocer. There was a general hubbub as reporters assumed the jury had reached a verdict. Instead, the note explained that a "peculiar situation had arisen" and asked the judge to come to the jury room. Instead, Judge Andrews ordered the jury into the courtroom.

They filed in quietly and took their seats. Rather than addressing their secret concern, he explained, "There is very little I can say in addition to what I have already said." He continued, telling them that the law required that any questions must be asked in open court; and if this problem concerned evidence, he would have it reread to them. "That's about as far as I can go."

The jurors glanced at each other, then stood without asking any questions and returned to their room. The courtroom once again was quiet. The general feeling was that the jury problem concerned an inability to reach a consensus. So it came as a great surprise an hour later when Judge Andrews was informed the jury had reached a verdict.

CHAPTER NINETEEN

The news spread rapidly, and within minutes the courtroom once again was completely filled and noisy with expectation. The Roosevelt team hurried back from their headquarters in the Onondaga Hotel. A telegram was waiting for Ivins when his train reached Utica, and he made arrangements to return immediately. The fact that the jury had been able to agree within such a brief time reinforced the presumption that the verdict must be for Barnes.

Minutes after eleven o'clock, Judge Andrews warned the spectators that he would not permit any demonstrations in his courtroom, "no matter what the verdict is." That said, he instructed the court clerk, Charles J. Clarke, to bring in the jury.

The waiting had been difficult for Roosevelt. By the end of the trial, he later told his son Kermit, "Both Barnes and his counsel, Ivins, began to show the strain and they did not wait to hear the verdict, I think from sheer nervous breakdown. I was pretty nervous myself but I stayed in the courtroom, for I was going to take the gaff without flinching if I had to."

If the jurors were surprised or even noticed that neither Barnes nor Ivins was in the courtroom, they showed no sign of it. They barely even glanced at Roosevelt, who sat rigidly as he watched them enter the courtroom.

When all were settled, Judge Andrews nodded to Clerk Clarke, who asked, "Has the jury reached a verdict?"

Foreman Somers responded, "We have."

The silence in the courtroom was so complete that even the slight squeak of a chair seemed jarring. The ripping whine of the pile driver that had disturbed the trial only weeks earlier was long gone and forgotten.

"How do you find?"

Roosevelt remained motionless, looking sternly and anxiously at the jury.

Several jurors conferred for a moment, then Somers stood up and said, "We find for the defendant..." but before anyone could react he continued, loudly, "with the suggestion that the costs be evenly divided between the two parties."

Judge Andrews responded to that suggestion with a puzzled look. At the defense table Roosevelt looked to his counsel for an explanation, but no one seemed to know quite what to do. At the announcement "for the defendant," his famous broad smile had instantly reappeared and he raised a clenched fist in victory.

But when Somers added his proviso, the Colonel creased his brows in wonder, then leaned over and told Bowers, "I don't want a cent of his money."

John Bowers rose and told the court, "I offer to divide."

Almost simultaneously William Barnum, for the plaintiff, stood up and thundered with palpable outrage, "I object!"

Judge Andrews banged his gavel and said, "The court is prohibited by law from accepting a verdict in that form." He shook his head in dismay, and said sternly to the jury, "The verdict is hardly proper. Gentlemen, you must retire and find a verdict, either for the plaintiff or defendant. A suggestion as to who is to pay the costs must not be put in."

Foreman Somers smiled knowingly at that, and requested a standing vote be taken. The court clerk began polling the jury. Juror Henry Hoag, a Republican, stood up and said strongly, "I find no cause for the defendant!"

No one quite understood what he meant. "You mean you find for the defendant?" Judge Andrews asked.

"I do."

Following Hoag, one by one, each juror stood and firmly repeated his response. Irving Mills, Franklin Rhoades, F. W. Pierce, Ray Tanner, each of them found for the defendant—until Clarke called juror number 11, a heavyset man named Edward Burns. In the jury room, it was revealed later, Burns had been the last vote for Roosevelt—on the condition that the court costs would be split between the sides. Burns had taken this stand on the inaccurate belief that the entire cost of the trial would be borne by the loser.

In reality, the taxable cost of the case, the expenses both men would pay the court, as opposed to all of the legal fees, was only $65.

When Burns was told it was not possible to make that part of the verdict, he switched quickly to Barnes, perhaps in hopes of forcing the compromise. When his name was called by the clerk, Burns hesitated for a few seconds then "electrified the courtroom" reported the *Times*, "by almost shouting, 'For the plaintiff!'"

A confused murmur spread throughout the room until it was gaveled silent. Bowers tried different means of sending a message to the jury that his side would be delighted to share costs. "We offer to stipulate," he began.

But each effort was cut off by the plaintiff's side, who did not want the jury to hear any such offer. Judge Andrews explained, "I can hardly instruct the jury as to what the parties may do amongst themselves. I simply say to the jury that they must find a verdict in the form I have given them."

After the twelfth juror pronounced his vote with the majority, the judge ordered the jury to return to their room until they agreed upon a unanimous verdict. The jurors stayed seated, looking at each other as if there were some alternative to resuming deliberations. When they accepted the reality that this was not over, the disappointed and clearly tired men filed out of the room.

As soon as the door was closed behind them, spectators began descending on the jubilant Roosevelt, shaking his hand, giving him manly pats on his back and offering their hearty congratulations. An attractive young woman told him she wanted to hug him. Roosevelt beamed and held her hands, thanking her. While not yet a victory, it was now clear that he would not lose, which was, in and of itself, a huge relief. He returned to the hotel to wait for a conclusive verdict, which everyone assumed would be quickly forthcoming.

The remaining members of Barnes's team sat rigidly, clearly stunned by this development. Until then, they had believed rumors that had the majority of jurors favoring their position or, like Roosevelt's camp, predicting a split jury.

When the jury failed to announce a verdict through the afternoon and early evening and then the night, they began to take hope that it would remain deadlocked. Juries are notoriously fickle and unpredictable, and the danger for Roosevelt was that the single holdout might garner more support for his position. Getting one man to change his mind is far easier than if two or three or four dig in and entrench themselves.

The attorneys seemed bewildered; Bowers told reporters that sometime in his past he had heard of a similar incident but couldn't recall when or where that was. All agreed this was an extraordinary event; none of them had ever seen a jury bicker like this out in the open for public view.

Suddenly that lone juror number 11, Edward

Burns, became an object of curiosity. The entire six-week-long lawsuit, which had been followed with great interest throughout the entire country, suddenly hinged on the firm belief of one man that the costs of the rancorous trial must be shared by both sides. Reporters quickly discovered that the Democrat Burns was a hardworking man, one of the longest-serving trolley motormen in Syracuse. He had run the very first car when the branch of the trolley line to Solvay had entered service, and prior to that he'd run a horsecar.

The hours passed slowly as the drama of the hold-out juror captured the attention of the newsmen. Could one man really stand in the way of a verdict? Was this a tribute to the American legal system or a troublesome defect that might someday destroy it? Should the weight of eleven men against one be sufficient? Even the United States Supreme Court, the highest court in the nation, required only a majority to reach a decision. And there were some states in which certain cases did not require unanimity from a jury. New York was not among them.

As the deliberations continued, it became obvious that Burns had become an outcast. When the jury was escorted to dinner at the Winchester Hotel, he walked alone, trailing and ignored by his fellow jurors—although reporters noted he smiled at them as he passed.

The jurors worked until 2:00 a.m. the following morning before being "locked up" again in the jail dormitory. At 6:00 a.m., Burns sought out Somers, the jury foreman. A few other jurors attended, some fully dressed. Others sat on the edges of their beds in pajamas and nightshirts, while yet others remained asleep. It was hardly the sort of proper deliberation with all jurors present. Nevertheless, it appears there wasn't much to discuss. Burns wanted to inform the foreman that he accepted that the other men were right and he was wrong, and that on what turned out to be the fortieth ballot behind closed doors, he would cast his vote for the defendant without qualifications.

After sending a note to the judge that they had reached a verdict, the now unanimous jury still had to wait several hours for the court to convene at 10:00 a.m. The men were anxious to complete their duty and go home. "I never knew a second could be so long," one of them said later. "If I looked at my watch once in those hours, then I looked at it a thousand times. It seemed that time itself went on a strike."

For one last time the courtroom was crammed—although neither Barnes nor Ivins had made it back to the city. "Every single inch of space was occupied," the *Herald* reported. "It was a peculiar crowd made up of all ages from boys with their first growth of beard on their unshaven faces to men and women in the twilight of old age." All of them, it was agreed, anxious to get one last look at Colonel Roosevelt before he left Syracuse. While the rumors held that the jury had decided for Roosevelt, there had already been one false alarm, and these people wanted to see it for themselves.

The rumors were bolstered when the session began; Wolff immediately objected to any verdict being received or recorded, claiming the previous day's spectacle, when the jury had been publicly polled, had made it impossible for the jurors to reach a fair verdict. Judge Andrews overruled the objection and asked Clerk Clarke to proceed. "Gentlemen of the jury," he intoned. "Have you reached a verdict? And if so, how do you find?"

Foreman Somers stood. "For the defendant."

"So say you all?"

The jury was polled. In his turn, juror number 11, Burns, arose and said, "I find for the defendant."

Wolff objected to the verdict, claiming it was not supported by the evidence. This gave Judge Andrews one final chance to impose his own verdict if he so desired. He did not. "Overruled," he said.

Roosevelt could barely remain in his seat as the judge thanked the jury for their time and dedication. When the judge gaveled the trial to an end, a cheer arose from the gallery. An instant later the Colonel had pushed his way through the throng of admirers that descended on him to offer congratulations and was standing in front of the jury box; with tears in his eyes he asked to meet with them in an adjoining room. Roosevelt was described by a *Herald* reporter as "happy as a kid with a new toy, he bubbled over with exuberance, years have dropped from his shoulders in the few brief seconds consumed before the jury delivered its verdict."

Roosevelt had one final question for the judge. "Would it be ethical for me to thank the jury?"

Perfectly acceptable, replied the judge. Then

Bowers asked his client, "Does that include Juror Burns too?"

The gleeful Colonel said happily, "It includes everybody having anything to do with the case." And then added, "Truth and righteousness again have prevailed."

No longer "the defendant," Roosevelt greeted each member of the jury as a good and loyal friend as they entered the room. "The Colonel went from man to man," the *Times* wrote, "grasping each extended hand through both of his and shaking it like a pump handle, meanwhile chuckling with joy." After having his photograph taken with each man, he finally made a statement, his voice cracking with emotion. "I have been more moved and touched than I can express by what you have done… I shall try all my life to act in public and private affairs so that no one of you will have cause to regret the verdict you have given me this morning.

"I thank you from my heart."

He promised to provide a signed copy of the trial transcript for each of them and concluded, "If you men ever come down to Oyster Bay, just remember that the latchstring is out for every one of you." He was, he said, perhaps with some hyperbole, happier than he had ever been before in his life. The recalcitrant Burns was right there in the middle of the postverdict debrief looking as pleased as every other juror to be spending time, up close and personal, with the former president.

While Roosevelt days later called the verdict "utterly unexpected," the jurors informed him that he had never been in serious jeopardy. The very first vote, taken within the first twenty minutes of deliberations, was actually 9 to 3 for the defendant; two Democrats saying they wanted to ensure there would be a complete and fair discussion of the evidence. The second vote, taken five minutes later, however, was 11 to 1, where it stayed for the next forty-two hours.

Bowers pushed his way forward, equally ebullient. "May a Democrat say something to the jury?" he asked, to be greeted with friendly laughter. Taking hold of Edward Burns's hand, he reminded the room of what the Roosevelt side believed was at stake in this trial. "The victory that Mr. Roosevelt has won is a victory for good government. In my opinion, it is the most important case that has been decided since the Civil War. The issue that I put to the jury was whether machine government or government by the people should prevail, and the latter has prevailed… The verdict certainly assures us that the Anglo-Saxon system of determining questions between litigants is rightly lodged in the hands of a jury of twelve men."

Teddy Roosevelt's walk back to the hotel quickly became a victory parade. Syracuse's men, women and children surrounded him, shook his hand and escorted him all the way back to his headquarters.

Later in the day Barnes was informed by telephone about the verdict and issued his statement: "The jury declared that I have no cause of action against Mr. Roosevelt," he wrote, "who charged me with acts I did not commit and therefore the public may have believed I was guilty of what I did not do, however the knowledge of complete rectitude of my conduct must content me, which is the only important thing in life."

The trial turned several of the jurors into passing celebrities. Somers was widely interviewed and told reporters, "We acted calmly and there was no animosity among the jurors at any stage. We did our best and try to decide the case on the evidence. And the judge's charge. The main issue was the question of veracity between the two men."

Asked if politics played any role in their verdict, he replied forcefully, "Not in the slightest degree."

A second juror immediately supported him. "Politics went out of the jury room like a dropping of a tender." As for the controversial printing evidence, "That was totally disregarded, with the exception of how it affected the credibility of the plaintiff." That, of course, was the legally correct way of admitting that the printing evidence had been devastating to Barnes's case, since it had left the impression that he was dishonest in his business dealings. It had battered his credibility. The fact that so much of that testimony had been ruled incompetent—meaning it could not be considered by the jury in its deliberations—after it was already heard in court, actually prevented the Barnes side from fully countering it.

Roosevelt left Syracuse early in the afternoon, arriving at New York's Grand Central Terminal at 7:30 p.m. He was met there by his son Ted and daughter Ethel, with her husband, and after a brief reunion, during which he displayed "bubbling good spirits," he spoke with the gathered reporters. "I have no need to say anything. I have said it all under oath. This is just a little family party." Then he drew on his vast store of appropriate anecdotes. "You may remember the advice a New Bedford whaling captain gave to his mate, advice I am very fond of. They had been having a quarrel and the Captain said, 'All I want of you is silence, and darn little of that.'"

His family had arranged a surprise at home; a magnificent horse was waiting for him. A day later, as Roosevelt tried to mount this steed for the first time, he was pitched off and suffered two broken ribs.

The Barnes team, meanwhile, called for a new trial, claiming that Judge Andrews had made serious errors in permitting testimony relating to the printing contracts to be heard by the jury. They announced they would appeal the decision to a higher court, and if necessary, to the United States Supreme Court.

During the next few days, the nation's newspapers editorialized about the verdict. They generally supported the decision, which as it turns out, had the effect of extending slightly more protection to their own stories. The *New York Mail*, for example, called the verdict "much more than a vindication for one man. It is a triumph for a cause, it is a victory for the people in their efforts to wrest control of their own affairs from the bipartisan alliance of bosses…a system graft upon American politics, where the bosses always win and the people always lose, no matter who is elected."

The *Times* reported that the jurors had "made

up their minds that one (Barnes or Roosevelt) was not telling the truth, and they concluded that one was not the Colonel." Roosevelt agreed with that conclusion, writing to his son Kermit, "The jury evidently decided primarily upon the estimate it had formed of me during the nine days I was on the witness stand and of Barnes during the four days he was on the witness stand."

As for the impact on the principals and their political careers, the *Syracuse Journal* noted that "If Mr. Barnes had wanted to put Mr. Roosevelt back on the political map, he could not have done more than he has done in this case… Whatever Mr. Barnes started out to do to Colonel Roosevelt has failed. He has not injured the Colonel in the least. On the contrary, he injured himself as a politician of national standing." While the *New York Tribune* pronounced its own verdict: "On the outcome of this case Mr. Barnes staked his political future, he has lost. Mr. Barnes having appealed to the people and lost, has little chance in any further appeal. The outcome is bound to be heartening to members of all political parties who have been fighting the kind of machine politics that Mr. Barnes represented. Mr. Barnes' case in court crumbled, Mr. Barnes politically crumbles, the political order in which he believed in so thoroughly is crumbling…"

Barnes did have some defenders. New York State assemblyman and now deputy attorney general Harold Hinman, who had testified for Barnes in the trial, said, "It hardly seems possible that a verdict against Mr. Barnes could be rendered by any fair-minded jury. There was no evidence to bear out the allegations made in Colonel Roosevelt's article. It may be that the jury was actuated by a desire to prevent a former President of the United States from being smirched in the eyes of the world."

While Roosevelt walked away from the trial politically unscathed if not emboldened, Barnes's political career was damaged and his power and prestige immediately diminished. Two days after the trial's end, the *New York Times* launched a biting attack on him, writing, "The disclosures regarding the interests of Mr. Barnes in printing contracts seem to have made the most profound impression on those who followed the evidence… There has been for years more or less scandal about the State Printing, and the existence of a 'printing ring' has been known to everyone who has followed affairs at the capital…"

But then the *Times* continued, carefully skirting the edges of the libel laws, to hint at something far more nefarious. "It was suggested here today by a person closely in touch with what was going on at the time of the Hughes racetrack legislation that the testimony brought out at Syracuse did no more than scratch the surface… It is common talk in Albany among friends of Senator Grattan that even though, as Mr. Barnes intimated on the stand, he was induced to prevail upon Senator Grattan to vote against the bill by Colonel Roosevelt himself, a very substantial 'campaign contribution' came to the Republican organization as a result of Senator Grattan's change of front. Senator Grattan himself is authority for the statement that he was approached with a money offer, which he turned down, and that, with every intention to support the Hughes measure up to the very moment when Mr. Barnes summoned him to his house and bluntly directed him to supply the one vote that was needed to defeat the bill, he was subjected for many days to importunities from men representing the racetrack gambling interests which almost drove him to distraction."

The point was as clear as the newspaper legally could make it: Roosevelt had been absolutely right. And the jury had gotten it right. Barnes was a corrupt politician and the leader of a corrupt Republican political machine. Barnes had brought this action against the wishes of his political cronies and the result had been precisely what they had feared: his career had taken a broadside while Colonel Roosevelt, as Republican leader Cornelius Collins had warned, was "dragged out of his political graveyard."

But the trial had taken its toll on each of the participants. Surprisingly, rather than being purely celebratory, at times even Roosevelt became melancholy about the whole affair. Two weeks later, in a letter to his friend, British journalist and editor of the *Spectator*, John Strachey, he wrote, "I have felt this libel suit which has just ended was really as much a fight for those who have fought with me during the last three years as for myself. It has justified in court by legal evidence what we said about boss rule and crooked business three years ago. I do not grudge the money it has cost me, but I think the service was really worth rendering; but I do very strongly feel that in a way it excuses me from doing too much more.

"There is an anecdote that has long been proverbial in our family. Doctor Polk, of New York, now an old man, was Inspector-General of the Confederate Artillery fifty years ago. Just before Appomattox, Lee sent him to the rear to hurry up the stragglers. He was sitting on a rail fence, with his horse-bridle over his arm when a lank, frowning, half-starved North Carolinian Infantryman trooped by, his feet going 'muck-muck' as he ploughed through the mud. Polk said in a perfunctory way, 'Hurry up, my man, hurry up.' Whereupon the North Carolinian looked gloomy at him, shook his head and remarked as he walked by, 'If I ever love another country, damn *me*!'

"…I think the people have made up their minds that they have had all they want of me, and that my championship of a cause or an individual, say in exceptional cases, is a damage rather than a benefit."

As this trial came to an end, the world continued to careen out of control. Roosevelt continued to rage against President Wilson's inaction, to which Wilson smugly replied, "…the best way to treat Mr. Roosevelt is to take no notice of him. That breaks his heart and is the best punishment that can be administered." But the Colonel's warnings proved prescient; when the German government announced early in 1917 it would resume attacking all shipping in war zone waters, President Wilson finally asked for a declaration of war. Two months later the first American doughboys landed in France.

Roosevelt's attempt to lead a volunteer force into combat, as he had done in Cuba two decades earlier, was squashed by Wilson, but each of his four sons served nobly: Archie lost the use of his left arm when wounded leading an attack on a German position for which he was awarded the Croix de Guerre; Kermit served with British troops and received the British Military Cross; Ted earned a Silver Star to go with his Croix de Guerre and suffered the effects of mustard gas; youngest son Quentin was killed when his plane was shot down behind enemy lines, and German airmen honored him with a military funeral. The Colonel was active throughout the war, doing whatever was possible to raise morale on the home front.

But he never forgot "the six weeks of great strain" in the Syracuse spring of 1915. This trial and the six-cent verdict he had won against the *Iron Ore* newspaper two years earlier were major milestones for Roosevelt. He updated his biography in the prominent *Who's Who* book, where famous individuals are chosen to submit summaries of their greatest achievements, not just to include the two trials, but afforded them far more space than the Panama Canal and many of his other major White House accomplishments.

The fate of William Ivins was far more immediate and tragic. The trial had robbed him of his strength and vitality, and he became seriously depressed. Within days of its completion, he collapsed and was found unconscious in his home. He recovered, and against the warnings of his physician began framing his appeal for Barnes. He was certain, he told his associates, that the Appellate Division would reverse the decision. He threw himself into his work, which proved too much. Two months after the verdict, on July 23, he died at age sixty-four. In his obituary the *Times* wrote, "The Barnes-Roosevelt case was blamed for breaking his health at the time."

Following Ivins's death, Barnes's appeal was never filed.

John Bowers's firm, Bowers & Sands, billed Roosevelt $31,159.64 for its legal work. Once a variety of other trial-related expenses were added, the final cost to Roosevelt may have gotten close to the total amount Barnes was seeking in the trial. Nevertheless, Roosevelt happily paid the bill, in full. Bowers continued his career, eventually being appointed to the nation's Draft Advisory Board by President Wilson. When he died on March 5, 1918, his *Times* obituary highlighted his trial summation as a "masterly oration" and lauded him for his defense of Roosevelt.

William Barnes never regained his full stature within the national Republican Party. His days of helping elect presidents were done, as was his own dream of holding elective office. But he did retain some influence within New York state politics. Incredibly, especially after Roosevelt's bitter attacks on the party machine, in 1918 Republican leaders offered him the party nomination for governor of New York. The Colonel was reportedly incredulous to learn that Barnes supported this suggestion. Barnes told reporters, "The people will vote for him because he is Teddy Roosevelt.

"I signed the call addressed to Theodore Roosevelt to enter the Republican primary because I believe Republican thought and activities should be raised to the level confronting the United States… We require above all else, in the highest affairs of trust and power, not only men of integrity and character, but primarily men who can see into the future and who will not be content with doing only those things which become obviously necessary. Had this nation been led by vision the war would have been already won."

This letter, signed by Barnes and other leaders of the party, was a complete vindication for Roosevelt. But he turned down the offer, responding, "My work is for the men who are fighting in this war."

But within months it became clear that Progressive Party leaders almost unanimously wanted him to make one more run for the presidency. In the wake of his somewhat prophetic predictions and warnings about the Central Powers and the war itself, there also was growing support among Republicans, as well. But Roosevelt still harbored the reservations he had expressed following the trial. He told his secretary, Joseph Bishop, in late December 1918, "I am indifferent to the subject. I would not lift a finger to get the nomination… I am not eager to be president again. But if the leaders of the party come to me and say that they are convinced I am the man the people want and the only man who can be elected, and that they are all for me, I don't see how I could refuse to run."

And then, Bishop remembered, the Colonel sud-

ONONDAGA HISTORICAL ASSOCIATION

Theodore Roosevelt in 1916, his reputation saved, once more ready to charge forward into political battle.

denly sat up, clenched his fist and declared, "And by George, if they take me, they will take me without a single reservation or modification of the things I have always stood for."

No one was to know how that might have ended. On January 6, 1919, weeks after making this statement, Theodore Roosevelt died.

In those years following the trial, Roosevelt had remained a major player in the national political scene, but never again dominated the headlines as he did in Syracuse in the spring of 1915.

* * * * *

BIBLIOGRAPHY

Backer, Alice. "Barnes versus Roosevelt." Master's thesis, Syracuse University, 1947.

Betts, Charles H. *Betts-Roosevelt Letters: A Spirited Discussion.* New York: The Lyons Republican Company, 1912.

Bishop, Joseph Bucklin. *Theodore Roosevelt and His Time: Shown in His Own Letters.* New York: Charles Scribner & Sons, 1919.

Blackstone, Sir William. *Commentaries on the Laws of England, vol. 1: The Rights of Persons.* Lexington, Kentucky: Republished First Rate Publishers, 2014.

Blackstone, Sir William. *Commentaries on the Laws of England, vol. 2: Of the Rights of Things.* Schwab, Germany: Republished Jazzybee Verlag, 2016.

Blakey, George T. "Calling a Boss a Boss: Did Roosevelt Libel Barnes in 1915?" *New York History* 60, no. 2 (April 1979): 194-216. https://www.jstor.org/stable/23169602.

Bliven, Charles Mason. "Pleadings Their History: Comparison of the Common Law and Code Systems Technicalities of the Code." Master's thesis, Cornell Law School, 1895.

Blume, William Wirt. "Origin and Development of the Directed Verdict." *Michigan Law Review* 48, no. 5 (March 1950). https://www.jstor.org/stable/1284842.

Burke, Samuel B. "Hearsay, a Brief History." Alagood Cartwright Burke PC. https://blogs.lawyers.com/attorney/civil-practice/hearsay-a-brief-history-33130/.

Coleman, Chas. T. "Origin and Development of Trial by Jury." *Virginia Law Review* 6, no. 2 (Nov. 1919): 77-86. https://www.jstor.org/stable/1064053.

Connors, Dennis J. *Crossroads in Time: An Illustrated History of Syracuse.* New York: Onondaga Historical Association, 2006.

Greene, John Robert. "Theodore Roosevelt and the Barnes Libel Case: A Reappraisal." *Presidential Studies Quarterly* 19, no. 1 (1989): 95-105. https://www.jstor.org/stable/40574567.

Grenig, Jay E. "The Civil Jury in the United States." *North Dakota Law Review* 92, no. 2 (2017): 365-395.

Hancock Jr., Stewart F. "Barnes v. Roosevelt." *New York State Bar Association Journal* 63, no. 8 (Dec. 1991).

Humbach, John A. "The Common-Law Conception of Leasing: Mitigation, Habitability and Dependence of Covenants." *Washington University Law Quarterly* 60, no. 4 (1983): 1213-1288.

Keller, Morton. *Regulating a New Society: Public Policy and Social Change in America, 1900-1933.* Cambridge, Massachusetts: Harvard University Press, 1998.

Liberty Fund, Inc. "1736: Brief Narrative of the Trial of Peter Zenger." Last modified April 13, 2016. http://oll.libertyfund.org/pages/1736-brief-narrative-of-the-trial-of-peter-zenger.

Mooney, William McKinley. "Boxing Lessons From Theodore Roosevelt: What I Learned About Keeping Fit from Our Great Fighting President." *Leslie's Weekly*, 133 (October 22, 1921).

Morris, Edmund. *Colonel Roosevelt.* New York: Random House, 2010.

Morris, Edmund. *Theodore Rex.* New York: Random House, 2010.

The New York Times, April-June 1915, Timesmachine.com.

Onondaga Historical Association. *Syracuse: Images of America.* With text by Dennis J. Connors. South Carolina: Arcadia Publishing, 1997.

The Roosevelt Panama Libel Case against The New York World and Indianapolis News. New York: Printed for the *New York World*, 1910.

Roosevelt, W. Emlen. *Roosevelt vs. Newett: A Transcript of the Testimony taken and Depositions read at Marquette, Mich.* Privately printed, 1914. http://www.theodore-roosevelt.com/images/research/scholars/trversusnewett.pdf.

Syracuse Journal, selected editions, April-May 1915.

Syracuse Post-Standard, selected editions, April-May 1915.

Wigmore, John H. "The History of the Hearsay Rule." *Harvard Law Review* XVII, no. 7 (May 1904). https://archive.org/stream/jstor-1323425/1323425_djvu.txt.

ACKNOWLEDGMENTS

I want to thank my father, Floyd Abrams, for his help in reviewing the manuscript and providing essential thoughts and guidance on some of the more complicated legal issues involved. Our last book was dedicated to him and he remains my great mentor.

A special note of appreciation to our always supportive editor, Peter Joseph, from Hanover Square Press who believed in us before the success of our last book. His smart suggestions and changes made this book that much better and knowing we have Peter behind us provides us with additional confidence and creative freedom. His team at Hanover Square, including Natalie Hallak, was also so helpful in bringing this to fruition.

I also want to thank my producer/assistant, Stephanie Alexander, for her tireless efforts helping me balance my time to ensure I could always focus on this project that was so dear to me. In retrospect, however, this project would not have happened at all without literary agent Frank Weimann of Folio bringing my co-author and me together.

And most important of all, there is that deft co-author, David Fisher, whose talents are truly boundless. David's complete absorption in the history and details made the book and this story come to life. With David's guidance, I have become a better scribe, editor and historian. He's a true pro and I'm now proud to call him a good friend.

Speaking of good friends, I want to thank David Goldin and David Zinczenko for always serving as smart, focused sounding boards for all my projects.

And then there is family: my mother, Efrat; my sister, Judge Ronnie, and her husband, Greg; and their girls, Dylan, Teddy and Finn. And, of course, the mother of the boy to whom I dedicated this book. I will always be forever grateful to Florinka for her advice to me in all my endeavors and, of course, her devotion to our son, Everett. While he adores his "nonna" Ilike and "nonno" Roberto, from Italy, and his Geeta, he simply loves Florinka more than anything else in the world.

—*Dan Abrams*

Bringing long forgotten history to life is always challenging, and this book would not exist without the assistance of several people. I would like to acknowledge my co-author, Dan Abrams, who is always there, day and often nights, to do all that was required to bring this story to the page, and to do so with never-failing enthusiasm. Working with him is a pleasure. We are fortunate to be working with our editor and publisher, Peter Joseph, whose gentle guidance is visible on every single page. And, as always, our agent Frank Weimann of Folio, who has been a friend for so many years, and took care of all that other business stuff quickly, efficiently and with great humor. We owe him a lot!

I would also like to gratefully acknowledge Gregg Tripoli, the Executive Director of the Onondaga Historical Association in Syracuse, N.Y. It is accurate to say that without his invaluable assistance this book would not have been possible. A bonus from the project is our friendship. While I am grateful to the entire staff at OHA for welcoming us (and cleaning up the mess we left) and assisting in so many different ways, I do want to express my special appreciation to Research Specialist Sarah Kozma and Curator of History (and ersatz cameraman) Robert Searing for going so far out of their way on our behalf. If you happen to be in Syracuse please stop by to step into history or visit online at www.cnyhistory.org. It's an amazing museum.

We also were fortunate to have the guidance of Ellen R. Fuller, law librarian at the Supreme Court Library in Syracuse, who helped us lay the foundation.

I also would like to express my gratitude to "Big John" and Susan Nicholson for their efforts on our behalf in the early stages, when it made a big difference. And to my friend Brian McLane, who lays the welcome mat for all who need it in Syracuse, my words will never sufficiently thank you for what you've taught me. Finally to my wife, Laura, for always being my biggest supporter and my best friend, thank you, thank you, thank you.

And you too, Willow.

—*David Fisher*

INDEX

Page numbers for photographs are indicated in *italics*.